The Fires of Yule

- A Keltelven Guide for Celebrating the Winter Solstice -

Montague Whitsel

ISBN: 0-75965-565-0

This book is printed on acid free paper.

1stBooks - rev. 9/31/01

This book was inspired by Brighid,
the Celtic Goddess of the Hearth,
and by the Whittiers;
who first haunted me in 1974
down at the old burned-out house
along the railroad tracks
south of the town where I grew up.

This book is dedicated to all those students
who inspired me as I inspired them,
together creating the spiritual landscapes
of Ross County
wherein we could dream of a better world
and work out the conundrums
of a spiritual life
in the contemporary world.

This book is also dedicated
to all those fictional characters
– like Cornelius Whitsel –
who have inspired my students and I
over the course of the last 20 years
and who have made the Yule
so vivid a reality
that we cannot approach the Winter Solstice
without dreaming again
of its magick, depth and mystic runes.

"Haunted at the girth of the open road
I summoned my spirits_
Yet who should come but the Elves
with their Fables of long gone Seasons of Yule!

Shaking boughs of Mistletoe at me,
these Elves let go their Reason;
the Fables deducting from their mystic syntax_
and I am transported to Another Country!"

- Cornelius Whitsel
Earthen Meditations (1986)

Table of the Season

To the Reader (About the "Keltelven Traditions")

The ancient Celts – and many of their modern descendants can also claim this – were a vividly imaginative people who could just as well converse with persons on the other side of the veil that separates *this world* from the *next world* as chat with their neighbors across a fence or sit around a hearth with friends and neighbors who came together to tell stories, play music, dance and relax after a hard day's work. They received inspiration from their belief in other worlds and from their interaction with heroes, saints and ancestors living in the Otherworld, where all souls go once they die.

The spiritual praxis presented in this book is deeply Celtic in that it grew out of years of 'interaction' with spirit-guides and mentors living in an imagined otherworld called Ross County; a poetic geography that was created as I told stories and engaged in spiritual instructions with students over the last 20 years or so. Within that "other world" – fictional, but also a "poetic nemeton of inspiration" if you want it to be – are Pagan characters initiated into what they call "The Keltelven Traditions."

The "Keltelven Traditions" are a fictional construct based on years of research into Celtic and other Pagan European traditions. They were created in response to the need to have a livable contemporary spirituality that was both grounded in the past and open-ended enough to allow its practitioners to continue to grow and change as they live their lives in the 21st century. As the text of The Fires of Yule has come to its present form, this fictional "tradition" has become a template and touchstone for my students and various friends who have sought to enrich their experience of the Winter Solstice Season.

The book you are about to read is written in the kind of Celtic mindset that permits of converse with people in "other worlds" (in this case a 'fictional' landscape) and thus when you read about "the Keltelven Traditions," remember that what you are reading about is a *fictional* construct. Only my students and I live a "Keltelven" life on *this side* of the veil between the worlds. All talk of Keltelven Druids and Bards, practitioners, books and communities in The Fires of Yule refers to *characters in Ross County* and *the fictional history and background* of these characters.

As you read <u>The Fires of Yule</u>, I invite you to imagine that Ross County exists! Listen to what is said in these pages about the Keltelven Traditions and imagine what it must be like for people to live out of the resources of this "ancient Pagan paradigm." By allowing yourself to believe in the imaginative reality of Ross County and by imagining the practitioners there who are initiated into this Tradition, you will be able to enter more deeply into the aura of the Fires of Yule that are always glowing in the Hearth of Wisdom at Alban Arthuan (the Winter Solstice). Those who dismiss the fictional dimensions of this book, saying, "Ross County isn't real!" or even "Fantasy isn't 'real,'" – will not get as far as those who allow that "To be Celtic you must imagine many worlds." So be it. I welcome you to Ross County!

Prelude to the Fires of Yule

"The Fires of Yule burn in the hearth of every human heart and in the eyes of children who certainly know what it means to await the arrival of Old Saint Nick as their patron saint and friend." (8)

- Egbert Whittier
The <u>Thirteen Dayes of Yule</u> (1800)*

As the Autumn passes and days grow shorter – as the last of the leaves turn from orange, red and yellow to brown and then fall from the trees – the spiritual imagination begins to turn toward the magic and mystery of Winter. For those of us who are practitioners of the Keltelven Traditions, this means anticipating kindling the *Fires of Yule* once again, awakening the magick of the Winter Solstice Season.

Keltelven spirituality is a way of life that draws its poetic depth and power from two ancient roots: the mysticism of the Celts – both Pagan and those who were earthy mystics of Christ – and the lore of the Elvenfolk. These two traditions came together at the beginning of the Middle Ages, as Mediterranean Christianity became the officially recognized religious power in Britain. Those who desired to maintain their olden faiths were driven underground. Beginning in the late 7th century – so our Keltelven Bards say – the Celts who wanted to preserve their traditional mysticism forged bonds with the surviving stone age peoples – the Elves – and

---

* *A Note on Quotes*: All of the quotes in this book are drawn from sources attributed to characters living in the fictional landscape that I call Ross County. This landscape has come into existence as I have taught Celtic spirituality –both Pagan and Christian – over the last 18 years, and as I have worked out the mystical logic of the Thirteen Dayes of Yule. The stories I tell about characters in Ross County complement the practical instructions.

Many of the characters living in Ross County are writers, poets, actors and musicians as well as mystics, magicians and contemplatives. These characters have written various 'books,' a list of which may be found in the Bibliography at the end of <u>The Fires of Yule</u>. As I refer to these books in spiritual instructions, it seems only right that I quote my fictional characters in the books that I myself write.

created a "New Pagan Path." This new praxis survived as an underground spiritual movement in Mediaeval Europe and persisted into the Modern Age.[1]

Keltelvens today – like most Pagans – consider the Earth to be the center of their spirituality. The pattern of the Earth's seasons is depicted as a Wheel with eight spokes. These spokes represent the primary festivals of the year. They include four druidic festivals (31 October-1 November, 2 February, 30 April-1 May and 2 August) plus the Equinoxes and Solstices.[2] By celebrating these festivals we stay in touch with the processes of life—death—rebirth that are constantly unfolding around us in the Earth.

Keltelvens understand the Earth and the entire Cosmos as infused with Mystery. The world itself is mysterious, full of things that cannot and will never be fully understood, despite the advances of science and philosophy, literature and religion. "Mystery," however, refers to more than just what human beings fail to understand. "Mystery" is that aura of Presence that has been called by numerous sacred names – the names of gods and goddesses, for instance – in the religious traditions of the world. The reality of Mystery, however, has never been fully grasped by any name in any theology or philosophy. Christians call it "God" while some Pagans call it "Goddess." Keltelvens – though we use any number of poetic names to refer to this reality – often call the Presence of Mystery "Spirit."

A Keltelven practitioner lives life "in the Earth *and* Spirit." Ours is a poetic path in which we dedicate ourselves to the pursuit of Truth, Wisdom and Beauty. We live life according to the three principle values of Honesty, Compassion and Creativity. We respect science as a way to knowledge as much as we esteem magick as a way to "get things done." We look to the ancient Celtic and Elven traditions as wellsprings out of which to source our lives, though we're not trying to 'reconstruct' an ancient way of life. Our spirituality is intended to help us to live life in our own contemporary world.

By celebrating the various spokes of the earthen year we acknowledge the mysterious presence called "Spirit" in all things. Though we celebrate the beginning of each New Year on 1 November, beginning at dawn on the day after Samhain (i.e., Halloween), the Winter Solstice (21 December) is our principal annual festival. Winter's Solstice is that point in the Wheel of the Year when we experience the death and rebirth of life in the Earth. As the Sun "dies and is born again" so we too can experience psychic and spiritual renewal.

Winter's Solstice is the vortex of personal transformation and communal inspiration. It's the most profound time of ending and new beginning in the round of the year. Keltelvens call the Winter Solstice Season "**Yule**." To the extent that it's related to the Sun, Yule is a time for lighting fires. Fire symbolizes the presence of solar power on Earth. **Fire** is also a primary icon of the Presence of Mystery during the dark days of December. To light a fire – whether a candle-flame, a hearth-fire or a bonfire – is to become aware of Spirit; active and moving in and through everything that exists.

Fire is one of the four primary forms of Spirit manifest (the other three being Water, Earth and Air). Fire gives light, warmth and energy to those near it. Though fire can lead to destruction if it's not well tended, it is primarily a symbol of life. To light a fire is to invoke the presence of Spirit, which is to be *awakened* to the way in which everything is infused and pervaded by Mystery. **The Fires of Yule** are icons of the Spirit in the midst of Earth. As the Sun's power decreases during December we light candles, decorative electric lights and fires in the hearth, all in the hope that when the Sun's power is regenerated – during the dark passage of Solstice Night; called **Alban Arthuan** – we will also experience a psychic and spiritual rebirth.

The Keltelven season of Yule is patterned around thirteen sacred days (13 – 25 December). The season is initiated by a celebration on the 6th of December (the Feast of Nicholas and the Elves), a week before the first of the Thirteen Dayes. This is the day when we finally start taking out the trimmings and making preparations for Yule gatherings. The celebration of Yule then gets under way on the 13th of December (Rowan Day), climaxing on the night of 21 December – the longest night – when the process of the Sun's diminishing power reverses itself.

After the Solstice, the spiritual renewal, transfiguration or psychic resourcement that we've been anticipating and striving for during the preceding weeks generally comes to fruition on or about the 25th of December, which is called "**Glastonbury Thorn Day**" in our traditions. The journey through the Winter Solstice is construed by Keltelven practitioners as an imaged journey *to* the Glastonbury Thorn, which is an actual old tree located on Glastonbury Tor; an ancient hill in County Somerset, England.

Keltelvens see Glastonbury Tor as an iconic destination of the Yuletide journey. We journey to the Tor in our imaginative keeping of the

Thirteen Dayes of Yule, and our arrival there is celebrated during the night of 24 December, which we call **Matrum Noctem**; i.e., "The Night of the Mother." Pathing to Glastonbury Tor in our spiritual imagination, we seek to find the Thorn Tree. The Stag-God Cernunnos[3] leads us through the star-lit darkness to the Tor and then to the Thorn. There we find the mouth of a mysterious cave. We enter the cave, wherein we find the "nativity" of our own rebirth. It is in this cave – the tunnels of which take us deep into Glastonbury Tor – that we hope to experience a degree of rebirth, rejuvenation or transfiguration each year as we finish our Yuletide journey.

As such, the journey of the Thirteen Dayes of Yule is not just a sentimental remembrance of some ancient event or story. It is a journey into transformative possibilities. Each year as we pilgrim through the Thirteen Dayes, celebrating the Solstice and then Glastonbury Thorn Day, we are hoping to experience a change in our lives. We go on the journey desiring to glimpse the light of illumination and taste the cranberries of wisdom. We are seeking to be reborn in the Spirit, and as such to become more "divine" in our human dwelling.

This rebirth is the actual Pagan mystery encoded in the stories of the birth of Jesus of Nazareth, who is the Christ of the Christians. As such, Keltelvens have always looked to Jesus of Nazareth in earthen ways as an icon of what the Season of Yule is all about. Though not "Christian" in any ordinary sense, the Keltelven Traditions recognize the mythic and psychic reality represented by the birth of Jesus of Nazareth 2,000 years ago. The Thirteen Dayes of Yule may therefore be construed in part as a "journey to the Nativity," where the child-god Jesus was born.

With the Nativity – located in the cave on Glastonbury Tor – as our objective, participants may think of themselves as following either the path of Joseph and Mary (Jesus' parents) or that of the three Astrologers (the "wise men" immortalized in the carol, "We Three Kings") through the Yule. As Jesus the Carpenter-God is imagined being born in the manger once again each year on 25 December, so we who are gathered to the Fires of Yule can experience psychic and spiritual regeneration.

Keltelvens understand Jesus of Nazareth as one of the *many* incarnations of Wisdom in the world. Because his birth is celebrated at the tides of Winter's Solstice it is appropriate – as people who accept wisdom wherever we find it – to honor Jesus of Nazareth as a Keltelven Lord of the Yule.

By introducing Jesus of Nazareth in these pages under the title of "the Carpenter God" or as "Christ our Stag," we do not mean to import any of the abusive legacies of institutionalized Christianity into our Pagan celebrations! We are *well aware* that the history of Christianity has all too often been a history of atrocities, oppression and hatred. However, despite the ways in which Christians have departed from wise living, there is great wisdom in Christ-centered mysticism and contemplative spirituality, and Jesus of Nazareth himself can be understood as an incarnate Wisdom-God.

By reclaiming Jesus as one of the gods of the Earth, Keltelvens seek to learn as much as possible about wise living from this legend. As people of Earth & Spirit we should be able to see that Jesus of Nazareth – as much as Cernunnos, Merlin, Bran[4] or the Irish hero Cú Chulainn[5] – can awaken us to our truest selves in the midst of life-as-it-is. The Keltelven spirituality of Yule therefore affirms the wisdom of Jesus of Nazareth by re-incorporating his tale into a Pagan framework.

The present book brings together all of the principal symbols, customs, rituals and stories necessary for a Keltelven kindling of the Fires of Yule. The Introduction will explore the nature of the Winter Solstice. Part I will outline the runes of the Keltelven Season of Yule. Part II will delineate some of the preparations necessary to fully enjoy the Fires of Yule. Part III will then lead you on a poetic and spiritual journey through the days of the Season to the Winter Solstice.

It is hoped that by reading this book you will find ways to resource your own experience of the December 'Holiday Season' and make of it more than the rat-race it has often become. Whether you are Christian, Secular or Pagan, by offering you our sacred kindling for the Fires of Yule, we hope that you will be empowered to engage in a more mystical journey through Winter Solstice Season! So mote it be. Blessed be and *Bon Voyage*! Amen.

- Montague Whitsel

An Introduction to the Winter Solstice Season

"From times before the Mists of Time, people have tracked their spiritual lives through the Wheel of the Year. The Solstices and Equinoxes were the four primary mystical knobs of the year's horizons, between which were the spikes marking the celebrations of the Cross-Quarter Days. ... The Winter Solstice, in ancient Anglo-Saxon spirituality, was the time when the Sun was reborn each year, beginning its spiritual odyssey, once more, through the Wheel of the Year." (89)

- Judas Sackneuseum
The Celtic Crossroads (1985)

"The Pagan Celts were witchy about *every* season they celebrated in the Earth. Everything came down to contact with spirits, questions of what magick and healing were possible, and whether or not there was a way to collapse the veils between the worlds long enough to taste of the wisdom that could open to you an enlightened state of consciousness." (16)

- Cornelius Whitsel
The Keltelven Traditions (1982)

All sacred seasons require doors and paths – ways in, through and out – by which people can experience their pilgrimage through mortal and earthen time. Symbols, myths, metaphors, customary practices (like decorating or singing carols) and even particular memories that connect us to the spirit of a season, may function as the doors and paths we need to find as we seek to participate once again in a sacred season.

Entering into sacred space and experiencing sacred time through these portals does not lead us out of the ordinary world in some naïve or escapist way. Rather, we *add* something to our experience of the world and venture more deeply into our daily experiences and responsibilities. We become aware of Mystery as present in the ordinary day to day dimensions of life. By experiencing sacred seasons, we find ourselves inspired to intuit ideals worth striving to enact in everyday life.

The end result of entering into sacred time is that our everyday lives can be gradually transfigured. The celebration of sacred seasons reminds us that life is more than our daily rounds of work, play and sleep. Sacred festivals awaken the human spirit to the way things *should* and perhaps *could* be. Their observance hints at how we might transform daily life into an image of the intuited ideal. A sacred season is a rune of life's mystery and a touchstone of human becoming.

The Winter Solstice is the primary touchstone that has given rise to the celebrations and myths of Yule, the legends of Christmas and many other observances in both the religious and the secular imagination of human beings around the globe.[6] By reflecting on the meaning of Winter's Solstice we can begin to recover the depth of spiritual meaning encoded in the Keltelven "Thirteen Dayes of Yule."

There are two Solstices in the annual turning of the Wheel of the Year, a Summer Solstice and a Winter Solstice. These natural turnstiles of earthen time arise as a result of the orbiting of the Earth – which is tilted on its axis – around the Sun. During December, those living in the Northern Hemisphere experience the Sun's energy diminishing. The days get shorter and the nights grow longer and colder during December because, as we swing around the Sun in our annual orbit, the top of the Earth tilts away from the Sun. The direct beams of the Sun's light strike our planet south of its equator, thus allowing the Northern Hemisphere to cool off and grow darker.

On 21 December the Southern Hemisphere is experiencing summer while the North – above the Tropics, at least – is entering into the Winter Season. Then, as the Earth continues in it's flight around the Sun, it leans more into the path of the Sun's direct beams and, by 21 June, the Northern Hemisphere is having it's Summer, while those living south of the equator are traveling into Winter.

All ancient peoples living north and south of the tropics experienced this astronomical ebbing & waning of the Sun's natural powers as a spiritual event. People in many northerly societies lit fires during December as a symbolic way to invite a rekindling of the Sun's power. They sought to aid the Sun's return to its former eminence through rituals and prayer. They performed magical rites that helped them participate in the mysticism of the Sun's death and rebirth during the year's longest night.

Throughout the Iron Age the Winter Solstice was celebrated across northern Europe and particularly in the British Isles as a great Festival of Light. The Celts were at their height in the Iron Age, and their Druids called the night of the Winter Solstice "**Alban Arthuan**." Though "**Yule**" is an Anglo-Saxon word for Winter's Solstice, it was later picked up by early Keltelvens in England and used to describe the days leading up to the Solstice.

The Season leading up to the Winter Solstice has long been a deeply mysterious time for those who live life in tune with Earth and Spirit. It can be approached as a doorway of death & rebirth, magick & transformation. The Winter Solstice is the vortex of a time devoted to spiritual awakening. Its symbols are touchstones of life's deeper and most pervasive meanings. The pivotal guiding metaphor of the Winter Solstice is the rebirth of the Sun. Out of this mythic event come all of the other mystical and poetic Yuletide associations.

As the solar year winds down toward the Solstice in December, the arc of the Sun's path across the sky declines toward the southern horizon (in the northern hemisphere) between 22 June and 21 December. After the Solstice, its arc begins to incline again, away from the horizon. The Sun then gains in strength and brightness from 22 December to 21 June. Pagans have often interpreted this celestial pageant as a sign of the Sun's death and rebirth between dusk on 21 December and dawn the next day.

Myths of the Winter Solstice encode symbols that enable the mystic, poet, magician and saint to path his or her way through the days and nights leading up to the death & rebirth of the Sun. Through these myths we may prepare our selves and our huts of dwelling for whatever might transpire during the Solstice Season. Rituals help celebrants map out their own path toward a symbolic death, through which they experience a hoped-for psychic and spiritual transformation.

Myths record and 'explain' the various kinds of experiences that people have had of Winter's Solstice down across the centuries. The tales we tell from year to year remind us of how the darkening of the world can be experienced in the context of earthen dwelling, opening both heart and mind to the Presence of Divine Mystery in the Cosmos and in Human Worlds.

We can experience this annual solar increase & decrease personally in our own lives. If we remain conscious of the patterns of solar ascent and descent in Nature as we path through our lives, we will find that we can move from a personal & communal experience of rebirth at Winter's Solstice to the henges of spiritual enlightenment at Summer's Solstice. Then, after High Summer, we will experience ourselves descending again into the re-creative darknesses of Autumn, back toward Yule.

During the mysterious passage of Yule it's often possible to find some new direction for our lives and re-orient our selves toward mystical goals. Most of the changes we experience as we celebrate Yule year after year are likely to be on a small scale, but major transformations can and have occurred as people go pathing a pilgrim way through the Yuletide. Keltelvens think of Yule as a time to forsake vices, cease neglecting one's destiny and abandon the sloth that arises through taking life for granted.

As the Sun descends and dies, so does the natural world. Leaves and plants wither, earth cools and Winter gains a foothold. But, just when all seems lost, the Sun is renewed, and life itself is given another lease. Another annual cycle of planting, growth, harvest and death is promised, foretold in the lengthening of the days after Winter's Solstice. Within a few weeks after Alban Arthuan, the Sun's warmth can be felt once again, rekindling hope's fires.

As the solar year ends, so our own life in this world can be experienced coming to a symbolic end. This experience frees us from the various shackles we've forged – for ourselves and others – during the course of the year. It liberates us as mortals from the prisons we've thrown ourselves into via the mistakes we've made, and via the conundrums of interpersonal misunderstandings.

Experiencing a psychic renewal at the tides of Winter's Solstice enables us to begin leaving our shattered intentions and ideals behind, more and more each year. We may now make a new start, liberated from sorrows, disappointments and frustrations. The rites and symbols of Yule are the runes through which this annual birth, growth, consummation and death may be realized, in both the individual participant and in the community. The Fires of Yule illumine the Way to the Sun's rebirth.

Winter's Solstice is a time of new beginnings when we can take our lives in hand, in spiritual terms, striving to put wrongs to right, seek out new paths, and make resolutions for the next solar year. The making of **resolutions** – which has come to be associated with New Year's Day in modern culture – would be more effective if re-linked with spiritual awakening in the tides of Winter's Solstice. Resolutions evolve out of our experience of dying at dusk on Solstice Night and then awakening – renewed and refreshed – in the increasing light after 22 December.

It is interesting to note that **the birth of saviors and gods of light** have been celebrated in many cultures on or around the Winter Solstice.[7] The Egyptian god Horus and the Celtic god Hesus were both born during the longest night of the year, and both their mothers were virgins. The Persian savior Zarathustra's birth happened as the Sun was being reborn on the morning after Wintertide. As his birth cord was being cut, those present with his mother heard angels prophesying. Angels were present at the birth of both Mohammed and Confucius, and there is a folk-story of Buddha being born out of his mother's right side. This was not exactly a *virgin* birth, but miraculous nonetheless. All of these saviors, gods and prophets are connected in one way or another with the light of solar forces. Adhering to their teachings brings a person to doors of personal transformation and enlightenment.

Early Christians came to identify the birth of **Jesus of Nazareth** with the Winter Solstice. They believed that, as the Sun is reborn on the day after the Solstice, so the Son of Wisdom is born in the flesh. This is an old, old story! Its basic elements and outline are much older than Christianity. Christians adopted the old Pagan theme of the death & rebirth of the Sun as a metaphor in which the birth of Jesus could readily be expressed. Jesus of Nazareth – who becomes the "Christ" [i.e., an anointed teacher of Wisdom, in Keltelven terms] to anyone who believes in him – was born of a virgin. Angels attended his birth, and he is identified with the Sun and the Son of Righteousness and is the "Light of the World." As such, his story is similar to all the other saviors and gods of light who are said to have been born at Winter's Solsticetide.

The connection between Christmas and the Winter Solstice becomes even more apparent when we realize that these two festivals used to be celebrated on the same day. Though Christmas now falls four days after Alban Arthuan, this has only been the case since the calendar was adjusted in the 18th century to make allowance for astronomical changes that had taken place since the calendar had previously been set. Until that time, 25 December had been the date of the Winter Solstice. Thus, when the early Christians chose a date for their savior's birth, they chose the Solstice. If we appreciate this, we will better comprehend the Pagan significance of Christmas for life lived in the Earth & Spirit.

Mid-December is thus one of the most positively magical times of the year. Things are possible during December's darkening days that are not even dreamt of at other spokes of the Wheel of the Year. We should use this magic as a vehicle for deepening our awareness of the world around us and preparing our souls for the ongoing pilgrimage of our lives. A seeker of Wisdom in the thrall of Winter's Solstice should consider their celebrations as a spiritual pilgrimage or even a quest, during which, through the disciplined use of the spiritual imagination, he or she may encounter one's own truest self along the way and in communion with Spirit.

How long has it been since you really paid attention to the shortening of the days and lengthening nights of December? If you need to reconnect with this natural event, get yourself a calendar or an almanac with the times of Sunrise and Sunset listed for each day. Over the weeks leading up to Winter's Solstice note the times of dawn and dusk. Mark 21 December on your appointment book. Reflect on the impact of this growing darkness on your own consciousness, moods and experiences.

One way of describing the journey to Winter's Solstice is to see it as something like preparing to go to sleep. We are entering the darkness of the longest nights of the year. Most people sleep at night and many people do, in fact, tend to sleep more during December than at other times of the year, due to light deprivation. In mythic terms, this sense that we are 'falling asleep' or 'getting tired' as 21 December approaches facilitates the kind of 'rest' that results in spiritual renewal and the reinvigoration of our natural energies. We must adjust to the lack of light by shifting our energies and slowing down a bit.

If we're too busy during December, we're going to feel it more than at other times of the year. One of the best ways to approach Winter's Solstice is to begin cutting anything out of the daily appointment book that doesn't *have* to be there. How many things do we really *need* to be doing? Are there meetings or tasks that we've agreed to, simply because we're used to chasing our tails and never sitting down to rest? When it comes to shopping for Solstice gifts and giving or attending parties, what counts as true generosity and hospitality? What really *needs* to be given?

Even after we've weeded out our daily schedules, however, there will still be plenty to do. Therefore, we should begin planning for Yule and the Solstice early. Start making a list of Solstice gifts in October or early November. You don't have to be 'in the mood' for the Fires of Yule to imagine what this or that person might need or want to receive. Then, as the days get shorter, you'll be better able to handle what needs done in a more solemn manner.

Approaching the Winter Solstice, though, is not simply a process of arranging, making preparations and then carrying them out. It's a time when we must light the Fires of Yule intentionally and await the manifestation of Wisdom – in the person of **Nicholas and the Elves**, in the Pagan advent of **Jesus** or as the indwelling of **Tailtiu**, the Mother Goddess of the Winter Solstice – near the Hearth.

The ancient Celts and the Elvenfolk lived in pastoral-agrarian communities long before the advent of television, malls, mass forms of entertainment and home-theater, and thus spent the Winter Solstice Season near the hearth in the gathering darkness, telling stories, praying, casting spells of good will, and awaiting the advent of Mystery in their lives. We can imagine that they were often snowed-in and unable to leave the house. They entertained themselves with sacred tales and rituals that led them through the descent into renewal on the morning after Alban Arthuan. Our traditions relate that the earliest Keltelvens often secluded themselves in communal houses – called **ráths** – in which they nurtured their own rebirth. This seclusion grew ever more intense as Solstice Night drew near. They would dream dreams and see visions, imagining *how life could be*.

Today, as we enter into the aura of the light cast by the Fires of Yule, we should seek to leave the rat race of the world behind – at least for a few hours each day – and dwell in the gathering darkness, illuminated by the Fires of Yule. The calendar presented in this book is intended to help you do this, in the hopes that – through your own divinations by the hearth and journeys in the Fires of Yule – you will experience an authentic rebirth in the days following 21 December. Nema. So mote it be. Amen.

"Awaken the Fires of Yule in your heart; Invoke the Christmas Spirit."
- The Yuletide Grimoire (1898)

I. The Keltelven Season of Yule

"Deep in the forests of Europe, along mysterious footpaths and hidden within the crags of mountains, the ancient traditions of the Pagans mingled. Druids and sibyls, shamans and priestesses of the Goddess all shared their traditions of native wisdom. There, in these secret convocations, the mediaeval Keltelven traditions evolved. Much of the contemporary keeping of Yule was forged during those dark times, when the wise ones of various ancient traditions had to find safety far from the main streets of early mediaeval society." (34)

- Cornelius Whitsel
The Keltelven Traditions (1982)

If we're going to kindle the Fires of Yule today, we're going to need a map that will enable us to unpack the mystery of this poetic time of the year, linking up all of the rich symbols and tales that have come to be associated with Winter's Solstice. Our traditions say that Keltelvens have celebrated the Winter Solstice – as (by no means the only) heirs of European Paganism – for over a thousand years. The present section offers an overview that should give you some idea of the flux and flow of Yule. Once you get the 'big picture' you will better see how to light the Fires of Yule for yourself and then journey in their light toward Pagan turnstiles of personal renewal and transfiguration.

The Keltelven pattern for celebrating the Season of the Winter Solstice has evolved over the last few centuries into a month-long praxis for seeking Earthen Wisdom in the embers and stars that are always glowing in the hearth of Yuletide. The liminal horizons of this hallowed season are defined by two sacred days: one to demarcate our entrance into the season (6 December) and another to mark our exit from sacred time (6 January). Between these two horizons the "Thirteen Dayes of Yule" are celebrated near the hearth of our gatherings and in the heart of every participant.

The Feast of Nicholas (6 December) is the day when the magical doors between the ordinary realm of everyday life and the extraordinary realm of Yule swing wide open. On the eve of this feast Nicholas – a mystic of Jesus of Nazareth now living in the Otherworld with Pagan Elves and Reindeer – makes a mysterious worldwide journey, visiting every hearth where people are hoping to light the Fires of Yule. He encourages us all to bless children, befriend the ostracized and provide for the needs of the poor of the world. On this day the Elves of the Earth also come out to play!

Epiphany (6 January) – a month later – is the day when we hope that our annual pilgrimage through the tines of Winter's Solstice will come to fruition. Coming twelve days after Glastonbury Thorn Day (25 December), Epiphany symbolizes consummation, completion and wholeness. On this day our spiritual quest for the embers of Wisdom in the Yule Fires comes to fruition. Our month-long journey is completed. We arrive at a place where we will hopefully – from one year to the next – begin to feel more 'whole' as incarnate souls in the Earth & Spirit. Thus it's a day when we arrive at the place where spiritual maturity may begin to become manifest.

The 6th of January is also referred to in Keltelven mysticism as **"The Hinterlands,"** for it's the day when the Elves of Nicholas leave the hearths of our homes and go back to their own abode. Once upon a time the Elvenfolk lived in the actual wildwoods of Europe and Britain, though now they dwell in imaginary Strangewoods in the Otherworld. These lands exist on the borders between *this world* and the next, just beyond the Sídhe,[8] and are called the "Hinterlands." Familiars, spirit-guides and ghosts who have visited our hearth during the preceding month now depart to their place in otherworldly realms as well.

These two feast days – 6 December and 6 January – encompass the magical power and spiritual potency of the **Thirteen Dayes of Yule** (13 – 25 December) in conspicuous temporal horizons. After the 6th of December the spiritual mood of Yule builds up for a week. Then, on 13 December – called Rowan Day – those intending to celebrate the season traditionally gather for a small meal. At this table participants dedicate themselves as pilgrims of Winter's Solstice devoted to discovering whatever the Spirit may have to teach them before Glastonbury Thorn Day (25 December).

Celebrants then observe each of the Thirteen Dayes, participating in traditional rituals, meditations and activities. Each day has its tree-name and also a name that describes the activities characteristic of it. (e.g., Rowan Day – 13 December – is also "Gathering Day.") Our journey reaches its initial consummation during **Solstice Night**. At dusk on 21 December all of our Yuletide devotions approach their consummation, drawing us into the aura of the Mystic Fires of the Sun's Rebirth. After this night we repose – basking in the light of the Fires of Yule – until the eve of the 25th of December.

The Season then rises to another crescendo in the mysteries of **Matrum Noctem** ("Night of the Mother"), which begins at dusk on the 24th and continues until dawn on Glastonbury Thorn Day. The night focuses on the ancient mystical pattern of Birth-and-Rebirth, during which participants may meditate on any appropriate manifestation of the Great Goddess as the one who births the entire universe and everything in it. The Earth Goddess is often known as "**Tailtiu**" in Keltelven Traditions, while another goddess – **Brighid** – is "Benefactress of Humanity," "Lady of the Hearth" and the great healer. She kindles hearthfire and keeps all spirits of dread and disdain at bay during the holy tides of Yule.

The journey through the Solstice is **a Journey to Glastonbury Tor**. Along this path Matrum Noctem is a time to enter into the womb of Mother Earth (at dusk on the 24th of December) and then undergo a ritual process of rebirth that will last through the night, coming to completion at dusk on the 25th of December.

Over the centuries Keltelvens have also evolved an earthy interpretation of the mystery of the Virgin Mary, the mother of Jesus of Nazareth, seeing in her journey to Bethlehem a paradigm of psychic renewal. Mary can be numbered along with the many other "virgin mothers" in Celtic mythology who give birth to god-like heroes. She is in the same company as Ceridwen (the mother of the Irish Bard Taleisin), the unnamed mother of Tuan mac Carill (who lived through the entire prehistory of Ireland in his former lives), and numerous other women who gave birth to god-like heroes without being impregnated in the 'usual' way. By meditating on Mary's journey we approach our own rebirth and spiritual awakening in symbolic terms linked with the mythic birth of Jesus of Nazareth. We see Jesus as a divinely conceived Son of Wisdom. Following Mary and Joseph to Bethlehem, where Jesus was born of the mythos, the Winter Solstice Season becomes **a journey to the Nativity**. The word "**Nativity**" intimates a primeval place of birth and rebirth. It names a particular "crosstroads" where Divine Mystery enters the world in human form. Though Christians have often shied away from the implications of their own celebration of Christmas because of its Pagan undertones, it's these dimensions that we as Pagans should be able to re-appropriate with ease and enjoy.

The spiritual trek we undertake from the Feast of Nicholas to Matrum Noctem is often thought of in Keltelven mysticism as *"climbing Glastonbury Tor."* The 25th of December is known in our traditions as **"Glastonbury Thorn Day,"** being named after a legendary tree that Joseph of Arimathea – an early Jewish mystic of Jesus of Nazareth – planted on Glastonbury Tor after a long pilgrimage to Britain.

Glastonbury Tor is an actual place. It is located in SW England and has been a site of Pagan and Christian pilgrimage for many centuries. The "Tor" is a sculpted hill of rock, riddled with caves. It has an ancient maze-like path etched into its slopes, which leads devout pilgrims from the flat ground around the Tor up to the top. There, an ancient hermit's oratory stands. The Tor is thought to be the burial place of Arthur & Guinevere, Joseph of Arimathea, and several other Celtic heroes and heroines. The Tor is also associated with the mystical isle of Avalon; the "Land of Apples" and a place of psychic rebirth. Pagan Celts once walked the maze-like path up and down the Tor at the sacred turnstiles of the year. Keltelven lore remembers that later Celtic saints of Christ also climbed the Tor on the Eve of Christmas in order to keep their vigil of the birth of Jesus and await the rising of the Sun on Christmas morning. As such, the Tor is an ancient crosstroads where Pagan and Christian mysticism intersect.

The **Glastonbury Thorn** is a renowned tree growing near the Tor. **Joseph of Arimathea** – who is said to have brought the Grail to Britain – is also credited with planting the original Thorn, which blooms at Christmas and has long been imaged as a tree of either the Hawthorn or Blackthorn variety. All Glastonbury Thorns in England today are descended from this original tree.

The Glastonbury Thorn may be tied into the vast network of Celtic tree-lore and is an instance of a Bilé (i.e., the "World Tree"). As such it connects the Earth beneath our feet with the Heavens above and functions as a doorway through which we may cross back and forth between *this world* and the Otherworld.[9] Those who visit the Thorn may commune

4

with heroes and ghosts, gods and goddesses, saints and martyrs. As such, it is a worthwhile mythic destination for those who go pilgriming through the Yule. Keltelvens often treat the journey of the Thirteen Dayes of Yule as a pilgrimage to the Tor, where they hope to find the Glastonbury Thorn on the eve of 25 December.

We then celebrate our progress through the Yule at a meal called **the Feast of Commonweal** on the 25th of December during which we re-dedicate ourselves to the spiritual ideals of equality, justice and peace for all the sentient beings of the world, animals and humans alike. This feast is usually held toward dusk in the afternoon. After the feast, a period of extended repose is indulged, during which we bask in the light of the Fires of Yule, allowing whatever spiritual benefit we've gleaned from the Season to sink in and imbue our lives with a renewed spiritual ardor and vitality.

The 25th of December marks a shift in the sacred journey; at this point we cease climbing Glastonbury Tor and begin our descent back into ordinary timespace. This descent will proceed slowly and last until Epiphany – 6 January – when the Elves go back to the Hinterlands.

"To climb the Mountain of Yule
with Nicholas at our side
is the Mortal Rune of Solstice Mystery
burning in our hearts
for the Coming of the Spirit of Life.
Strange are the patterns
Of the Stag's hoof-prints in the soul's snow."

- The Yuletide Grimoire (1898)

During the evening of Glastonbury Thorn Day, the olde god Cernunnos pays celebrants of the Yule a visit as an icon of the benefits we've reaped during this particular trek through the Solstice. Cernunnos is the Celtic Lord of Wild Animals and is the harbinger of bounty, wealth and prosperity. By showing up after we've come down from Glastonbury Tor, he symbolizes spiritual bounty in our midst. Cernunnos is called "The Gifting Stag" in the afterglow of the Fires of Yule and is believed to stay near the hearth through the 26th of December. Children may first glimpse him looking in at windows. Adults may hear him scratching the walls of the house with his antlers. The antlers of the Great Stag symbolize fertility, power and wisdom.

For those who honor Jesus as a Wisdom-Teacher, Cernunnos is "Christ our Stag." Understood in Pagan runes, Jesus represents the fruition of our spiritual desire for Wisdom, Truth and Beauty. He is the teacher and son of Wisdom, and his horns are full of enlightening insight.

Decorations usually begin to be taken down soon after 26 December, and – so our traditions say – they must all be stored away and out of sight by dusk on 6 January. If they're not, prank-playing Elves and other spirits may come around to tease and trouble us. Also – so our Druids say – benefits we have reaped during the Yule may begin to dissipate if we attempt to perpetuate the Winter Solstice Season beyond the tines established for it by the runing of sacred earth-time. After this day, life returns more or less to normal, though we are hopefully changed somewhat by each year's pilgrimage to the Nativity.

Before you begin your own journey through the Solstice to Glastonbury Tor and the Nativity of rebirth, meditate on this pilgrim's schedule. There are runes hidden in this pattern that – when touched by inspired understanding – reveal deep spiritual treasures. The overall pattern of the Season is called "**the Holy Calends of Yule.**" A 'calend' is a special date on a calendar. Learn these calends, and meditate on what they entail:

The Holy Calends of Yule
Feast of Saint Nicholas (6 December)
First Day of Yule (13 December)
The Winter Solstice (21 December)

The Triad of Glastonbury Tor:

I. Matrum Noctem (24 December)
II. The Feast of the Thorn (25 December)
III. Gifting of the Stag (26 December)
The Hinterlands (6 January)

Reflect on what each of these calends might mean in the context of the whole Season of Winter's Solstice. You will then learn their *deep meaning* by celebrating the Season as a kindler of the Fires of Yule. To acquaint yourself ahead of time with the basic pattern will help facilitate the process. You might begin to meditate on these calends by marking them on a calendar or in your appointment book. Then, learning about each of the Thirteen Dayes will flesh out this basic pattern.

The primary experiences you will have of the Winter Solstice from year to year will transpire in the context of the "Thirteen Dayes." You should learn the names of these days and become familiar with their progression. The Thirteen Dayes are at the heart of the Season of the Winter Solstice, and each day is named for a particular tree associated with the Yule as well as given a "common" name:

Day 1 – 13 December – Rowan Day – Gathering Day
Day 2 – 14 December – Cedar Day – Lighting Day
Day 3 – 15 December – Balsam Fir Day – Arts & Craefts Day
Day 4 – 16 December – Hemlock Day – Storytelling Day
Day 5 – 17 December – Ivy Day – Mother of Hearth Day
Day 6 – 18 December – Frankincense Day – Vision and Quest Day
Day 7 – 19 December – Mistletoe Day – A Day in the Quiet
Day 8 – 20 December -- Holly Day – Day of Hunting Fire

Day 9 – 21 December – Alban Arthuan – Winter Solstice

Day 10 – 22 December – Yew Day – Spirits of the Hearth Day
Day 11 – 23 December – Silver Fir Day – Nemeton & Heath Day
Day 12 – 24 December – Bayberry Day – Hearth of the Heart Day

Matrum Noctem (Night of the Mother)

Day 13 – 25 December – Glastonbury Thorn Day – Christmas Day

As you celebrate these days – on your own journey to the Solstice and then on to the Tor of Renewal and Transformation – you will find that the names, activities and associations are not assigned at random. Though they may at first seem merely decorative, keeping the Thirteen Dayes will reveal patterns of ever-deepening spirals to you in the Deep Heart of the Presence of Mystery. They will guide you to the fountainstones of new beginnings. May Nicholas, Cernunnos, Jesus and the Elves lead you to the Fires of Wisdom. Nema. So mote it be. Amen.

II. Preparations for Entering into the Aura of the Fires of Yule

"The Hearth is the heart of a home. Dwelling near the hearth we become more ourselves; more human – and humane. The Hearth contains the Fires of Yule, in the flames of which our visions of new life and the fantasies of children both dance. Dreams of sugar-plums and a world free of hate and despair both emanate from the light of the hearth!" (39)

- Robert Werner
Wintering Upon the Way (1970)

Many of the customs connected with Yule and the Winter Solstice have been so secularized in our culture – turned into the glitz of mass-marketing and used to sell merchandise – that we scarcely even intuit the meaning they once conveyed in an authentic Pagan context. Who knows why we put up "holiday trees" anymore, or even why we give gifts on the morning of 25 December? Why do we "go home for the holidays" or put lights in the windows of our apartment or house?

So much has been lost – in the secular rat race called "Christmas" – that many people are abandoning it, and with good reason. The Winter Solstice still happens, however, as a cosmic event, and if we want to reconnect with it, we need to prepare ourselves in certain ways for the darkening of the days leading up to 21 December.

Now that you've seen an overview of the Winter Solstice Season, we must now consider a few topics that will be difficult to discuss in the actual process of our journey to Glastonbury Tor. This section will better prepare you to kindle the Fires of Yule and enjoy the spiritual depth of this mysterious season in all of its inspiring wonder.

First, we will reflect on the "Spirit of Yule" as a metaphor for the power of Mystery that is manifest during Yuletide. Next we'll explore the meaning of decorating as a spiritual act, recovering the Pagan meaning of specific decorations. Then we'll re-imagine what it means to keep the

Yule as adults, as the "Christmas Season" in secular culture has been reduced to an entertainment for children and contains very little to attract adults. As many people have no family and others find themselves alone at Winter's Solstice, we'll address how to keep the Yule in solitude. Finally, we'll explore a Pagan appreciation of the mythic birth of Jesus of Nazareth.

A. The Spirit of Yule

"Have you ever been inspired to do a kind deed or give a good gift to someone anonymously?" 'Tis the Spirit of Yule! Have you found yourself taking notice of people less fortunate than yourself? Have you wanted to do a service for someone you normally don't care much for the company of? 'Tis the Spirit of Yule! Have you heard Elves rushing around on the roof, long after all the walnuts have fallen from their boughs? 'Tis the Spirit of Yule!" (206)

- Egbert Whittier
The Thirteen Dayes of Yule (1800)

Mystery pervades the Earth and every season is infused with Spirit in a unique way. Spirit inspires the actions, stories and rituals that characterize each season of the year and leads us into the vortex where mystical insight becomes possible. Mystery presences, and then, in the particular season of the Earth in which we're dwelling, we suddenly discern the runes that will map out the Way to Wisdom.

The Spirit of Yule is a wintry manifestation of Mystery. It inspires a desire in us to be transformed. It encourages a person to seek their own truest identity and act according to their own best intentions. It inspires us to remember the wildness, innocence and openness of childhood and reflect on what we may have lost as well as what we've gained as we've grown up and taken on adult roles. The Spirit of Yule breathes whispers of rejuvenation, which communicate the possibility of transformation.

An encounter with the Spirit of Yule may reveal our lack of concern for others or a nonchalant unfamiliarity with life's more difficult challenges. We often become callous without recognizing our own hardness. We respond to being hurt, abused, mistreated and disappointed in ways that lull us into complacency. By awakening to the Spirit during the Yule this outer shell of psychic and emotional armor may become more or less translucent in the aura of the Hearth's luminous light. It may even crack our shells of defensive self-preservation open, revealing a fire still incandescent in our souls.

Only by seeking to be united with this Spirit at the doors of December do we find the stamina and heart to be pilgrims in the Yule, seeking the Fires of the Winter Solstice each year. Those who burn out in mid-season or who never really get into the mood for December's Dark Journey have not yet allowed themselves to re-link with the mysterious powers haunting the Earth at Winter's Solstice.

This particular manifestation of the Spirit is ignited in the world each year by a spark thrown on the Hearth by **Brighid**; the Keltelven Mother of the Spirit of Yule. She dwells in hearths and in the warm light of candles and even in glowing electric lights. Brighid sends out a beacon to the lost and comforts those who are learning how to recover their compassion, integrity and generosity as the Winter Solstice approaches. Brighid may inspire strange acts of kindness and hospitality as a way of kindling the Spirit of Yule in us. Giving gifts to people in need is one way in which we can seek the kindling wood of Yule. If we attribute our gift-giving to Nicholas and his Elves, rather than taking credit for it ourselves, we will make the Fires of Yule burn brighter.

The Spirit of Yule works through the natural regenerating effect of the darkness of December. As we enter into this originating darkness, we tend toward a more restful state, taking solace in the company of others, all the time seeking to go home again, symbolically, to where the first fire was lit in the hearth of our hearts. The Yuletide journey is about homecoming, both in the Spirit and in domestic, familial terms. **Homecoming** happens in our domestic lives and also in our spiritual experience. Our desire to return to the hearths where we've kept Yule in the past is actually a reflection of our deep need to rekindle our own humanity. Though we cannot return to the past, we can always turn to Brighid and resolve to live more as a firebrand of the Spirit in the World.

The Spirit of Yule is kindled through our own awakening to the various symbols of the Winter Solstice Season. Snow on the fields, Holly bushes dotted with red berries, Ivy and Evergreens are all symbolic trajectories through which we can establish links with Yule's Spirit. To imagine a Stag standing in a wintry scene intimates the Spirit of Yule coming to us in human dwelling. Cernunnos is the spirit-guide of pilgrims in December. He comes to inspire a sense of wonder in our hearts and kindle a desire to follow him, off into the wildwoods where the pilgrimage to Glastonbury Tor can be dreamed. Images of Nicholas and of Elves can prepare the hearth of our hearts to receive the brand of the Fires of Yule. If we set up an image of any of these symbols as November turns toward December, our eyes will become doorways through which the sparks of the Spirit may reach the hearth of our hearts.

Storytelling is one of the ways in which we can kindle the Spirit of Yule. As we live our lives, the human spirit collects stories and associates them with particular earthen tines of our existence. Stories store wisdom, insight and the impact of various experiences on the human soul. By telling stories we can enter into the impact certain events have made on us. The Yule is filled with stories. Traditional ones – like Charles Dickens' <u>A Christmas Carol</u> (1848) – are paradigms of what it means to experience the Winter Solstice Season as a pilgrimage to rebirth and renewal.

We might also sing songs that have come to be associated with the Yule. Keltelvens have long experienced music as a primary manifestation of Spirit. The Elves sing songs – out at the Sídhe and in their ráths in the Hinterlands – and when they sing of the Yule, our spirits hear the tunes. Music carries **shunnache** (i.e., spirit-energy),[10] and to 'hear' a song with our soul is to be infused with this energy.

As we sing and tell stories about the coming of Winter's Solstice, Keltelvens also dance to invite the Spirit of Yule to enter our places of dwelling. To dance is to participate in the rhythm of the cosmos. Every season of Earth & Spirit has its own rhythms, harmonies and cadences. The rhythm of Yule is generally encoded in songs called 'carrols.' It is a solemn yet joyful rhythm that can ignite, suddenly – like a damp haystack onto which a torch has been thrown – sending up sparks that can ignite other Fires of Yule.

Storytelling, the singing of seasonal songs and dancing are the primary activities by which we can quest for the Hearth of the Spirit of Yule. As we make these willing gestures, longing to be home-gone, the Spirit comes and lifts up our mortal consciousness to the wonder of Yule!

Tining toward the nadir
of Spirit in the depths of Earth,
Elves haunt us,
our own faults taunt us –
and yet Brighid calls us onward;
into the holy snows
of enlightenment and renewal!
Amen.

B. The Spirituality of Decorating

"The Divine Mother is here, but we don't usually see Her.
Elves and Faery walk among us, though we don't often
sense their reality. Decking the halls makes the spiritual
reality in which we normally live manifest to our senses."
(2)

- Catharine Abbot
What is Decorating? (1987)

Another way in which we begin to awaken ourselves to the presence of
the Spirit of Yule is through altering our surroundings with symbols, icons
and other artifacts that stir up our seasonal imagination. The presence of
images and statues during sacred times stimulates an awareness of the
sacred and prepares us to experience it. Decking the halls with greenery
and festooning places of public life with lights and shiny ornaments are
traditional ways of preparing for the Winter Solstice.

Decking the halls, however, is much more than merely creating a
festive or 'party' atmosphere. There's a spiritual discipline and also an art
involved in trimming that most people have all but forgotten. We must
therefore remind ourselves of what it *means* to trim and decorate our
places of dwelling and the offices, stores or factories where we work.
Decorating is an outward preparation for Winter's Solstice. It usually
begins as much as a week or so before Saint Nicholas Eve, when the urge
comes over us to go and get the trimmings out of their boxes.

13

To begin decorating is to acknowledge that you either sense the season changing, or that you would *like* to be more aware of the imminent arrival of the Spirit of Yule. By decorating we proclaim that a magical time is unfolding around us. Some people begin decorating at the end of November, while others prefer to wait until the Feast of Nicholas. As soon as you start to trim, however, you should begin to meditate on the meaning of the season you are entering. Decorating transforms our lived worlds.

As you un-box the trimmings, think about how you might want to trim your place of dwelling *this* year. Involve everyone you live with in this discussion. While the old standard ways of decking out the house or apartment for the Fires of Yule may still work, it's easy to get into a rut. Therefore, allow that as you grow older and as times change, the way you decorate may need to change, either subtly or suddenly. No two Winter Solstices are identical, so why should our decorations always be the same?

If you keep the Yule with other people – either family or friends – everyone will probably have their favorite decoration, while every cherished trimming will have its detractors. Try to balance individual preferences against the needs of others. Make every attempt to mix the old with the new, so that there is continuity in your choice of decorations, as well as new variations and possibilities. No balance is ever perfect, so each year we get to try again.

There are two pitfalls to avoid regarding trimming. First, you must avoid turning decorating into a sentimental escape into yesteryear. We do not live in the past, and yet the present grows largely out of the past. Therefore, while you should not neglect to use old trimmings, don't think you *have* to use them just because they're *old*! Decking the Halls should not turn the house into a time bubble. When you finish trimming, you should feel at home in your house in your own place and time in the world at large.

Likewise you must also avoid the urge to bow down to the latest fad in decorating just because it's what everyone else is doing. There's no virtue in decorating in a completely new way every year just for the sake of keeping in step with your neighbors. There's a certain value in continuity with the past and also a benefit in using new trimmings. The primary question is, "Will trimming this way help me/us to awaken to the mysteries of the Season?" The trimmings you use will probably end up being a mixture of old and new, representing your own connection with the past as well as your desire to move forward.

It's perhaps best to begin decorating slowly. The place of dwelling should be transformed according to how the Spirit of Yule is becoming manifest. Trimming too fast too early can result in getting into the mood too quickly, and then 'losing it' before Glastonbury Thorn Day. Trimming too late may have the opposite effect.

Consider not trimming all at once. Putting every ornament, candle and swag of evergreen up at one time may make the shift into mystical space-time too abrupt. Children rarely mind getting everything decorated all at once, but as we become more spiritually mature, we begin to pace ourselves in order to experience the full import of the whole act of decorating. In our culture of fast food and satisfaction-on-demand, it's good for the soul to learn to wait upon what is worth waiting for!

Ultimately, *decorating* is *a way of transforming the place of human dwelling* so that the Spirit of the Season can become manifest among us where we live. Decorating is a way of opening our hearts to receive the Spirit, intuiting the tines of Wisdom. If we have trouble getting into the mood to celebrate Yule, decorating can kindle intuitions and memories that will help open us up to the earthen season.

'Decking the Halls' is a way of envisioning the spiritual nature of existence. Trimming is a matter of turning the house or office into an image of Paradise, making the spiritual realities that are usually invisible all but evident to our senses. The glittering tinsel and shimmering lights, the sparkling ornaments and the aromas of scented candles are all elements in an imaginative re-construction of the real Spirit-infused world, which we can't normally see because we've become too dull-witted to notice it.

Decorating usually begins with outdoor trimming. We need to prepare the exterior of our lives before the Fires of Yule begin to burn in our inner hearths. After the exterior of the house or apartment is decorated, begin trimming indoors. As you do so, leave a place for the Yule Tree, which will be set up last, usually on 14 December (called "Lighting Day" or "Cedar Day"). We often need to move furniture and small tables in order to get the Yule Tree to its station, so make allowance for these moves as you're decorating. Sometimes, however, the place where the tree will be set up is subtly revealed through the process of decorating, rather than being agreed on ahead of time.

As part of your indoor decorating, set up a table where you can go to meditate, relax and pray, away from the hustle and bustle of the day's routines. This is the Yuletide version of the meditation table that Keltelven practitioners set up as a kind of "home altar." All the various tools of our arts and crafts as well as icons of the various seasons are kept on the meditation table throughout the year.

As Yule approaches set up red and green candles on the table and set out icons, statues and other symbolic items that inspire the mind to meditate on the Winter Solstice. These may include pine cones, pieces of pine branches, silver bells, electric candles, small electrically lit houses or models of other structures, such as churches or cathedrals, and – on the 6th of December – an icon of Saint Nicholas (i.e., Santa Claus).

You might also create a **dolmen**[11] on the Yule Table by bringing three fair-sized rocks and a larger flat stone into the house. Set these up on the table, with the three rocks supporting the flat stone. The dolmen should occupy no more than a quarter of the table. Some people like to set up their dolmen underneath the table. Put a candle in an altar glass inside it to represent the illumination of the Spirit of Yule. The dolmen represents the place in your hut of dwelling where *this world* and the next intersect.

You may also set up a **Year Wheel** on the meditation table. This is a circular base with four candles in it. The candles represent the equinoxes and solstices of the year. Light one candle at a time, starting with the one positioned on the table aligned with the east. This candle represents the Vernal Equinox. Then, in a few days, light the next candle, which is aligned to the south. This one represents the Summer Solstice. After a few more days, light the candle in the west representing the Autumnal Equinox. Finally, on 21 December, light the candle symboling the Winter Solstice, which is aligned to the north. Use three red candles and a green one in the Wheel, or vice versa. Use the odd colored candle to represent the Winter Solstice (the one aligned to the North).

Lighting the four candles represents a meditation on the journey you have made through the year since the last Winter Solstice. Light each candle in turn, and reflect on the year that is passing. What were its high and low points? Were you devoted to your work this year? Did you heed the gods and goddesses with love and curiosity, or did you stray away from the most mysterious paths? What resolutions might you want to make this year as you approach the Winter Solstice? After Alban Arthuan you will set up four fresh candles in the Wheel of the Year and meditate on bringing all of your experiences from the previous 12 months to Glastonbury Tor by 25 December.

While most of the decorating is done in a few days time, you might continue adding to the basic trimmings little by little throughout the Yule. Most of us wake up to the presence of Mystery and the nearness of Paradise a little bit at a time. Like waking up in the morning, spiritual wakefulness is a personal process. If we're awakened too quickly, we're likely to become irritable. Spiritual awakening must be nurtured as though you were helping a child learn some new lesson about life.

After the initial stage of trimming is finished, meditate on your expectations and hopes for the Yule. What do you want to learn? What do you want to experience as you make your way through the Solstice Season to Glastonbury Tor? Reflect on your own memories of Yuletides past, both good and bad. Seek a direction in which you can be edified, and through which you might bless and edify others.

After you've trimmed, take a walk outside and look at your house or apartment window from the vantage of passers-by. Once you get the trimmings up indoors, take a little time before or after a meal to just sit and enjoy them. A few minutes of meditation on the Spirit of Yule a day makes a world of difference. As the lights of Yule blink and shimmer each night, meditate on how they transform the house into *another place*. We often put up trimmings and then forget to enjoy them. This is a waste of time and effort. Decorating is not some inane job that you can forget about after it's done. By decorating we are in the process of transforming ordinary reality into an image of Paradise as it presences to us in our mortal realms. Imagine what it would be like to live in Paradise all year round! Though this kind of wakefulness is difficult for ordinary human beings to maintain, we can encourage ourselves to be more awake via a pattern of regular devotion and meditation on the *actual mystical nature* of Reality.

At the end of the Season – by 6 January – you will have taken down all of the decorations, but you should not forget where you are living just because the trimmings are no longer apparent. We decorate in order to awaken ourselves to the deeper dimensions of Reality. After the trimmings are taken down, there's always a tendency to slip into a kind of dull mood or even depression. If this happens, then you've been sled-riding through the surface glitz of the Season and not really experiencing its inner meaning. To take down the trimmings is to return from Paradise, in a way, but it is also to be given the chance to take off the training wheels of the self and live life to the fullest without the props.

> Let us go wandering in the Spirit,
> singing holy Pagan carols
> so that the squirrels and gods
> will hear our tune!
> Mystery is breaching the walls
> of our resistance
> with strange spells of Yuletide ambiance!
> *Imbas*! *Imbas*! *Awen*! Amen!

C. Celebrating the Winter Solstice as Adults

"The belief that 'Christmas is for children' betrays a covert failure of adult faith in our culture. Certainly, Saint Nicholas is the patron of children, especially of orphans and the poor. But there is no spiritual reason why Christmas should not be celebrated earnestly by adults. When I hear that 'Christmas is for children' I really hear an admission that adults no longer have a living and viable faith in the mysteries that the old mystics and poets believed could become manifest in the world at Winter Solstice-tide." (192)

- Robert Werner
Wintering Along the Way (1970)

Though the secular 'holidays' of December have become a time focused almost exclusively on children, the Fires of Yule burn just as brightly for adults as for the young. In fact, the traditional Winter Solstice Season is geared for adult celebration. As you approach the lighting of the

Fires of Yule, you might meditate on what it means – as an adult – to celebrate the Yule.

This meditation might begin with the question of *why* the secular Christmas celebration has become so focused on children? I would argue that the transformation of Christmas into an entertainment for the young is due to the growing inability of adults to believe in anything that thrusts the imagination beyond the realities represented by the evening news and the stock market report. A crude and un-spiritual "realism" has overtaken western culture in the last century that has repeatedly dealt mortal blows to the adult capacity to participate in imaginative ideals or to have mystical experiences.

As a result, "Christmas" – with all of its emphasis on Elves, Santa Claus, and imagined situations of human transfiguration – has come to be something many adults can't even *make* themselves believe in anymore, so they surrender "Christmas" to their children. How many times have I heard someone say, "Oh, I just celebrate Christmas for the kids, but I won't do all of this anymore once they grow up." This confession clearly alludes to our society's spiritual poverty. Any culture that cannot see beyond the ordinary realities of everyday life to imagine how things *could* be – much less how they *should* be – has lost its moorings in Earth & Spirit. When only the children can believe in mysticism, magick, miracles and faery tales, it won't be long before the society loses its verve for life. The superficialities of so much art, film and theater today is a clear indication that our society is now all but spiritually bankrupt.

Of course, the Season of Yule *should be* enjoyed by children. The myths of the Winter Solstice evince a sincere interest in the welfare of children, and in Keltelven Circles the children are always included in the wonder, fascination, magic and imaginative visioning that the Fires of Yule generates. However, it's adults who provide a context in which the young can celebrate sacred seasons, and if the adults cannot appreciate the mysticism of the Winter Solstice, the children won't be able to glean much depth from it. If they grow up only to learn that their parents never really believed in the spiritual magick of Yule, what's to keep them from being disillusioned as well?

One of the ways in which we can learn to celebrate the Yule as adults is by adopting Saint Nicholas as an exemplar of the kind of hospitality and generosity that needs to be practiced in our world today. Keltelvens have adopted Saint Nicholas as a mentor of a kind and compassionate heart. The historical Nicholas – who lived in the 4th century in Asia Minor – was a patron of children, affirming the worth of the young in a society that didn't much value their existence. Young people still need the patronage of Nicholas, especially those who are neglected, abandoned or abused. And there are far too many unfortunate children in our ever-so-civilized world. If as adults we can meditate on Saint Nicholas as a saintly hero and imitate his example, the children around us are going to learn to appreciate the depth of spiritual value represented by the Yule more than if we just pretend to believe *'for their sakes.'* If we treat Nicholas as a spirit-guide during our Yuletide journey, we will set a better example for the young.

The irony here is that young people are often more ready to embrace the mystery of the Season of Yule than are adults, and thus – in one sense – adults can learn how to be more childlike by observing the young as they prepare for the Winter Solstice. Children are generally less burdened by disappointment, frustration, grief and pain than we are as adults. Adults carry a much deeper burden of experiences – both positive and negative – around with them. The various experiences we've had during the year make it either easier or more difficult to keep coming to the Fires of Yule with a joyful spirit. The turmoil, trials and disappointments we've undergone can mount up and become a barrier to waking up to Mystery's Presence in the Earth.

Adults can also fall into celebrating holidays for less simple, less direct reasons. It too often becomes a time for chumming people up, inviting them to parties and laying on the schmooze, just so we can manipulate them or get something out of them. The "holidays" in contemporary society have become a time to use the ideals of generosity, kindness and hospitality for political maneuvering and for setting agendas while we drink the eggnog and devour the festal turkey. But this is *not* the meaning of the Keltelven Winter Solstice Season!

For many people, the secular holidays become equated with seeing family and parents and spending especially meaningful time with their children and spouse or life-partner. Then, when parents die or children grow up and move away, or when a divorce breaks up a family, "the holidays" become something people just *can't* or don't *need* to celebrate anymore.

As people attempting to live in communion with Earth & Spirit, Keltelvens struggle to celebrate the days and nights of Yule for more simple and direct, mystical reasons. We need to strive to love the Season for its mythic content and not for the baggage – no matter how valuable it may be – that we've imported into the Yuletide Season for various well-intended reasons. Obviously, it *is* important to spend quality time with family and friends at the tines of Winter's Solstice, but we need to do this *in part* because of a deeper spiritual realization, and not just because it's the prescribed thing to do.

Can we learn to love others and other things in our lives because of what the Winter Solstice stands for; because we're seeking a mystical rebirth and therefore trying to live more compassionately, reclaiming the kindness and spirit of hospitality that seems to evaporate throughout the year? There's something wondrous *going on* in the Earth & Spirit as the days of December grow dark. Can we learn to experience the Yule as a holy time and *therefore* get together with others, practice hospitality and nurture a renewed sense of the love of life *as adults*? We are always having to take our spiritual bearings and return to the true meaning of Yule as the Winter Solstice approaches. Some people have experienced such disillusionment, grief and tragedy in the course of trying to live life well that they are tempted to give up and refuse the Spirit of Yule a place near their hearth!

Many things can lead us to such a point of resignation. The pain of broken relationships, lack of good health, and the experience of a loved one's death may make us unwilling to open up to the magick of Yule. We may have experienced a particularly devastating series of events and feel that we can never again kindle the Fires of Alban Arthuan! The Winter Solstice is real, however, regardless of how we feel, and if we fail to keep the Yule, then the tragedy of pain or grief will have won the battle against hope and life. We need to prepare to celebrate the Yule *as adults* and get ready to abandon despair!

By *intending* to celebrate the Yule we can often find our way back to the paths along which our grief and disappointment can be worked out. The Spirit of Yule can heal us of the losses and hurt we've experienced, perhaps not in just a single Season, but certainly in time. If we can't 'go on' with Yule after the death of a loved one, perhaps this is a sign that we've lost our spiritual focus in all the distractions and dustbins of life's alleyways, and forgotten the *meaning* of earthen seasons.

Have we thrown the meaning of Yule out with the table scraps of our lives, and put relationships, our job, or material pleasure and possessions in the preeminent place? If so, perhaps it's time to get centered once again in the real mystery of the actual Winter Solstice Season that unfolds around us – in Nature as the arc of the Sun across the southern skies declines toward the horizon – during December. Preparing for the Thirteen Dayes of Yule can help get us back on track spiritually.

There's been a lot of attention in recent years to the phenomenon of '*holiday depression*' in our culture. Depression can be biologically based and therefore be subject to medical treatment. However, depression can also be spiritually rooted. 'Holiday depression' can be linked to a failure to be aware of what's going on in Earth & Spirit. As the days get shorter, the human eye receives less light, and our moods may begin to change, growing darker with the days. This en-darkening is not bad in itself, but may have negative results if we fail to be aware of what's happening, and if we don't work with the darkness by engaging in some kind of preparation for Winter's Solstice. It's for this reason that Yule has always been celebrated as a "festival of lights" down across the centuries. Lighting lights can help to counterbalance the darkness.

Winter's Solstice comes, whether we're aware of it or not, and it cannot be ignored. Trimming and then meditation on the lights of the Season help ease the tendency to be depressed or fall into lethargic moods.

Spiritual depression can also be caused by failing to connect with the magick of the Season; by not throwing off our burdens and surrendering our fears and grief as the Solstice draws near. We can become so inundated by all the hype our society generates as the secular holidays approach, that we get derailed. We then fail to arrive at Glastonbury Tor where we *might* have been able to refuel ourselves spiritually had we not neglected to keep the Yule in our Hearts near the hearth of home. Then, once the holidays pass and the trimmings come down, we experience the world as a bleak, futile wasteland (so it may seem without all the lights and glitter) allowing depression an anti-spiritual abode in our heart.

Spiritual depression can also arise as a result of emotional or psychic exhaustion. Every effort should be made, while keeping the Yule, to *slow down*, if possible, and get beyond the propaganda intended to induce us always to buy, buy, and then buy some more. We might graciously limit our gift giving, at least where other adults are concerned, to one or two well-chosen gifts from each person to each person. When *are* we going to learn that neither the price of a gift nor the amount of gifts constitutes true value?

How can we enjoy the Winter Solstice if we're always rushing about trying to buy the kids more gifts than we did last year? How can we discover the mystery of gift giving when we're preoccupied with placating everyone on our list with some trinket, regardless of how expensive it might be? We need to turn off this compulsory buying, and we will only do this if we can discover and meditate on the real intent of gift giving as this is inspired by the mystical logic of the Winter Solstice Season!

Holiday depression can sometimes be averted by giving anonymous gifts to strangers, by participating in a 'Toys for Tots' or 'Angel Tree' program in your area, or even by volunteering to play Santa Claus at a mall or hospital. We are generous and hospitable beings. When we fail to share what we have with others, even if the only thing we can give is a smile or a handshake, spiritual inertia sets in. Depression follows. By anonymous acts of giving and simple hospitality we can divert the tendency to spiritual depression. Even if we don't 'believe' in what we're doing, a generous act can begin to generate a renewed sense of hope and well-being. The act stimulates the imagination we need to be inspired to celebrate through the Yule and arrive at Glastonbury Tor.

We also need to learn to turn off the television and radio for a few hours each day during Yule, in order to stem the tide of commercialism. Listen to uplifting recorded music or watch inspiring videos during this self-liberation. Finding entertainment that will stir the embers of the Fires of Yule in our hearts as adults will not be easy. Most of the TV and cinema productions released for the 'December viewing market' are geared for children, and are not going to be very inspiring to us as adults. On the other hand, movies and TV shows for adult audiences usually just further all the clichés of violence, sexual innuendo and intentional stupidity (the contemporary excuse for comedy) that permeate so much of mass entertainment. Therefore, you must go looking for the real gems of entertainment; those that glow with an ambiance kindled in the Fires of Yule.

Once we liberate ourselves from the popular rat-race called "the holidays" we will find that making a Journey to Glastonbury Tor means becoming *like* children in our orientation toward life, rekindling dreams and hopes. This is not the same as becoming childish or giving up our adult sense of the world and watching cartoons all day. To be child-like is to let go of cynicism and despair, learning to be more spontaneous, playful and intuitive. We can do this by learning to imagine the stories of Yule and meditating on their truth-value *as* stories. We can become childlike by learning to play games again, and then treating whatever rituals and customs we might engage in as playful acts that make the Spirit of Yule manifest in our hearts and in the Hearths of Home.

Becoming child-like means nurturing a less burdened heart. Making the pilgrimage through the Winter Solstice as adults means that we have to travel the path as who we are and not just as the guardians and parents of children. We're not just 'tagging along' for the sake of our kids! We're also seeking deep spiritual resourcement for ourselves!

D. Celebrating the Winter Solstice Alone

"Solitude is a spiritual discipline. ... Though it should be practiced voluntarily, we are sometimes cast into the situation of being alone in life, for a more or less long time. If this happens, though it may be painful, we can and should use this time as an opportunity for solitude. Accept the state willingly and turn it to a good end. It would be better to do this than to experience profound loneliness without spiritual consolation!" (21)

- Catharine Abbot
A Yuletide Handbook (1986)

As adults in our contemporary and highly mobile society, we often find ourselves unable to get home during Yule. Jobs keep us where we live, and where we live is all too often far away from family and old friends. If you can't get 'home' for the Winter Solstice, use the following calendar of days to celebrate the Season where you are. Kindle the Yuletide Hearth wherever you find yourself dwelling.

Life and society also tend to isolate people, and many of us find ourselves with no one to turn to during the holiday season. Untimely and inevitable deaths leave people suddenly alone with no family, few acquaintances and even fewer friends. Life itself is still a gift, though, even if we're so unfortunate as to have no close companions with which to share it. Ideals may get tarnished, aspirations may get frustrated, and we may lose everything we thought made life worth living, but Yule still comes, caroling around on the Wheel of the Year. There's always another opportunity to light the lights, listen to music and prepare a feast; even if the only feast we can afford consists in heating up a frozen dinner and eating it all by ourselves by the light of red & green candles.

We have to be careful when dealing with the value of being alone versus the value of being with other people. Our society is extremely extroverted, and tends not to understand people who like to keep to themselves. For some people, to be alone is a curse. Others are more solitary by nature and actually prefer to keep holidays by themselves. Some people need time alone in order to recharge their psychic batteries and get up the energy to rejoin the flux and flow of daily life. If so, keeping Yule alone might be a blessing. Extroverts may not understand you, but that doesn't matter. Just try not to upset those who need to be around people all the time in order to be happy.

Most people in our society are afraid of being alone. Far from being introverted, our culture is compulsively gregarious. We don't just get together in order to enjoy one another's company, but rather to *avoid* being alone. When we find ourselves alone, most people have a tendency to become unfocused, doubtful of their own worth and tempted to do things they *wouldn't* do if other people were around. We need to experience spiritual Solitude purposefully if we're going to embrace our vulnerability and the lack of rootedness this weakness portends.

However you end up alone during the Winter Solstice Season, you can still enter into the mysterious aura of the Fires of Yule by participating in the symbols, trimming and making your own personal meditative journey to Glastonbury Tor. If you're alone, practice the disciplines of solitude and find your own Yuletide Hearth. Solitude is a spiritual state of being alone in which we can better seek the Presence of Mystery in Earth & Spirit.

To dwell in Solitude is to learn to trust in the process of life as well as trusting our own will, compassion and creativity. This is a healthy experience for adults who know that – sooner or later – life tends to rear up and give you a good swift kick. We can't preen ourselves on other people's good opinion of us when we're alone, and we can't take refuge in noise, meaningless activities and other subterfuge when we're not running with the pack. We usually have to be quiet when we're alone, and silence frightens most people almost as much as being alone does. It's only when we're quiet, though, that we can listen for the whisperings of divine revelations haunting our hearts.

If you happen to find yourself alone at Winter's Solstice, don't despair. Allow yourself to miss the company of those you would rather be with, but keep the Thirteen Dayes of Yule anyway. Use it as a time to center down, get quiet, and wait for the shining glimmers of truth to enlighten your heart. Participate in the activities indicated for each day of Yule, and meditate on the symbols described in the following calendar. Most of the activities can be engaged in even if you're alone. Those that don't lend themselves to solitary practice can be imagined. By doing this, you will find a deeper ground of communion with Earth & Spirit than can ever be discovered simply by being 'one of the gang.'

E. A Pagan Appreciation of Jesus of Nazareth

> "Holly and other evergreens are symbolic of the presence of the god-force in the Earth. As the Pagan Celts came to find wisdom in the teaching of Jesus of Nazareth, these symbols came to represent the mysterious presence of the god-man who was encountered in the forests of Celtic countries and who taught Wisdom's runes freely." (91)
>
> - Cornelius Whitsel
> The Keltelven Traditions (1982)

Talking about celebrating the Winter Solstice as adults, it always occurs to me that we need to grow out of our spiritual immaturity. We often act like mystical toddlers, walking around with our religious toys, claiming "mine are better than yours" and going off in a huff if someone tries to broaden our horizons!

As Pagans, Keltelven practitioners believe that Wisdom is a manifestation of the Presence of Mystery in Earth & Spirit, and that we must therefore "accept and appreciate Wisdom wherever we find it." This dictum – which is part of a larger rann in a Keltelven Book of Shadows – applies to spirituality and religion as well as to other aspects of life. Many religious traditions – even the patriarchal "World Religions" that have persecuted Pagans and attempted to wipe out *our* Wisdom – contain seeds of Wisdom or they would not have been as popular as they have been over the centuries.

The Keltelven traditions draw on the *entire* ancient Celtic legacy. As such they have developed an interesting take on the relationship between Pagan mysticism and Christianity. During the 4th to 7th centuries CE a great many Pagan Celts took up the teachings of Jesus of Nazareth and became Celtic followers of the Christ as the Stag of Wisdom. This primitive form of Christ-Following was innately Celtic and not yet Romanized *or* institutionalized. It affirmed the equality of men and women,[12] the goodness of Nature as God's Creation,[13] and maintained a high degree of social and economic justice in its communities.[14] These early Celtic Christians often interpreted Jesus of Nazareth in terms of the old Celtic myths of the heroes, the gods and the goddesses. Many of the saints lived out themes that had earlier been connected with one or more of the great heroes & heroines of the Pagan Celtic Tradition. They lived a life full of mystery, magick and hope, seeking Wisdom in Christ at every crossroads of life.

As the Keltelven traditions emerged, the earliest Henges and Dens, Groves and Circles absorbed the wisdom of Christ's mystics as well as that of the earlier Pagan Druids and Gwrach.[15] Over time the myth of the Virgin Birth of Jesus got integrated into the Keltelven celebrations of Yule. Three elements of this story have become standard metaphors for the journey through the Winter Solstice to Glastonbury Tor. First, the *image of the Star* – which guided the Astrologers from the East to Judea and then to the manger where the child-god Jesus was being cared for – has become an icon for the *awen* (i.e., inspiration) that directs us in Yuletide paths. We can imagine ourselves as *like* the Pagan Astrologers who journeyed across the wilderness to the land of the Jews, there to adore a divine-child of wisdom.

Keltelvens have often heard echoes of their own mythic heroes in the biblical tales of Jesus' birth. When the hero Cú Chulainn was born, wise men and women flocked to the house of his mother Dechtire and gave gifts to the infant who was destined to become the ultimate hero of Ulster.[16] Many people desired to foster the future hero. When the Astrologers arrived at the stable behind the inn in Bethlehem where Jesus had been born, they lavished gifts of gold, frankincense and myrrh on him.[17] When Joseph and Mary took their newborn child to the Temple in Jerusalem for circumcision, a prophetess named Anna proclaimed that he would grow up to be "messiah" of the Jews, and then the prophet Simon declared that he could now die, as he had seen the face of his 'savior' at last.[18]

As often happens in Celtic tales, Mary conceived the Hero Jesus in her womb without the usual intercourse with a human male. As such, Jesus is truly a god-child who makes the Mystery of the Universe manifest among us. Like so many other heroes in Celtic mythology, one particular man comes forward and claims Jesus as his own, to raise him and give him a name. This man was Joseph the Carpenter, who was already engaged to be married to Mary at the point when she became pregnant through the magick of "the Holy Spirit." Together they became a holy couple, and pledged themselves to care for the god-child, who was destined (according to ancient prophecy) to be born in Bethlehem.

A second theme from the mythology of the birth of Jesus that plays a prominent role in the Keltelven mysticism of Yule is that of *the journey of Joseph and Mary to Bethlehem*.[19] Their journey from Nazareth to Bethlehem is an archetypal pilgrimage. Keltelvens often imagine themselves journeying with Mary & Joseph on the road from Nazareth to Bethlehem, where they are present – on the night of 24 December – when Mary gives birth. This event is experienced as intimating our own 'nativity,' as we hope to undergo a rebirth by the morning of Glastonbury Thorn Day (25 December).

The biblical myth indicates that Jesus was born in a 'stable,' probably located in a cave in the hillside behind an inn in Bethlehem. Mary and Joseph had gone to Bethlehem in order to be part of a census that was being taken, and the inn was full, so that they had to stay with the horses and cows and other barnyard animals. The birth of Jesus among the animals can also be understood in Pagan terms, as indicative of his closeness to Nature. He is not born in a "house of the world" but in a "hut of earth." He was born among humble, earthy people. As such, he comes into the world as a native of Nature and will become a divine critic of the world of the savvy and the well-dressed, the rich and the arrogant.

The last major theme from the birth myth of Jesus to serve as a metaphor for our journey through the Season of the Winter Solstice is that of *the shepherds in the field* who came to see the god-child in the manger.[20] They had a vision of angels singing of the birth of a savior coming to deliver his people from ignorance, and this vision inspired them to go into town and visit the child. Some of us begin the journey to Glastonbury Tor late, while others may not get into the mystical mood of the journey until Solstice Night or even later. For these people the shepherds leaving their fields after the god-child is born can indicate that it's *never too late* to get to the nativity where our own rebirth can unfold.

In each of these three themes – as in many other aspects of the birth-mythos of Jesus of Nazareth – we can detect Pagan elements that are edifying in their connection with our celebration of the Yule Season. To adopt these themes is *not* to import any of the arrogant religious absolutism that has so often characterized the Christian religion into our hearth-circles! Nevertheless, Keltelvens have always held that, as Pagans, we should be more open-minded than those whose religion makes them narrowly exclusive in their beliefs. Therefore, we accept Jesus in Pagan swaddling as a guest at our Yuletide festivities, even though most Christians generally will not let our Pagan Wisdom illuminate their hearts.

Having discussed these preparations for keeping the Yule – (a) the Spirit of Yule, (b) the spirituality of decorating, (c) celebrating Yule as adults, and (d) solitary celebrations of the Winter Solstice, and finally (e) a Pagan appreciation of Jesus of Nazareth – we are now ready to turn to the actual calendar and begin entering into the mystery, magic and mysticism of the Yule.

As the first days of December arrive, take a moment to stop in your daily rounds and acknowledge that the season is shifting, the days are darkening, and that Yule is just a couple of weeks away. Reflect on how you might best kindle the Fires of Yule *this year*, given what the last eleven months have been like and where you are in the midst of your life. Then recite the following "Invocation to the Spirit of Yule:"

Invocation to the Spirit of Yule:

Spirit of the Yule, hear me as I call_
come to my Hearth, illumine my Heart,
and call to me all those memories
                that will make me merrie and wise!

Here I am, Spirit of the Yule!
Come! Spirit of the Hearth of Love!
Come! Spirit of the Heart of Mystery,
                and open our sleepy eyes!

Here I come with a'Yuling desire_
Open my eyes and let me see
                the mystic paths of Paradise!

Spirit of Yule, hear me as I call_
for I long to be giddy with Your Wine
                and inspired by Your Rhyme!
Call me to Your Circle and call to my Hearth
all those spirits
                who will aid me in my journey
to Glastonbury Tor! Amen.

Having spoken these words, you are ready. Abandon mundane distractions, seek the glimmering icons of holy fire on the distant imaginary horizons where the Autumn Sun is setting, and take your first steps toward the Illuminations of Winter Solstice. Holy Fire, here we come, as pilgrims once again and for evermore, with Cernunnos as our guide and Holly to mark the threshold of the Heart's Door!

Saint Nicholas Eve (5 December)

Over the heath and through the wood
all wassailed of the glistening snow,
Saint Nicholas came with Reindeer
and a troop of Elves in tow!   1

Past the WellSpring of the Saints,
he came with Holly & dried Bay_
to winnow the wights out of the World,
and with the Spirit's Children to play!   2

He slung his sack with some delight
across a horse-and-rider fence,
and came approaching toward the house
making folly of mundane sense!   3

He had a broom of thistle & heather,
and a cap full of pomegranates_
Within his sleeves were glowing secrets
from which True Hopes originate!   4

Climbing the chimney, he set about
divining the household's aura_
And then he slung about the doorposts
– Ivy Wreaths of Christed love!   5

The Reindeer were yet invisible,
the Elves were gasping in giggles_
as snow began to cover the Night,
and the Spirit spread out Her riddles!   6

Three windows with a candle's glow
each beckoned from above the portico!
They summoned the Saint to gift the pockets
of those who laid their heads
upon the pillows of finely quilted beds!   7

"Hurry! Hurry! _We dare not delay," he cried!
The Reindeer knocked upon the door,
the Elves they climbed the lattice!
Saint Nicholas turned into a mist,
and slipped in through old keyholes!   8

Around the house the Visitor flew
with Holly boughs and sweeping Yew,
He took the staircase with abandon
while seeking out the chosen few!   9

He found their chambers open wide,
with hearts yet empty from inside!
He left them Pomegranates of Faith
and the Apples of his starry sleigh-ride!   10

"Hey, wait! _Santa, is that *you*!?"

_One small voice dis-spells the wraith,
and into deep crevices of the Night –
Saint Nicholas and his Elves depart,
putting our fears, unseen, to flight!   11

Off across Fields-of-Life they fly,
leaving hoof-marks in frosted snow;
White tails frisking prayers like Art,
the Moon chasing them with Her glow!   12

·And in their stead a blessing's found_
Runes of Life in the Fruit of Faith!
Mystery is once again unbounded!
Amen.

Come, Saint Nicholas! We await you!   13

A. Feast of Nicholas and the Elves (6 December)

"Over the hills and not so far away, the Spirit of Yule will play, with hopes and dreams of things to come, making mead of all our fears on the run!" (iv)

- Robert Werner
Wintering Upon the Way (1970)

"The figure of Santa Claus has one foot in Pagan tradition and another in Christian tradition. It's impossible to sort him out and make him serve one spirituality or the other! This can either be seen as a problem – by religious purists – or as a blessing. If Santa Claus is as Christian as he is Pagan, then we can see the myth he represents as bridging traditions and opening lines of communication between modern Christians, wicche and any other group that honors the legend of Santa Claus in any of its manifestations." (29)]

- Catharine Abbot
Weaving the Christed Way (1989)

The Feast of Nicholas and the Elves is a doorway through which we pass into the realm where the magick of renewal and transformation becomes possible. At this tine in earthen seasons the Presence of Mystery embraces us. Coming a full week before the first day of Yule (13 December), this celebration allows people time to shake themselves and get ready for what's just over the mystic horizons. On the Eve of 6 December, the portals of the Solstice Season swing open. As we approach the Hearths of Yule and prepare to kindle the Season's Fires, we listen for the ghostly bells of self-renewal beckoning to us. On the Eve of Saint Nicholas, we become aware of ourselves as invited guests of the Season.

The innate natural magick that begins to stir on the eve of the 6th of December has been likened to a firebrand thrown on damp, forgotten hearth-fodder. We often neglect what is sacred and wonderful in life. Nicholas reminds us of just how far we've wandered from the Hearths of Yule during the intervening eleven months since the last Feast of Epiphany.

The focus of this first day of the Season is on *the arrival of Saint Nicholas*. Nicholas was an historical person, born in Asia Minor in c. 370 CE. He was orphaned at birth and grew up knowing Jesus as his foster-brother. He became the patron of all lonesome, abandoned or abused children. He gave anonymous gifts to needy children, and when he died he crossed†over into the Otherworld, where he continued his benevolent ministry.

Keltelven lore indicates that Nicholas was joined by 12 Irish Elves in his ongoing ministry to children from his home in the otherworld. These Elves came to Asia Minor on a quest. There they met Nicholas near his hometown of Myra. By the time of their meeting, Nicholas was already acknowledged as a living saint. Finding Nicholas to be wiser than his years, the Elves pledged themselves to him in willing service. They delivered gifts and ran errands for him, thereby helping him expand his ministry until it nearly filled out the extent of his heart's compassion. Nicholas and the Elves lived together in a cave a couple of miles outside Myra. This cave had once been the treasure-stash of a local bandit who had donated many riches to the boy-saint after Nicholas had healed him of a sword wound.

As the time of the saint's death approached, Nicholas and his Elves made a pilgrimage north, attempting to get back to Éire. During this journey they were encountered on the shores of a northern sea by Christ Jesus their Stag. Jesus led them across the Sídhe to a place "at the top of the world." There they found a workshop and a circle of twelve *ráths* (i.e., faery huts) already prepared for them. They settled down at this esoteric place and began their compassionate and philanthropic work.

This new home in the Otherworld has come to be known as "the North Pole" in modern times, though to the Elves and Nicholas it was "**Tara Lough**," named after the Elves own home back in Éire. At this new home in the Otherworld the Elves and Nicholas listened for the wishes of needy children around the world all year long. They then planned acts of open-handed charity for each coming Yule.

Over the centuries, Nicholas came to be known by many names in many countries: *Sinter Klaas*, the *Weihnachtsmann*, Father Christmas, Grandfather Frost, and eventually – in the United States – **Santa Claus**. In all these guises Nicholas continued his benevolent ministry of anonymous gift giving, throughout the Middle Ages and down to the present day. Each year on the eve of his feast, he and the Elves crossover into *this world* and begin inspiring Yuletide cheer in those who are willing to awaken to the magick of the Winter Solstice Season. They then crossover again from Tara Lough during Matrum Noctem to deliver gifts to children in every land where his existence is accepted. They leave Tara Lough by a series of long-established 'roads' between the worlds, and return by dawn the next morning.

On the day that Nicholas and the Elves first crossedover, Jesus the Stag-of-Wisdom also gifted them with *eight magnificent Reindeer*. These animals drew the saint's wagon across the Sídhe and into the Otherworld, eventually bringing them to Tara Lough at the top of the world. As they are of divine origin, these Reindeer have the uncanny ability to find 'thin places' between the worlds.[21] Being creatures of the Otherworld, they can also fly. Thus Nicholas and his Elves can pass back and forth from Tara Lough at the top of the world, travel through the vales of mortal time and then go back again each year. The same eight Reindeer have pulled Nicholas' wagons and sleighs since his crossingover. They have recently been joined by *a 9th Reindeer*, whose name is famous.[22]

This is the basic gist of the Keltelven story of Nicholas, which has been embellished and handed down over many generations. It is still being augmented in new circumstances according to spiritual revelations that we intuit during our Yuletide celebrations. By learning the basic story – and thus tying the historical Saint Nicholas with his mediaeval and modern manifestations together in a coherent narrative – we begin to make some sense of the role Santa Claus now plays in our contemporary Yuletide Imaginations. Once we can imagine the whole story, we'll be more likely to encounter Saint Nicholas and be inspired by him on the eve of 6 December.

As dusk approaches on the eve of 6 December, Nicholas can be imagined as beginning his annual visitations. He leaves his workshop at the top of the world and, with his Elves, journeys around the world singing spiritual songs in the hopes of awakening all those who desire to be attuned to the power and light of the Winter Solstice Season.

All through the night, Nicholas and the Elves cast spells of compassion over the world as they circle around it. They chant invocations of earthen love and spiritual illumination over every known land. They touch down here and there, giving token gifts to those children and some adults as well who find it difficult to awaken to the wonder of the Winter Solstice. They make every attempt to invite everyone they encounter to kindle the Fires of Yule. Nicholas and his entourage pay particular attention to the downtrodden, leaving runes of hope for the lost and the alone.

We begin to observe this feast – as mortals pilgriming to Glastonbury Tor – as the sun sets on 5 December. Hold a special meal and dedicate it to Nicholas. This meal doesn't need to be elaborate or large. The point is not to eat a lot, but rather to pass through a door into the horizons of the Winter Solstice Season. Serve symbolic foods, such as crabapples – dyed red and green with food coloring – and cranberry sauce, walnuts and gingerbread.

Crabapples are sacred to the Spirit of Yule and are connected in symbolism with the deer, who love to eat them. To have crabapples adorning your dinner table this night is to invite the deer to come near the house and visit mortals in their dreams. This also sends out a symbolic invitation to the Reindeer of Nicholas at Tara Lough saying, "come and visit us!"

Cranberries are red and come ripe in late Autumn. They are one of the red berries associated with the Earth Goddess Tailtiu as well as with the divine birth of heroes and gods and thus with the Virgin Mary at Winter Solsticetide. They are sour to the taste and as such represent the discovery of wisdom via the hardships of life. As they grow wild in bogs, they are related to water as the source of life, and by extension, they intimate wakefulness and rebirth. As we are seeking to be spiritually awakened during Yule, we should meditate on cranberries in some form at the Nicholas Eve Feast.

Walnuts are symbols of Wisdom, which is always a hard nut to crack. Their outer shells represent the difficulty of penetrating the meaty marrow of a parable, rann or sacred riddle, and their fruit represents the nutritious and sustaining power of true Wisdom. To see Walnuts – and other nuts – on the table on Nicholas Eve is to be reminded of the Wisdom that is waiting to be discovered within the paths of Yule. To hold a Black Walnut during meditation and smell its aroma is to ask for a taste of Wisdom.

Ginger is a symbol of spiritual awakening, as it raises the metabolism and is said to enliven the spiritual senses of mortals in *this world*. Ginger kindles the Fires of Yule in the human *coích anama* (i.e., "soul house"). By eating food with Ginger in it on Nicholas Eve you are asking to be given divine fire for the Pagan pilgrimage to Glastonbury Tor. One rann in the Keltelven Book of Shadows (1948) says that "Wisdom is Spicy and comes from a Good Mother's Kitchen."

Light the first green and red candles on the table where the meal is set. As the sun goes down, light a candle scented with Hollyberry, Cinnamon or Balsam Fir extracts. These three fragrances are iconic of Yule. Smelling them in the air alerts your mind to the approach of sacred time, and helps you to augur the beginning of your own sacred journey through the Solstice Season.

Hollyberry is another of those plants with red berries that symbolize the Goddess of Birth and Rebirth, and thus it is indicative of the Virgin Mary's presence near the hearth at the tides of Winter's Solstice. The scent of this candle may be thought of as the "perfume of Brighid." When it is burning we may well become psychically or poetically aware of Brighid's presence, for she is "Guardian of the Hearth."

Cinnamon is a scent signifying knowledge. During the Winter Solstice Season it stands for the heightening of our awareness of the mystery of birth and rebirth. It is used in magical spells, prayer and rituals to enhance our ability to *see* the spiritual reality in ordinary things. As well as being put in candles to scent the place of dwelling, it can also be used to flavor food. Leaves from the Cinnamon tree can be added to wreaths that decorate the doors and windows of the house.

Balsam Fir is one of the many evergreens associated with Yule. It is connected with creativity and life-giving inspiration, and to smell its fragrance on Nicholas Eve is to be awakened to the various roles that evergreens and pines will play in the coming three weeks (see 15 December, "Balsam Fir Day" for more lore on this evergreen).

Either before or after the evening meal, tell a story or two about Nicholas. This will kindle the spiritual imagination and attune it to the coming Season. You might read Clement Clark Moore's poem "*A Visit from Saint Nicholas*" (1822) and let your imaginations ramble in its wonderfully simple rhythms. Though Moore wrote the poem for children, it's crammed with interesting details. The names of the Reindeer, for instance, go back to various pre-Christian mythologies, and the imagery of the sleigh is drawn from Norse legends of the benevolent Hrolf; a spiritual warrior who rescued travelers from avalanches and snowdrifts. Meditate on the generosity of Nicholas and his psychic reality and presence in the world as the evening unfolds.

During the evening, nurture an awareness of the presence of the Spirit of Yule by watching a favorite seasonal movie on TV, video or DVD. Pick a film that lifts your spirits and contains some scene that strikes you as embodying the spirit of Nicholas's benevolence or some other theme connected with Yule. *The Santa Clause, Hook, Home Alone, Bernard and the Genie* and *Scrooged* all communicate something of the Spirit of Yule, as do old favorites such as *Miracle on 34th Street*" or even zany classics like *Christmas in Connecticut*.

During the evening, while watching a film or telling more tales of Nicholas, serve a traditional seasonal drink, such as warm cinnamon apple-cider, eggnog or simply a mug of hot cocoa. **Apples** are symbols of wisdom, and eating one while meditating symbolizes our desire to wake up to the wisdom inherent in the season. Apples are among the favorite foods of deer. Dip apple snits in your cocoa and imagine the Stag of Yule coming to the windows of your place of dwelling!

Meditate quietly on stories you've heard or seen during the evening, and then go to bed. During the night, listen – with an imaginative flair – for sleighs or wagons going by outside. Be aware of any 'noises' you might happen to hear as you drift off to sleep. If the sound of some vehicle seems unusual, for instance, imagine that it's Nicholas in his sleigh visiting your street. He may be in his old horse-drawn wagon or perhaps the reindeer-drawn sleigh, but in these days allow that he might also be traveling in a rustic automobile or an old pick-up truck. He may even come to your town in a "hot-rod sleigh," as one popular country song portrays him. Whatever you hear, interpret it according to the runes of the night. You will then be more likely to dream of being visited by the Saint.

Imagination and dreams are two of the best ways to enter into the Spirit of Yule. While this might seem like strange advice, Keltelven mysticism has always emphasized the importance of the imagination.

Those who cannot imagine that there is a 'reality' beyond what is reported on the evening news will never be mystics. Imagination is the primary vehicle through which the Presence of Mystery becomes apparent to us. Gods and Goddesses speak to us in and through our Imagination. Contemporary society has shut down its imagination and therefore lost its faith in the Mystery of 'God.'

Everything in the spiritual life requires that we re-imagine the world around us, learning to perceive it in altered ways. Yule is perhaps the most imaginative time of the year, as it enjoins us to re-connect with our own best intuitions of what it means to be human(e); reviving compassion, generosity, and hospitality as the paths to our own transformation. Imagination – when employed under the yoke of the Spirit – will lead us into awakened states where Mystery can be experienced in salient ways.

Drift off to sleep wondering what the advent of Nicholas will mean in your house and to those with whom you are living. Nicholas will visit everyone who has an open mind and who goes to sleep anticipating dreams of their patron. Nicholas will comfort the sick and entertain the sad. Though gift-giving is now connected generally with Glastonbury Thorn Day (25 December), Nicholas may leave small trinkets for children with specific needs and for adults who are feeling lost or alone.

If you are going to become aware of Nicholas' visit you must learn to re-imagine the ordinary. If you wake up during the night, pretend that a noise has awakened you. Get up and go from room to room with a flashlight looking for evidence that Nicholas was there. Look for a chair with a warm seat, or a rocking chair that is still rocking gently, its occupant having just left after hearing you up and about. If you have children, peek into their room to see if Nicholas might be there. This act is a rune that teases the adult imagination to awaken to the Season's enigmatic magick.

If in the old days you heard sleigh-bells at midnight on the 5th of December it was a sure sign that Nicholas was near by. **Bells** were often rung to purify the air, getting rid of nasty or malevolent 'spirits' (i.e., energies that negatively affect our moods and mental states). Whether or not you imagine that you hear bells, sit up in bed and say the following invocation:

"Hail Nicholas,
Come to this house,
I bid you!
Bless our hearth and the hearts
that gather 'round it.
Come back to us,
when the Season is full of light,
and haunt us!
Amen."

Now go back to sleep, if you can. If you have dreams of Nicholas on his journey around the world, consider yourself 'visited.' Some people try to imagine – before they fall asleep – Tara Lough at the top of the world and all of the activity that has gone on there during the year before they fall asleep. This is a good way to induce dreaming. Don't think of troubles at the office or of problems you may be having, or *these* will be the subjects of your dreams. Always meditate on what you want to dream about as you wait to fall asleep.

You might get up on purpose in the middle of the night and *ring a few small bells*. Walk around through your place of dwelling, from room to room, shaking the bells so that they sound like sleigh-bells. This ritual acts as an invocation meant to attract Nicholas and the Spirit of Christmas to your dwelling. If there are children in the house, this will also help inspire *them* to the threshold of Yuletide imaginings.

Then, at dawn on 6 December, get up and *ring a hand-bell*. 'Cry in the Season' by announcing that Nicholas has indeed been in the house! Then, either before or after breakfast, engage in the old ritual of "**Tracking the Deer**." Go out to look for unusual sleigh or tire tracks in the mud, on the lawn or in the snow. If a strange set of tracks *are* discovered, follow them to see where they lead.

Going out to track the paths of Nicholas' sleigh is a form of ritual play. As an adult this will rattle the cages of your mundane horizons. As you play seriously at this ritual you might be led up the street or back an alley to a neighbor's house. If you live out in the country you might be led out across a creek or a field, into the woods and not so far away, where the trail finally vanishes in the mud or snow. This ritual, when undertaken in a state of spiritual expectation, stimulates the psychic powers and attunes participants to the presence of the Spirit of Yule.

If you *do* find yourself following a certain set of actual tracks – such as bike, ski or sled tracks in new-fallen snow – regard them as runes bearing a message from Nicholas. Seek to learn from them something about how you should keep the Yule this year. Where sleigh or tire tracks cross one another, you might try to see runes in the markings and from them figure out the best options in decisions that will affect your immediate future. Identify each track intuitively with one decision or another, and then follow it to see where it may lead, if anywhere. Is it deep and sound or just a skid mark?

This art of "divining by the tracks" focuses our intuitions and enables us to see that life's paths may be changed, deepened or enhanced. The tracks in the snow, mud or grass are made at random, and only become meaningful through *our interpretation*. We are not predestined to any particular end. You can change your mind. No track in the snow *must* mean something 'negative.' When we read natural phenomena as runes we necessarily read our own pre-dispositions into them. 'Fate' is the chimera of those who are not creative enough to re-imagine their own lives in the freedom being human gives us!

If it's impractical to go out looking for actual sleigh or tire tracks, this ritual game can also be played in the house. If you have children, initiate the game by leaving a pair of old winter boots outside one of the children's rooms. A trail of "clues" – usually in the form of small Yuletide trinkets – should be left around the house. These will lead curious children to a door where they might – if they're stealthy enough! – catch a glimpse of Nicholas as he's leaving the house. If there's snow on the ground, you might anticipate going outside for the game, having left a trail of English or Black Walnuts with ribbons tied around them – or some other such "clues" – in a trail around the yard. You might even make a trail with a pair of skis, if you want to get elaborate, and leave the walnuts in the tracks.

An adult may elect to play the role of Nicholas. This person will ring the bells at mid-night and then at dawn lead the rest of those who have slept in the house out on a more or less elaborate quest to find some gift that Nicholas has left you. This gift might be a book of magical Yuletide tales, a new CD of seasonal music or some other offering that can be enjoyed by everyone.

Finally, if you're keeping this feast alone, set up a living diorama of Nicholas' visit. If you have a hearth, place an old pair of boots to one side of it and a gift on the other side. The gift should be wrapped. It might be something you bought yourself or it can be an old icon of the season, like a book, toy or image of Nicholas that you already own. Whatever it is, select something that will help you wake up to the Presence of the Spirit of Yule. Make it look like someone was sitting there by the hearth during the night. Go to bed, and when you get up in the morning, this scene is there to greet you. Come to the hearth and 'discover' the gift. Open it just as you would any other gift.

The pretense of wrapping the gift and setting out the boots and other props is essential. If you have no hearth, set up this diorama outside your bedroom door. By acting out the story of Nicholas' visit, we become aware of the spiritual reality of the Season. The Spirit of Yule is *already present*. All we need to do is wake up and begin participating in it as pilgrims in Yule's wondrous domain.

On 6 December, set out any images you may have of Nicholas; including statues, greeting cards depicting the saint, or even a stuffed or electrical Santa Claus. This image will function as an icon of the Season, drawing your attention to your pilgrim path, leading you on to Glastonbury Tor. It should be set out on a mantel or on some coffee table or shelf where it will readily be viewed by anyone passing through the room. Choose this image with care, as it will influence the tone and temper of your journey through the Solstice to Glastonbury Tor. It shouldn't be either hooky or sentimental. Neither should it have a "sugary" appearance or be such that it appeals only to children. The icon of Nicholas will help to awaken your imagination, and thus it should be something attractive yet challenging to look at.

Icons are symbols of what they represent. We learn – as we get used to their presence and discern how to use them as foci for daily meditation – to see *through* them to the reality behind the surfaces. A good icon inspires those who look at it to want to live life more fully; more genuinely. The object of meditating on an icon is not merely to adore the wood or plaster image as a merely aesthetic object, but rather to pass through the aesthetics to the mystic reality that it symbolizes.

Sometime before dusk, hang **bells** on the front and back doors of your place of dwelling. If you can acquire a leather strap with bells on it, so much the better. These bells will jingle every time you open the door, reminding you that you are to practice *hospitality* and *generosity* toward strangers and friends who come to your door. Then, during the evening of 6 December, attempt to finish whatever trimming needs done. If 6 December falls on a weekend, you may have most of the day to do your trimming. In olden times the place of human dwelling was decorated simply but elegantly with holly, mistletoe and pine or fir. Today we add lights, tinsel and ornaments, electric candles and other trinkets. Aim for simplicity in your trimming, without diminishing the luxurious aura of the Yule.

Once you've finished decorating, attention must turn outward, to the good of others. Nicholas' Feast is a day for examining our possessions, estimating our material 'surplus,' and making plans to give away any abundance to the poor and unfortunate in our community and in the world. This benevolence can be undertaken on the personal level or engaged in by the whole family or by Pagan communities. If you live with other people, you may want to make a group donation to some local charity. Better yet, get involved with a food bank or homeless shelter during the Winter Solstice Season, when regular staff often want to take time off, and when wintry conditions increase the demand for these services.

If you haven't done it already, set up the **meditation table** for Yule during the evening of 6 December. This table is always decorated according to the seasons, with stones, leaves, images, candles, and other items arranged on it in such a way that they stir up the imagination with associations appropriate to each particular Earthen time. It is sometimes covered with ceramic tiles or a plate of glass to make it more fire resistant. An old coffee table makes a good meditation table. You should set it up in a corner of the house where people can go to it, either alone or together, to meditate and pray.

During the Winter Solstice Season this table is called the "**Yule Table**." As you undertake the journey to Glastonbury Tor, begin decorating the table with icons of the Season. These may include an image of Nicholas, apples, small bells, sprigs of Holly, Mistletoe or pine, red and green candles (not one or the other, but always at least one of each), model sleighs, a Stag's antler, and anything else that might awaken

43

you to Yule's emergent earthen and mystical powers. These icons will create an appropriate psychic mood in the house and help prepare us to pass through the portals of rebirth and transfiguration.

Before you retire to bed on 6 December, light the candles on the Yule table for the first time and reflect on the sacred journey that is ahead of you. You are now a pilgrim in the tides of the Winter Solstice! Remember paths you have followed in years past and imagine how you might want to wander through the turnstiles of the Season this time around. This meditation on the path is your official *bon voyage*. A day ago you were trying to find the place from which you would depart on your way to Glastonbury Tor and the Nativity of Rebirth. Tonight, if you haven't already left, it's time high to go! As you leave, say:

"Nicholas, Saint of Charity,
guide my steps this Season,
and let me come to the Manger
of renewal and transfiguration!

There we shall find succor and blessing,
as well as Gifts of the Spirit!

Be with us, Cernunnos, as we go,
and guide our hands
to acts of benevolence and love!
Together we shall go
    with Hope as our Star.
Amen."

You call upon Cernunnos as the Stag who will be your official guide between 6 December and the 26th of December, at which point he then departs from our world and returns to the wildwoods on the Otherside. After Nicholas Eve you have a week to distill the significance of your experiences during this initial 24-hour period and approach the Day of Gathering. Use this time to meditate on the meaning of the Solstice Season and allow the Spirit of Yule to ignite the Fires of Inspiration in your Heart.

*Natural Meditation: Meditate on the phenomena that indicate the mystical approach of the Yuletide season: snow, ice, deer, and garlands of evergreen, Holly and Mistletoe. Reflect on whatever associations each of these natural phenomena have gathered in your Christmas experience and Yuletide imaginings.

Scriptural Meditation: Focus on the Journey of Mary & Joseph to Bethlehem (Luke 2:1-5) and on the journey of the Magi to the Nativity (Matthew 2:1-13). Allow yourself to become a traveler with these ancient pilgrims, pathing toward the place where Jesus as a Pagan Son of Wisdom will be born in your heart. Imagine the trials the parents of Jesus and the Magi underwent in order to get where they were going, and interpret any trials you might be facing as you embark on your own Journey to the Nativity.

---

* **A Note on the Meditations**: Keltelvens believe that Wisdom comes two us in "two shoes:" Nature and Word. We therefore indulge in a natural meditation and a narrative for each of the days of the Yule Calendar. The "narrative" we use for Yule is the biblical story of the birth of the god-child Jesus, found in the first two chapters of Matthew and the first two chapters of Luke in the Christian Bible.

These meditations are intended as suggestions and may be used to lead you into other, deeper meditations along the way. They may be used in the morning or evening, or at any time during the day when you need to center down and recollect yourself.

B. The Thirteen Dayes of Yule (13 - 25 December)

"We are all on a journey leading us to the Hearth of the Heart. One of the most profound places where this becomes evident is in the pilgrimage of Yule."

- Gawain Smythe
The Way of the Bards (1996)

Glastonbury Thorn Day is now about two weeks away. Getting there will hopefully be an adventure! There is always spiritual joy inherent in pathing a sacred destination, though we must be persistent, so that the desired spiritual reward doesn't elude us. We come to the brink of the Yuletide journey in a different mood and state of mind every year. Even after years of keeping the Thirteen Dayes, you may still wonder just how to enter into the mysterious calends of Yule this time around! The more dedicated one is to the path, therefore, the more one will get out of the journey.

The spiritual door swung open at Nicholas' Feast has enabled us to glimpse the light of the Solstice. That light shines as a beacon of potential personal transfiguration. It illumines our horizons at night, showing us the way to go as we path through the Thirteen Dayes, and as a **Star** of spiritual insight it can be seen shining in the night sky above us as we begin our journey. This is the Star that the Astrologers from the East followed on their way to visit the god-child Jesus 2,000 years ago. This Star we must now follow, night after night during the Yule, seeking runes of authentic Heart & Hearth as we approach Glastonbury Tor.

Like either Joseph & Mary or the Pagan Astrologers from the East – we now begin our actual journey to the place of nativity (i.e., rebirth & transformation). As we enter into the aura of the Thirteen Dayes, **Cernunnos** – the Stag God – also comes to lead us along toward our goal. He is the "Lord of the Wildwood" and – in Keltelven myths – the "Keeper of Pagan Wisdom." Each day as you begin your pilgrim's work, chant:

"Cernunnos, Stag of the Heart,
Come to us, we pray you!
Fill our Minds with Insight,
Flood our Hearts with Earthy Intuition,
and charge our loins with the Strength of Courage!"

Cernunnos guides us through the Season, from touchstone to touchstone, from wellspring to henge, and from dolmen to Spirit-filled cromlech, if we allow him. He is the servant of Nicholas, the Son of Brighid and the Daghda[23] and the friend of all pilgrims – Pagan or Christian – on their way to Glastonbury Tor. He knows all of the various ways in which mortals can possibly be led and by looking for his hoof-prints as you go, he will keep you from getting too lost or losing your way.

Each evening – at sunset – invoke Cernunnos as your guide and lift your eyes up to the light of the imaginary Star. Then, having discerned the next step or two of your path complete your day's devotions through the various rituals, the telling of stories, and the enacting of dramas appropriate to each of the Thirteen Dayes.

The Keltelven Yule is replete with icons by which we can map out our progress and reflect on our motives and ultimate goals. The basic agenda we now observe evolved as a way of ordering the various rich symbols, associations and expectations usually associated with Winter's Solstice into a meaningful praxis. Each of the Thirteen Dayes takes us to a new locus of spiritual intuition where we can taste a little more of the wisdom life that is waiting for us beyond Glastonbury Tor. Each day has *two names*: a mystical name and a practical name. The **mystical name** connects the day to some primary symbol of the Winter Solstice Season, giving it its general tenor and breadth. The **practical name** identifies some specific activity assigned to each day as a way to crack open its secrets. The mystical name lends the day its symbolic locus in the broader context of the Keltelven Traditions, while the practical name connects it with specific spiritual disciplines. By reflecting on the meaning of each day and engaging in some particular activity, you will eventually arrive at Glastonbury Tor.

You don't have to devote whole days to the keeping of Yule. It's not necessary to take time off from work to celebrate the Thirteen Dayes. What *is* important is that you focus on the symbols of each day and

meditate on the path you are following as you go about your daily rounds.
If you do only this much, the Spirit of Yule will discover a berth near your
hearth and indwell your daily life with Her power and renewing influence.
So mote it be. Blessed be! Hurrahya!

The Caroller in the Stream (13 December)

Down by the swinging Bridge of Willow
the children were playing – snowy mellow;
when into the Stream a Caroller came,
wading quite near
_in the frost-bidden hollow!   1

The Caroller in brown tatters
Shadowed fishes in the Ice Stream –
all gone yellow!
The children were all playing at *snowman tag* –
but gave out a cry at the Caroller's
brusque arrival!   2

He stood with Holly-berry prophecies
on the far bank of the swift flowing stream_
He took up his stance upon a slick stone,
and waited_ for distant Elven-bells to ring!   3

The children, all playing in the stream,
were calmed by his presence – ever-greened!
Songs seemed to come to them upon the water;
like offerings to the Ever-Ambient One!   4

Silvery, like the spirit-tongues of Fire,
the Caroller swooped his lop-sided hat awry!
Jiggering He waded, tall and oddly lean_
toward the gaggle of children playing!   5

Strains of tunes came into their cold heads_
leaping trout & salmon cried out for cadence!
Their scales then sang ebullient harmonies
in the timbre of unsung and stranger meetings!   6

"Gathering Teaberries, we greet the Yule!"

Eyes meeting over slow-motioned waves,
the children playing in the stream
saw the Caroller with a gift of Gleaming Sight,
take up his Rustic Accordion!   7

Round & round in the Stream He went,
with Christmass cacophonies in style.
Delicious the tunes stirred up the waves,
where the Willows were all bending down.   8
"O Cheery-red cheeks, welcome the New Child!"

Children playing, in harmony staying,
sang along in spiraled melodie.
Then dancing across the Yule-tide Heath --
they came to certain fortunes _still glowing.   9

Round & round the glad children went –
with a hickory-dickory-dock in their carols!
"Christmas is coming!" _they all sang out,
as the Caroller offered up his prayers!   10

"Green and bustle, Gold and Holly_
I sing the songs of Yuletide's Grail!"

The Willows sang, the Holy-tree swung,
'til all the ripened fruits were un-hung!
The children playing were then declaring:
"'Tis the spell of Christmass cheer!"   11

"Come, let us dance the acorns of Yule!"
The Caroller jigged, up and down,
He went to his own tune of wyrrd merriment!
And then when he stopped, Tall Pines whistled,
calling to their Lover in Heaven's Tines!   12

Visions of blinking lights ablaze
[and some glowing, all ruby and blue −]
sent their spirits up in a Yuletide craze;
where Holly & Ivy danced ever-true!   13

Round & round their lively feet swam_
with trouts in holy lace and golden reflections,
where stars were swirling down to Earth,
like Angels for the Shepherds of the Jews!   14

And then_
Rockety-springerly the Caroller jumped_
leaving the waters − and his boots!
The Hymnody rose and fell, and swelled again −
before this Stranger dis-appeared!   15

And when the children turned around_
Yuletide was Shining in Silver Delight!
Ghostly the Waters rushed down, the Aged Willows
sent forth their wishes in billows!   16
"Yuletide is Here! _Mirth and Good Cheer!"

Children playing in the stream of Yule,
stood on thresholds of GOD's New Hearth!
There they wished their day away − dreamy mellow −
and stood proudly upon Her Heathen Stoop!   17

Visions of the Caroller jigging round
Then sent the children flinging themselves down
upon the Ground of Yuletide Being −
where every ribbon is eventually found!   18

"Christ has Stag-gered us into a truer Song!"

Playful they went to the streamy shore,
with rocks and dreams and things!
And in their watery & imagined celebrations
they sang true praises to the Grail of Love!   19

"This is the Harbinger of the Yule!"
"Come, Christmass spirits, revel in abandon!"

Pine-scented rosaries of the Heart
announced the coming of the Holy Season –
as out of the Stream the children climbed,
returning to mortal wayes of walking!   20

"And we saw an old codger in the crick,
singing songs, and playing up a trick!"

And Then_
there at the place of epiphanies
they built a waterfall of stone and memory!
Galloping, giggle-ing,
praying through their joy,
they prepared a Manger in Nature's Ring!   21

Wading in the pool behind their dam,
children playing were always saying --
"Here is where the Caroller appeared,
and here is where we danced the Ring!"   22

"Yule!" "Yule" "Time to play the Fool_
like Christ in gowns of red & green!"
"Let's all sing the Tune of Christmas-weal,
inviting the Stranger to our Fire!"   23

Runes of Christed Hospitality rose
there in youth-full Imagination's dell.
Tunes of Hope stirred Solstice Solemns,
conjuring visions of a New World Tree.   24

And as their minds were whirling 'round,
all their reticent sins fallen down
upon the Holly Byre; quite a Heathen Pyre! –
they built oratories of new dreams
within the brambles left on the shores!   25

Wreaths of Christmass folklore rung
the bells of spiritual re-cognition!
Then in the coming of Night's Pure Gleam,
The haunted children prayed in the Stream!   26

"Holy, Holy, was the Caroller,
who came with mirth and holy desire!
Holy the Stag of Christmass-tide,
who lifted high our fire-brand!

Holy, Holy, the Caroller,
who is Christ upon the Pagan Heath –
He came to Children, unexpectant,
and mixed love into life's full sheath!

Holy, Holy, those who see Him_
coming 'cross the Rood!
Holy are the poor and abused,
who'll taste His Sacred Bliss!"   27
Amen.

1. <u>Rowan</u> <u>Day</u> *(The Gathering Day, 13 December)*

"At the base of the berries of the old mystical Rowan tree is the sign of balance and protection honoured by many ancient peoples: the Pentagram – a five-pointed star. Thus to the Bards these berries are indicative of the protective powers inherent in Nature." (32)

- Gawain Smythe
<u>The</u> <u>Way</u> <u>of</u> <u>the</u> <u>Bard</u> (1996)

Gathering Day is a time to formally "establish" the hearth as the focal center of your Yuletide journey. Home is where the Hearth is, and for Keltelvens this means anywhere we are able to experience the presence of the Living Fire of the hearth-goddess **Brighid**. When you get up on this first morning of Yule, go to a hearth and kindle a new fire in it as a symbol of the Fires of Yule. **Brighid** – the protectress and benefactress of human dwelling – will then infuse the hearth with her presence and invest its fire with an aura of domestic magic. This "new fire" may be anything from (a) a candle set into the hearth and lit to (b) a small fire kindled with small sticks of fragrant woods or even (c) a full-sized blaze. If the first day of Yule is a workday, however, you'll probably not want to be setting any large fire in the hearth. Therefore, light a symbolic one, and douse it after breakfast.

Many people today live in apartments or houses constructed without fireplaces. If this is the case, you have four options. First, you might simply choose to *imagine* meditating near a large open hearth in some house that inspires your Yuletide Heart. *See* yourself in the act of lighting a fire in this imaged hearth. *Feel* the heat from it and reflect on the light it generates. Return to this imaginary hearth whenever you want to re-center yourself in the Spirit of Yule during the day.

Second, you might light a few candles on the Yule Table. *The Yule Table often functions as a symbolic hearth* for those who have no fireplace in their place of dwelling. Meditate on the flickering flames of the candles and imagine what it would be like to sit beside a hearth. Thirdly, you might go to some public house that has a hearth, and meditate there.

Many family restaurants and pubs have decent fireplaces near which you can have breakfast. Lastly, construct an artificial fireplace along an exterior wall of your house. Put electric logs in it and use this construct as an icon throughout the Season.

However you "establish the hearth," the external act should prefigure an inner reality. Anyone you live with and anyone else with whom you will be keeping the Yule should join you near the hearth on this morning. Center and meditate together on the warmth and light of the fire. Then say together:

> "Hearth of Yule, Hearth of Life,
> Come to us, relieve our strife!
> Set a flame of love to burning
> within our hearts
> that are churning
> with desires for holy renewal!"

If possible, have a meal near the hearth before going about the day's work. Center yourself in the mood created by the hearthlight. Pray for the energy and discipline to carry the peace you have found near the fire with you the rest of the day.

This is a day for *gathering memories of former Yuletide seasons* and summoning the spirits of Winter's Solstice to your place of dwelling. Yule has long been a time of *homecoming*, when friends and family gather together with the rest of their kin near a hearth. It is also a season for *entertaining the ghosts who haunt us* and who help us to return to the spiritual center where we most belong. Yule is an hospitable refuge of fond memories. It is a time for easing one another's pain and suffering, as well as praying for the relief of our distress and anxiety and the restoration of wellness.

Gathering Day is designated for consciously making new beginnings. To begin the journey is to come home to where Spirit is already present. Keltelvens believe that, if we lose awareness of the Presence of Mystery, it's not because the Spirit has left us, but because we have wandered away from our truest home.

After breakfast, embark on your daily rounds. Whether you must go to work or school, or whether you'll stay around the house and engage in domestic chores, try to keep the morning's meditations in mind. During the day, look for signs of the Season. Establish the Hearth in your own Heart as an inner place where the light of the Fires of Yule can burn and shine. Gather your dissipated spiritual sensibilities and strive to be more aware than usual of what's already happening all around.

If you have a chance, engage in the old rite of *"gathering the Rowan."* The <u>Yuletide</u> <u>Grimoire</u> (1898)[24] says, "On this day, go out to a wooded place and procure some Rowan." The wood of the **Rowan** has long been known for its protective powers and its ability to help mortals identify and eliminate evil or disruptive influences in daily life. The word "Rowan" is related to the Norse word for "a charm" and is connected with the word for "magical letters" (i.e., "rune"). Rowan branches may be used to make healing wands.

This association of the Rowan with protection and healing arises from a peculiar mark on the tree's fruit. At the base of the red Rowan berries, opposite the stem, you will find a small five-pointed star. This star is known as a **pentagram**; a symbol that has long been interpreted as a manifestation of psychic protection and spiritual balance. Keltelvens interpret the pentagram as a symbol of life's cycles and use its five points to meditate on the "Five Virtues" (Humility, Compassion, Hospitality, Discernment & Service).

Rowanberries mature in late Autumn and grow in clusters. They remain on the tree and maintain their color into early Winter. The most common variety of Rowan in the eastern U. S. is the *American Mountain Ash*, sometimes called *Roundwood*. There is also a *European Mountain Ash* and a *Showy Mountain Ash*, though these are less common the further south you go. These trees tend to like the moist soil of valleys and slopes, and are often found growing in and around coniferous forests. They may also be found growing in yards, as small, bushy hybrids of various species have been developed.

Try and locate a Rowan tree out in the woods before 13 December so you won't spend the whole of Gathering Day searching for one. When you find a Rowan, all you really need is two small twigs. Bind these together with red or green twine or wool yarn, and then hang this rustic talisman over the lintel of the main entryway of your place of dwelling. If the Rowans are plentiful, gather a handful of twigs and divide them up according to how many doors there are in your abode. Affix a small bundle of Rowan twigs over the lintel of each doorway. Rowanwood is aromatic and will lightly scent the entryways of your house for several days. As you hang each twig, repeat the following prayer-charm:

"Bough of Rowan, berry and star,
take your stand, stay where you are;
Bless all those who pass this way,
and protect all those who leave each day."
Amen.

One small branch of Rowan may also be kept to light the hearthfire at twilight, both today and on Solstice Night (21 December).

As well as hanging Rowanwood above doors, you might also make a **Rowan Cross**. Tie two small twigs of Rowan together with red or green twine or wool yarn. Hang it around your neck as a protective necklace and as a sign that you invoke Cernunnos – Lord of Wild Animals – to assist you in your pilgrimage to Glastonbury Tor.

The Rowan Cross should be equal-armed, as it symbolizes the Earth. Throughout the coming days, hold the Rowan Cross in your hands during periods of morning and/or evening meditation, allowing the power of the wood to seep into your spirit's veins and draw your attention to the light of your own Inner Hearth. As you meditate, say the name of each friend or family member who comes to mind. This act casts an aura of protection around them, and also links your hearts together in benevolent connection. If you're keeping the Yule with other people, pray a blessing over them while holding a Rowan Cross. This will bring people together in fortunate ways and thus make for blessed Yuletide gatherings. If you don't want to wear the Rowan Cross as a necklace, lay it on the Yule Table where you can use it as an icon for meditation each day until 25 December.

These small, equal-armed Rowan crosses may also be hung over fireplaces and placed in dresser drawers, hung over stoves and kitchen tables. As such they symbolize the belief that the edges and boundaries of human spacetime are holy, and that anything may happen in such vortices of transition, where mortals are either entering or leaving holy crosstroads. Everyone passing into and out of the house beneath the

56

Rowan will receive a blessing from the crosses. Spirits & ghosts coming into the house – through windows and down the chimney – are likewise blessed by the presence of Rowan. Spirits of a 'dishonorable nature' are kept out of the house by the presence of these crosses.

At dusk, light another fire in the hearth. If you're going to be around through the evening, this might as well be a full-fledged blaze. If you have a functional fireplace, procure some aromatic woods to burn during Yule. **Cherry**, **Ash** and **Blackthorn** are traditionally associated with the Hearth of Winter's Solstice and in particular with Rowan Day. If possible, kindle this fire with a sprig of Rowan. This fire symbolizes Brighid's protection of our place of dwelling. She watches over us through the fire in the hearth, warming us via the fire she simultaneously kindles in our hearts. As the new logs catch on fire, say:

> "Brand of Rowan, Fires of Yule,
> blaze and furnish us with Light;
> warm our hearts,
> and preserve us from the Ghoul."

"The ghoul" here refers to an old Keltelven belief in a "force of chaos" that symbolized everything that threatened human safety, security and wellbeing during the winter months.

If there is no hearth in your place of dwelling lay out small twigs of sacred woods on the Yule Table and light a candle with a Balsam Fir or Hollyberry scent. Light a few other candles on the table and say the incantation kneeling before them. Throughout the rest of this calendar, when an activity is suggested involving the hearth, you may adapt it to be enacted near the Yule Table.

As well as kindling this blaze in your hearth, light a few candles on your Yule Table at or soon after dusk. A **Candle flame** symbolizes solar energy that has come to the Earth from the Sun. Fire is related to spirit, breath and life. The candle flame represents a fire under the control of a well-directed human will. It also symbolizes the human spirit, the energy of which is akin to the power of fire.

Celebrating the Yule is always a matter of a willing communion of our souls with Earth & Spirit. The Spirit does not force us to keep the Yule – or any sacred season, for that matter – and so we must *accept* the psychic invitation to celebrate, meditate on holy things, and be renewed. Holy Fire comes from the Presence of Mystery and yet human beings are able to create, manage and use fire to either positive or negative ends. The candle is symbolic of the positive uses of fire by humankind.

Sharing a meal is another sign of the cooperation between human beings and the Spirit. As we must eat, we work to prepare food and set a table, but it is the Earth Goddess who ultimately provides us with the raw materials of a meal. The meal held on Gathering Day is named after **Saint Deirdre** (713-752 CE), an early Keltelven sister of Christ our Stag, who lived in Northumbria. During the tides of Yule, Dierdre made healing crosses out of Rowan and gave them as gifts to people who were unwell. She used them to cast a spell of blessing on her neighbors and friends during Matrum Noctem. She blessed enemies and strangers in the name of Christ her Stag.

Deirdre gathered the poor of her area together, including orphans, those who were neglected, the outcast and even those who were considered to be "enemies of the public good," and helped these people establish a hearth for themselves out in the wildwood or at the edge of local villages. She went to visit those who had become estranged from one another during the year, seeking paths of reconciliation where it was possible. She went to chieftains who were at war with each other and invited them to a common meal where they could discuss their animosities and where a truce might possibly be reached before Winter's Solstice. She brought hostile parties together in situations where peace of mind and good will could be nurtured. She is known as the Mistress of Reconciliation in Keltelven lore.[25]

Her feast on Rowan Day is held around the time of dusk. Begin by saying a blessing over the food to be put on the table. Then invite Saint Dierdre to be present with you by reciting the following invocation:

> "Dierdre of the poor,
> bless our table by your light!
> Dierdre of the outcast and unwelcome,
> Be welcome at our table,
> with all thy guests!
> Illumine our hearts with gracious weal
> and inspire us to common hospitality. Amen."

As a Christian Saint Deirdre evinces the ethic of hospitality so central to Keltelven spirituality and Celtic peoples in general. During the meal, meditate on the spirit of this open-hearted Pagan woman and discuss ways to advance the vision of good, earthy hospitality as the days of Yule are celebrated.

During the evening, take a little time to sit and enjoy the fire in the hearth or watch the flames of the candles that are lit on the Yule Table. Aesthetics is an important part of spiritual preparation, and we must not neglect the sensual as we seek to approach the Dolmens of the Spirit.

As mid-night approaches, arrange mementos of people who have died during the previous year on the Yule Table. This symbolizes our willingness to remember them and accept the presence of these souls near the hearth. The visitation of spirits and the souls of the dead will be celebrated on *Yew Day* (22 December). Beginning tonight, though, we prepare ourselves for the task of hosting our ghosts.

You may want to keep a little notebook – called a "**Mourning Book**" – on or near the Yule Table. In its pages you should keep a list of anyone you know who has died during the year, as well as an ongoing list of ancestors and relatives of former generations who stand out in your mind as people you want or need to remember. As the years pass, a series of pages will develop recording the names of those who were remembered at the Yule Tables of past seasons. Finally, make a list of your greatest losses or disappointments during the previous year.

This book will become a source of connection between those dwelling near the hearth during the tides of Winter's Solstice, on both *this* side and on the other side of the veil between the worlds. When you go to meditate or pray at the Yule Table, open the Mourning Book and read over the names you find listed in it. You might take one name each day and pray for that person's well-being in the Otherworld. You might also read over entries written by other people keeping the Yule with you. These entries may be written in cryptic or enigmatic terms, and should always remain anonymous. Pray only for the concerns that you are moved by the Spirit to mention and pass over the others. Reading these entries forges garlanding links of compassion between the celebrants of the Yule.

Even if you are keeping the Yule alone, make a Mourning Book and write out your concerns. Pray for these as you are led, from day to day and use this list to reach out to other people in a similar situation. No matter how we suffer or what afflicts us, we are never alone. Even if we're involuntarily keeping the Yule by ourselves, we can enter into spiritual company with other people through prayer.

The names recorded in the Mourning Book remind us that, although there is a veil between this life and the next, love never dies, and the connection between people who love survives the event of death. At certain times during the year – especially at Samhain (31 October)[26] and during the Yule, the veil separating *this world* and the Otherworld grows thin and our loved ones can come back to visit us. "At Winter's Solstice we all come home. Even the dead are welcome here" (<u>Yuletide</u> <u>Grimoire</u>, 1898).

This is perfectly natural according to Keltelven mysticism. Keltelvens – like the Celts and the Elves before them – believe that death is a transformation; a passage from one stage of our existence into another. When we die we *discarnate* and go on a journey into the Otherworld, which is sometimes called "the AETHER" in Keltelven mysticism.[27] Life in the Otherworld is simply a continuation of the life we have been living in *this world*. Whatever spiritual progress we have made *here* becomes the basis for our existence *there*.

The wiser we have become *here*, while incarnate, the easier it will be to travel and experience life to the fullest in the Otherworld. Those who have made little or no spiritual progress in *this life* may well fall asleep at the point of death, not to wake up until after an extended incubation period (like what a caterpillar goes through, as it becomes a butterfly). Those who have led wicked lives in *this world* may disintegrate in the transition called mortal death, ceasing to exist altogether. Thus the dead who return from the Otherside during Yule are not to be feared; only those who survived death – by being seekers of wisdom in this life – can return to haunt us.

"On Gathering Day
Shall all the Spirits of Kith and Kin
Return to the Hearth."

Natural Meditation: Focus on the Rowan Cross and the earth-power it represents; protection against evil forces, empowerment of the human soul, security through the wintry months, and the connection between the divine (the vertical axis) and the human (the horizontal axis).

Scriptural Meditation: Focus on the Annunciation of the Angel Gabriel to Zechariah concerning the birth of John the Baptist to his aged wife (Luke 1:5-25). Imagine being encountered by an Angel. A biblical Angel is not sweet and cuddly, but a higher form of spiritual life in which 'GOD's' Will is manifest.

2. <u>Cedar</u> <u>Day</u> *(Lighting Day, 14 December)*

"Ever since I was a boy, Cedar trees have stood in our social hall in honor of the Winter Solstice. Cedar wood hath a purifying agency. The smoke from cedar sticks, when burnt in the hearth, doth purge a house of evil influences. The aroma of Cedar will heal thy children of sneezes and sores and keep evil fevers at bay. Keeping a piece of fragrant cedar wood near your bed will drive away bad dreams, and attract the faeries to your mind's world!"

- Egbert Whittier
<u>The</u> <u>Thirteen</u> <u>Dayes</u> <u>of</u> <u>Yule</u> (1800)

Though the exterior trimmings have been lit since Nicholas Eve or even earlier, and while the Hearth has already been established, the 14th of December is still known as "Lighting Day." There's a great deal of light to be let into the place of dwelling during Yule, as the Sun's power wanes. Thus on this day we focus on light, lighting, and illumination, as we progress toward Glastonbury Tor, following Cernunnos our Stag and the mystic Star.

There are two primary kinds of light in Keltelven philosophy: *Sunlight* and *Moonlight*. These two lights inspire complementary kinds of wisdom: *Solar* and *Lunar*. **Enlightenment** is connected with the Sun, while **Illumination** is connected with the Moon. Whereas the hearthfire is thought of as a chunk of the Sun fallen to Earth, candles have often been linked to the Moon as the mystical source of illumination.

Candles have a long pedigree in Winter Solstice lore and decorations. They have been in use since before the time of Christ. The first crude candles were made of fats wrapped in husks or moss. Later, chandlers discovered how to affix long wicks inside tin molds. Hot tallow and beeswax were then melted and poured into the molds. Today most candles are made from paraffin, which is an oil by-product, though you can still occasionally find beeswax candles in specialty stores.

Illumination is the primary goal of those entering the candle-lit chambers of Yule as pilgrims on their way to the Winter Solstice. After the Solstice, Enlightenment becomes the goal we seek as we wend our way to Matrum Noctem and the mysteries of the manger of psychic and spiritual rebirth. The journey through the Winter Solstice Season, therefore, is at first a *Lunar* and then a *Solar* pilgrimage.

For Lighting Day, try to obtain an interesting candle, perhaps made of beeswax or tallow. Set this candle out on the breakfast table in the middle of a **Yule Wheel** (a round holder with a place for four candles) or in some other appropriate holder. This candle may be surrounded with small sprigs of pine and should be lit during breakfast. Later move it to the Yule Table. Whether carved, specially molded or made of tallow or beeswax, allow this candle to remind you of the transforming powers of Yule.

If you can't find a beeswax or tallow candle, you might chose one scented with **Pine**, **Hollyberry** or **Cinnamon**. These scents are all connected with light and wisdom. A candle is a symbol of the materiality of life (the wax) being turned into spiritual energy (the flame). If you are going to be at home for the day, light a "day candle" (one in a glass container that will burn all day) at dawn, and let it burn throughout the day as a symbol of the spiritual light coming into the house.

This is the day when Keltelvens bring their **Yule Tree** into the place of dwelling, and so the 14th of December is called **Cedar Day**. Cedar – both the wood and the scent – has long been connected with the Winter Solstice. Cedar is deeply rooted in the cultural soil of western religious symbolism. Solomon – the wise king of the Jews who lived in the 10th century BCE – built a Temple in Jerusalem of Cedarwood.[28] As the Temple was a house for Yahweh (i.e., "God") to dwell in among his people, Cedar came to be the primary building material for chapels and oratories in later traditions, including among Celtic followers of Christ. Legends say that the gifts of gold, frankincense and myrrh brought by the Pagan Astrologers to the infant Jesus were carried in boxes made of Cedar. Keltelvens therefore keep magical grimoires, prayer books and the various paraphernalia of their arts and crafts in Cedar boxes. Devotions during Yule are often accompanied by the burning of Cedar-scented incense.

Cedarwood has any number of uses during Yule. First, the Yule Tree might be a Cedar. Second, Cedar boughs are used for decking the halls and making wreaths. Thirdly, Cedar branches are chipped up and scattered around the Nativity scene (which depicts the Birth of Jesus and thus our own rebirth). Cedar boxes may be given as gifts, and finally,

Cedar paper may be used for lining dresser drawers as Yule begins. As such, our dwelling is perfumed with Cedar in both obvious and subtle ways.

As this is the day when we invite the **"Evergreen Guest"** into the place of dwelling, those who have embarked upon the pilgrimage of Yule should have finished all necessary preparations. The place of dwelling must be fully decorated before the Yule Tree is brought in, as we are preparing the house for a representative of the Spirit of Yule. The Yule Tree is sacred to our Wisdom-Stag Cernunnos. In the presence of this guest we will experience a transformation of dwelling. The Light of the Season will then become visible to all who come to dwell near the Hearth.

Evergreen pines and firs growing wild in the woods were anciently seen as embodying an assurance from the god of the wilderness that mortals would always have access to the life-force during the cold, dark winter months. As pines remain green, so life survives the depths of wintry darkness and numbing cold. Green is a primary symbol of the life-force. As such, evergreens also remind people that life survives the sleep of death. When a pine or fir-tree is cut down and brought into the house, it symbolizes the tenacity of life. Through it Cernunnos becomes present among us. Many mystics claim to have seen the face of Cernunnos in the boughs of the Yule Tree. The Yule Tree also becomes a door through which souls and spirits may pass back and forth between the worlds.

The Yule Tree always used to be set up near the hearth as a symbol of the Goddess dwelling among us. The hearthfire is a masculine symbol, whereas the hearth itself is seen as feminine. The hearth is the "locus" of Brighid, daughter of the Great Triple Goddess,[29] with its womb-shaped orifice open for the masculine powers of the Sun – in the form of fire – to enter. The hearth holds the power of rebirth – including the rebirth of the Sun at Winter Solstice – within it. If you don't have a hearth, set up your Yule Tree near the meditation table, which embodies the powers of the hearth during Yule.

The Yule Tree also symbolizes the mystery and magick of the natural world. When the Tree is brought in its natural and mystical powers suffuse the place of dwelling, triggering implicit cadences of spiritual regeneration as if a set of wires were finally attached to a psychic battery. Its presence then becomes a catalyst for meditation, celebration, and mystical experience. Keltelvens have often had encounters with Brighid, Cernunnos, Christ, Mary, and saints while sitting near their Yule Tree.

Going out to find a tree has always been a kind of mini-quest within the larger pilgrimage of Yule. Try to be conscious of what you are doing, and don't get frustrated if at first no tree seems to 'offer itself' to you. If you have to deal with irate fellow consumers or dishonest tree sellers, take it all in stride. Journeying from one tree lot to another, from one side of town to the other, looking for just the 'right' tree for your place of dwelling usually demands patience. It always involves an intuitive if not an imaginative effort to locate just the right tree. If you find your tree without much bother, be thankful! The pilgrimage ends in either bliss or fiasco depending on the tree you either do or do not find.

In Olden Dayes – and perhaps not so long ago – those keeping Yule together would go out into a wildwood at daybreak, carrying axes and dragging a byre on which to haul the tree back home. This was a ritual anticipated by young and old alike; it was not just 'another obligation' to be fulfilled because Alban Arthuan was coming. Spiritual preparations only become obligations when people no longer believe in what they're doing. Having found just the right tree, it was hauled home and invited into the house. This scene is still depicted on holiday cards. If you have such an image, use it as an icon for meditation on Cedar Day. What does the image of the child or family dragging the evergreen tree through the snow signify to you? What does it mean to bring the Yule Tree to the place where you live near the hearth?

Carrying the Yule Tree across the threshold is a momentous act. The Evergreen Guest should be invited into the house with a word of welcome and petition. Pronounce a benediction of welcome over the tree at the door, saying:

> "Tree of pine, kin of fir,
> we hail thee to our halls full of Earthen glow!
> Come ye in, now, bless this dwelling,
> with all your power; and all our woes be now quelling!
> So mote it be."

Everyone says "Hurrahya," and then the tree is brought through the door and set up near the hearth (or Yule Table). It's important to formally *invite* the tree into the house for by this symbolic act you are welcoming all of the mystical and natural powers connected with the tree to come to your hearth.

Once set up, the Yule Tree becomes the spiritual and aesthetic center of Yuletide dwelling. All of the decking of halls and festooning you've done – whether you live in a mansion or a two-room apartment – should now be centered around Tree and Hearth. When someone enters the house, their attention will be drawn to where the Tree is standing. Let anyone who will salute the tree say, "Hail, Ever Green Lord!" This vow acknowledges that Cernunnos our Spirit-Guide is dwelling with us.

As well as symbolizing the presence of the Wild Lord in the house, the Yule Tree also represents everlasting life – as it doesn't shed its needles – as well as the power of potential perpetual wakefulness – called **Ceugant**[30] – to the Presence of Divine Mystery. This 'perpetual wakefulness' is the dream of all mystics – to dwell in an unbroken communion with the Spirit in *this* life – and is the ultimate goal of the authentic spiritual journey, both in this life and in the next.

Today there is a real turn toward the use of *artificial trees*. All I can say about this is that it can be either good or bad, depending upon one's motives and the way these tree-substitutes are treated. It is possible that, while the live evergreen is a symbol of something spiritual that cannot really be put into words, the artificial Yule Tree becomes the symbol of the evergreen. If you experience the power of the live evergreen *in* the presence of the artificial tree, then it's probably sufficient to have an artificial one. Just because something is 'artificial' doesn't make it 'unholy!'

The cost of live trees in urban areas may also make the choice of an artificial tree necessary, if not always desirable. Allergies may also prevent the use of live trees. Elderly people may need to put up smaller artificial trees, as all the work it takes to put up and take down a live evergreen may be too much for them. Meditate on the nature of the Yule tree as a symbol, therefore, and decide for yourselves whether you need a live tree or whether you can celebrate just as well with an artificial tree.

If you decide to use an artificial tree, use your imagination to participate in setting it up. Getting the artificial tree out of its box and putting it together can be equal to the quest for a real tree, providing that you engage in it with a lively sense that your place of dwelling will

66

awaken to the Spirit of Yule once the tree is in place. Artificial trees are –
in essence – large *icons* of the Season.

After the tree has been invited into the place of dwelling and set up,
water it and let it alone for a while, perhaps as long as a couple of hours.
This allows the branches to drink in the fresh water and relax, returning to
their normal position, after being dragged, shook and even bound with
twine for the trek to your place of dwelling.

If you leave the tree in the room by itself for a while, its energies will
link up with the psychic and spiritual energy of your place of dwelling and
begin its transforming work. To this end, turn off the lights and close the
door to the room where the Evergreen Guest has been set up. Depending
on the time of day or night, go and eat a meal or have a dessert or snack
and then come back later to trim the tree. Entering the room after the tree
has been left alone in the dark you may well be struck by the fragrance
with which your guest has scented the room. This aroma works on our
aesthetic sense to stimulate Yuletide imaginings and helps awaken us to
the fact that Mystery is present to us in mortal time.

As you trim the tree, think of it as symbolic of the Cosmos, with the
severed trunk actually extending down through the floor in its tree-ing
power, taking root in the earth (down in **Annwn**[31]) below where you
dwell. Imagine the top of the tree touching the gateway to the heavens
(**Gwynnyd**[32]), which is an old metaphor for the doors of the Sídhe leading
into the Otherworld and Paradise. The trunk then becomes the Staff of
Life, the branches and needles representing all living things on their way
through this present life. The Yule Tree is thus a symbol of the eternal
ordering of the universe, in which life springs up from the Earth (**Abred**[33])
and reaches toward the heavens. The upward sweeping boughs represent
the movement of the Spirit of Life encouraging us to ascend into more
mature states of spiritual consciousness (**Gwynnyd**). We are all like the
needles of the Yule tree; connected to Life's Source in our present
condition, blessed with animating sap, and yet with an innate desire to
journey on from here.

As the years pass we may imagine ourselves existing higher up on the
boughs of the tree, drawing ever closer to our ultimate spiritual goal.
Look at the tree, with all of its ornaments, as representing a Spiral Ladder
into the Divine Heart of the Hearth (**Ceugant**). Once the tree is decorated,

meditate on your own spiritual journey. Where are you situated in the boughs of the Tree *this* year?

The spiritual life is a journey. It involves a process, and leads from a place of psychic infancy to where we are as mature as we can be as mortal, finite creatures. We never really arrive at our destination in this life and yet progress is always possible provided we remain devoted to pathing Wisdom in everyday life, in our mystical experiences and in mundane tasks as well. 'Pathing' is the essence of a mystic's experiential praxis. Each year at the tides of Yule we recollect ourselves, taking stock of the progress we've made during the year. The Solstice is then a time for new beginnings. We hope to experience a rebirth by the 25th of December that will enable us to rededicate ourselves to the Path.

Tree-trimming may continue through the evening, though it should be finished before mid-night (halfway between dusk and dawn, *not* 12:00 AM). If we're alert to what's happening around us spiritually, trimming can become a mystery-infused few hours. As you trim, share stories of decorating from years gone by, remembering some of the Yule Trees that have been guests in your house.

If you feel playful, imagine Elves coming to help with the trimming. Someone may want to 'talk' with the Elves and share with the rest of you what the Little Folk are saying and doing. Elves have a long association with the Yule Season, and are not just figments of a childish imagination. Elvenfolk are among the most magical inhabitants of the spiritual worlds of Keltelven mystics. Elves are woven into the symbolism of the Solstice Season, just as surely as the Yule Tree, gifts and all the various traditional decorations. They accompany Nicholas on his rounds, and visit the home of every mortal seeking to discover the authentic runes of Winter's Solstice. They sometimes play tricks on us. They may tease and lead us into embarrassing circumstances. All these tricks, though, are meant to jar our sensibilities and awaken us in the illumination of the Fires of Yule.

Every Keltelven hearth may have its favorite imaginary elf. This may be an elf you heard about as a child or one you have become acquainted with since those days. The elf that haunts your hearth should be given a name suited to its character. If so inspired, tell new stories about it from year to year. These stories help the sleeping Mystic Mind to "wake up" to the Presence of the Spirit of Yule in the world. In this *waeccan*[34] state we hope to be ferried through the Yule.

When you finish trimming, turn off any tree lights that may have been turned on during the decorating and then wait for midnight. Everyone keeping the Season together should now gather around the tree. Then, light the lights and sing a carol. "*O Tannenbaum*" is a good song for the occasion. If someone among you plays a musical instrument, ask them to accompany your singing. Otherwise sing the song a cappella. If you aren't terribly musical, sing along with a recording or simply listen to one. The point is that *music* should accompany the lighting of the tree lights.

After the lighting ritual, put on a CD of seasonal music and stay up for a while, meditating on the various lights and other trimmings on the tree. As a traditional beverage, you might want to make up a bowl of hot cider-wassail for the occasion. One old recipe for it says:

> "In a large crock, heat a quart of apple juice laced with three cups of rum, and 2 twined cups of orange juice. Throw in six baked lady-apples, six small oranges, also baked, and three whole cloves to make it cheery! Serve hot and add cinnamon sticks to taste!" (The Thirteen Dayes, 1800; Appendix)

Sing songs, dance around the Christmas Tree (or in the center of the room where it stands), or simply sit and relax somewhere while others dance and sing. Once you have imbibed as much of the light of Cedar Day as you think you can relish at one time, wander off to bed.

> **Natural Meditation**: Focus on the symbolic nature of evergreens, generally, and on the symbols inherent in the Yule tree. At each stage in the process of finding, setting up and lighting the Yule Tree, pause to consider its significance.

> **Scriptural Meditation**: Focus generally on the presence of Jesus – as a Son of Mother Wisdom – in the Yule Tree. In the morning, meditate on the Annunciation of the Angel Gabriel to Mary concerning the birth of the Messiah (Luke 1:26-38), which may later be connected with the hanging of

an angel ornament on the tree or the placing of an Angel on the treetop.

Evening devotions should focus on the angel's visit to Joseph, and his response to Mary's being called to be the Mother of God (Matthew 1:18-24).

3. *Balsam Fir Day (Arts-and-Craefts Day, 15 December)*

"The ancient Bards of the Celts took branches of Balsam
Fir and waved them in the air at sacred prayer circles.
They thought of it's fragrance as making the presence of
the Muse – and later the Holy Spirit – known to mortal
senses." (36)

> - Gawain Smythe
> The Way of the Bards (1996)

We all know how much work goes into keeping Yule and experiencing
the Winter Solstice. No sacred season is without its holy labor. One of
the first things we need to do, therefore, as we wake up from the dull
round of the world's obsessive superficiality is to find a path of
moderation, balance and hearty compassion by which to path through
sacred seasons. Part of being a pilgrim on the way to Glastonbury Tor
involves learning how to discern between essential and superfluous
activities. We must weed out our appointment books and holiday
organizers if we're going to discern the Wisdom of Yule. There is work
that needs done, there are arts and craefts that must be employed, and if
our effort is not going to be wasted we must discern what is necessary and
what is not.

Approaching Winter's Solstice is an aesthetic adventure through which
we hope to experience personal (and even communal) transformation,
recovering the glimmers of our own best self-understanding. Keeping the
Yule well requires that we exert ourselves in devout ways and follow the
runes of the season in directions that will get us to the goal we're seeking.

There are practical arts and craefts that human beings use on a daily
basis that make a livelihood possible. There is also a range of mystical
arts & crafts that enhance the meaning and quality of daily life. These
latter include the arts of magick (**draíocht**),[35] divination (**taghairm**)[36] and
herbal arts (**corrguine**)[37] as well as some more basic craefts such as the
making of tools, candles and other paraphernalia for the mystical arts.
Through all of these various arts & crafts we seek to achieve wisely
compassionate ways of dwelling in the Earth & Spirit. While practical
arts & craefts generally establish the material basis of a good life, magical-

71

mystical arts & craefts help to improve the quality of life and expand our spiritual horizons. Though it is possible to 'survive' from day to day and establish a material kind of security on the basis of practical arts, the mystical arts add to the depth and ambiance of life.

The arts & craefts associated with the keeping of Yule are acknowledged and consecrated on the 15th of December. Today we dedicate our work – both practical and mystical – to the discovery of whatever Wisdom might emerge from our pilgrim journey into the darkness of the Solstice. On this day we should meditate on the value of the work we put into celebrating the Yule. How do we do what must be done in a devout way? Whether we're cooking, shopping, making gifts or engaging in divination in an attempt to discern the path we should take to Glastonbury Tor, everything we do comes under the aegis of either **Brighid**, as mistress of the kitchen, or **Lugh**, as master of the workbench.

Reflect on the work you *must* do, what you *can* give up doing, and what you can't *avoid* doing, and then engage in a *blessing of work*. Promise to flee from unfruitful or unnecessary labor, and then dedicate yourself anew to the "arts & craefts." During a morning meditation, say:

> "I give myself to the work
> that I am called to do,
> and promise to do neither more nor less.
> In this holy season,
> let me be
> sanctified to Wisdom's Walk."

There is both false and true work, and by this prayer we hope to make out which is which. We must continually discern the nature of the demands being put on us by other people, the media, and even by our own conscience. To do this, gather first at the kitchen table, light a Balsam scented candle and say:

> "We offer all our kitchen arts
> to Brighid who is the housewife
> of all creation.
> Gift our hands and minds and backs
> with the power to carry out
> everything needful
> for the keeping of this Season."

Then go to the worktable or to wherever you engage in craeft-work (perhaps at your office?), and say:

"We offer all our work
to Lugh, who is the craeftiest of all.
Bless our hands and eyes and minds for this work
and let it be
sanctified to walking in Wise Paths.
So mote it be."

Lugh and Brighid are the primary deities presiding over the arts & craefts during Yule. They represent various powers of the Spirit manifest in personalized form. For the Keltelven mystic, meditating on an image of Lugh or Brighid or calling on them for inspiration is a way of invoking the power of the Spirit of Yule on the 15th of December. When you invoke their names, the Spirit lights a Holy Fire in the devout minds and hearts of mortals. Warmed by this fire, you will then be better inspired to carry out whatever tasks may be at hand today and throughout the rest of the season.

Lugh gained admittance to the divine household of the Tuatha Dé Danann (the ancient Irish gods and goddesses) by being omnicraefty. Every Celtic deity had a trait or talent by which they were known; Lugh, however, could do it all! This was his claim to fame. Lugh's annual festival is held on 1 August (Lughnassadh). By calling on his name we indicate our desire to learn craeftwork.

Brighid is one of the primary ancient Celtic names of the Goddess. Brighid had many forms and manifestations, and may be thought of as an omnicraefty goddess. She's one of a triad of goddesses connected with Alban Arthuan, her two sisters being **Nerthus** and **Coventina**. During the Yule Brighid is Mistress of the Kitchen. She is the Lady of Inspiration in the glow of the Winter Solstice fires. She is versed in the healing arts.

Lugh & Brighid both visit the huts and hearths of those who are keeping the Yule in authentic earthen ways in the Spirit. They each carry a Balsam Fir bough when they come visiting. These function as natural icons of their divine identity. If we dream of them, we will recognize Lugh or Brighid because of the Balsam Fir branches in their hands. Dreamers

73

who have been inspired by these omnicraefty deities may wake up in the morning smelling the scent of Balsam Fir in their bedchamber!

Lugh comes in the early hours of 15 December and blesses the Keltelven worktable, leaving his power in the woodworking tools and the bellows, as well as in the farming tools. He may also be seen as blessing our PCs and other high-tech machines, though these are modern tools. Brighid comes to bless our kitchens, inspiring cooks and their assistants to create seasonal foods as Alban Arthuan approaches. She invests the kitchen utensils, the microwave, refrigerator and the stove with her artful power.

Each of these deities is thought to leave a twig of Balsam Fir in the house during their visit. Brighid leaves hers on the kitchen table while Lugh leaves his on a workbench, or perhaps on the hearthstones. These tokens let mortals know that they have been visited. After such visitations, the scent of Balsam Fir pervades the house, and so Arts & Craefts Day is also called **Balsam Fir Day**.

Balsam Fir is one of the many evergreens brought into the house and used in making swags and other decorations. The trees grow from 40 to 60 feet high, and their needles are pungently fragrant. The wood of the tree yields a fragrant resin. Its red berries and dark green needles make it an appropriate symbol of Yule.

At dawn on this day, use sprigs of Balsam Fir to enhance the centerpiece on your breakfast table. Light a candle scented with the fragrance of Balsam Fir. If you have one or two small Balsam Fir branches, attach one to the front of your Yule Table. If you have a worktable, light a candle on it scented with Balsam Fir. Take a bough of Balsam Fir and dip it in warm water. Then spray the doors of the house with the water, saying:

"With this water I douse thee,
with love and the Yule Spirit's power,
to let all positive creative spirits
come through you,
and drive away unwonted forces!"

This invocation is meant to attract "spirits of skillful endeavor" to your hearth.

Balsam Fir enhances the quest for Wisdom through the practice of traditional arts & craefts. To keep a small branch of Balsam Fir in a jar of water on the Yule Table is to invoke artistic and crafty talent. Those who work near it should imagine themselves invested with its power. After keeping the Yule for several years the simple scent of Balsam will be sufficient to inspire you to engage in creative acts.

A lone Balsam Fir in the wildwoods is a place where the Elvenfolk are said to romp and celebrate the Winter Solstice. Such trees often become sacred sites of mysterious encounters, well known to the mystics of the area, who frequent them regularly. Seek them out as places of inspiration! Offerings of fruit and baked goods may be left at them for the Good Folk to find.

If you know of a place where Balsam Fir grows, go out to it on this day and meditate near it. Break off a small sprig and hold it in your hand, praying for restored creative powers, saying:

> "Holy Balsam, bless my wits
> and make me craefty!
> Bank a fire
> of holy work within my heart
> and let me drink
> of Your Psychic Power!
> Amen."

A Balsam Fir tree has a triangular outline when it's found growing out in the open, unencumbered by nearby trees. Because of its symbolic shape, Balsam Fir has long been prized as a Yule Tree. The cone-shaped triangle is associated primarily with Moon-power; the source of all creative inspiration in the Earth. Keltelven Bards, it is said, once built their beehive-shaped (i.e., triangular) oratories near Balsam Firs in order to be close to a natural vortex of lunar inspiration.

Balsams are generally straight, their branches splaying out in whorls from the trunk. The cones, which are erect when mature, are composed of thin, close scales, each scale bearing two winged seeds when ripe. An old rann urges that you should hold three Balsam Fir cones in your hands during meditation to restore your creative powers. You might keep three such cones on your Yule Table. Then, when the hustle & bustle of life gets you down, return to the table and meditate while holding the cones.

Balsam Fir Day is a kitchen and workshop day. Those who are good cooks spend what free time they have making any foods that can be prepared ahead of time for later feasts. This might include making minced-meat for pies, baking fruitcakes and making various kinds of seasonal candy and cookies. **Yule candy** – especially the old rock-drop or snowdrop variety covered lightly in confectioner's sugar – is easy to make, so that even those not usually proficient in the kitchen can help.

Candle making is also traditionally associated with Balsam Fir Day. Candles are vehicles of light and the flame they hold makes us aware of the presence of Faery Light[38] and the supernal Light of the Spirit in our lives. Tapered candles are made using traditional dipping methods. Pillar or column candles are made using plastic or metal forms into which hot wax is poured. The process of candle-making requires great care, though it's fairly easy once you learn the basics. If you make candles on this day, decorate some with seasonal motifs. Designate a few of these for burning before Glastonbury Thorn Day. The rest may be put back for feasts and celebrations in the coming year. If you practice this craeft year after year on Balsam Fir Day, you'll eventually reach the point where you're *making* all of the candles you burn during the Yule from one year to the next.

Painting Yuletide icons is another craeft associated with Balsam Fir Day. These icons are usually made of plaster, plastic or ceramic. They represent various sacred characters, such as Santa Claus, the Yuletide deities (Lugh, Cernunnos, Brighid and Nerthus as well as the god-child Jesus), Reindeer, Elves, and various ancient saints or deities. Unfinished figurines can sometimes be purchased in craeft stores or, if you're bolder, made at home. As with candle-making, any number of good guides for making plaster statues and then for painting them are usually available in hobby stores.

Choose a figure with which you feel connected spiritually. Try to paint a different figure each year. Use the preparation and painting as a time to center yourself and meditate on the sanctity of arts & craefts as well as on the character whose figure you're painting. Those who are not engaged in the arts of the kitchen or candle making may find this a good meditative way in which to be devoted to the Yuletide path on Balsam Fir Day.

The creation of sacred figurines should be done with great care and devotion to the ideals represented by the various characters you paint. Set out finished figures around the house or put them on your Yule Table as icons. Images on the meditation table invoke the presence of the reality behind the image. As you set each icon up on the meditation table, say:

"Holy One [or *name*],
visit us in this place of dwelling
and bless those who are seeking
the hearth of Christmas.
Guide us with Inspiration,
lead us with forbearance,
and help us to reach
our destination!
Amen."

One day may be enough time for *some* people to paint a single figure. For others, however, this may take much longer! If so, work on your figurine as an active meditation day by day until Matrum Noctem.

Each evening at dusk, light a candle near the icon and invoke the presence of what it stands for. If the icon is of a fictitious character or of an animal, their presence will be felt differently than if the icon represents an historical figure – such as a saint – who is now living in the Otherworld.

Balsam Fir Day is also a time for thinking about the gifts you are going to give and is also when you might work on hand-made gifts for friends and family. Such gifts are invested with a degree of love and intention, generosity and good that purchased gifts rarely carry. The creation of such gifts is devoted to Lugh and Brighid as well as the welfare of the intended recipient. You might want to craeft small trinket toys to be put in stockings and addressed from Santa Claus to the children. There is something still almost magical in receiving a homemade gift from the Old Saint.

If you're keeping Yule with a group of people (family, friends or a Pagan community) you might want to put on a **Nativity Drama**. This play – usually acted out at mid-night on Matrum Noctem – re-enacts the story of the birth of Jesus of Nazareth and thereby represents our own desired rebirth at Glastonbury Tor. If you intend to put on a nativity drama, you might want to finish up your plans for the play and even practice it once or twice on the 15th of December.

Though this day is dedicated to practical work and to mystical arts & craefts, we may also approach it in a metaphorical sense as a time "to craeft ourselves into works of divine art," as it says in the <u>Yuletide Grimoire</u> (1898). Begin this work by meditating on the image of rebirth encoded in the rann that, "as Spirit has given herself to us in the Earth, so we should return our lives to Her every year at Alban Arthuan." This self-craefting is a *"mystery"* in which we discover the presence of the Spirit within us. Women discover the Goddess-within, while men discover the God-within. Meditate saying:

"Make my life a work of art
worthy of mere mortal contemplation,
and pleasant to Your Eye,
O God/Goddess, my Source and Inner Light.
Nema."

As you meditate, consider how your life is arranged and what you might need to do to bring it more into accord with the aesthetics of Divine Presence in the world where you live. This is a not a meditation on mere fashion, as if the outward appearance is what makes something truly aesthetic. True spiritual beauty arises from "the right alignment of all the parts of our life in a single whole," and from "the outward manifesting the inward," as the <u>Yuletide</u> <u>Grimoire</u> (1898) says. Thus the artistic meditation for today involves bringing our lives together in a coherent vision of *Slán* (i.e., wholeness).

One of the best ways to "to craeft ourselves as images of Divine Mystery," is to engage in *hospitality and service*, "humbly and with devout willingness and joy." Imagine ways to render a service to others without making a pretense of it. There are innumerable ways to practice the art of service. Pray about what those around you might need, and then seek to contribute to the fulfillment of these needs in largely anonymous ways, without getting in the way of other people or simply robbing them of the opportunity to do things for themselves. Service does not mean taking other people's legitimate work from them and doing it yourself, as if you're doing them a favor. Look for genuine need and not just for something *you* would *like* to do. True service begins in craeft and ends in art.

As this day ends, look back on what you have done or left undone and pray for an infusion of divine art and craeft. We never wholly become the people we *could* be in this life, as we are always evolving. The point is to get a little closer to *Slán* – 'wholeness' for ourselves and in the company of others – at each station along the Way.

> **Natural Meditation**: Focus on the giving of gifts during the Yuletide Season and then on the relationship between the gift of life that we receive each time we are born into *this world* and the gift we can make of ourselves to others. Meditate on the nature of work and art and craeft and the relationship of each to the others. Meditate on the Balsam Fir tree and imagine yourself *as* a wild Balsam, full of creative power and energy.

> **Scriptural Meditation**: Focus on the Visitation of Mary to Elisabeth (Luke 1:39-45). Meditate on the Divine craeft involved in the creation of the life unfolding in Mary's womb. This is a sublime mystery! Then meditate on Joseph – the carpenter foster-father – who remains at home in Nazareth while Mary goes on her first journey; i.e., to visit her cousin Elisabeth and share the news of the divine conception in her womb. Imagine the things that might have gone through his head as he continued to work while his wife-to-be was away.

4. <u>Hemlock Day</u> *(The Storytelling Day, 16 December)*

"The Bards are the masters and mistresses of the art of telling tales. They must memorize literally thousands of verses in order to be initiated at the Hemlock Door, and they know the pattern of every true story by heart. Thus the Keltelven bards are the keepers of the Hemlock Door of narrative inspiration." (2)

- Gawain Smythe
The <u>Way</u> <u>of</u> <u>the</u> <u>Bards</u> (1996)

Stories play a crucial role in the keeping of Yule and in the experience of Winter's Solstice. The telling of tales is best undertaken with others, but if we're keeping the Yule in solitude we can still experience the power of stories. True stories lead to changes in the way we experience the worlds where we live. If it's worth the time it takes to tell, a story either shows us something new or reminds us of something we'd known – once upon a time, perhaps – but that we've since forgotten.

Until we figure out which stories move us, we really won't know who we are or why we're living the way we do. Stories reveal the secrets of life. Most people live out their own stories unconsciously. One of the main disciplines of Keltelven initiates involves them in becoming more aware of the tales that make our lives meaningful *for us*. This discipline is practiced with enthusiasm during the Yule, when there are a wide variety of penetrating and insightful stories to tell.

There's something about life itself that's like a story; – namely, that it has a *beginning* (birth), a *middle* (the life we are living) and an *end* (death). Though most of us have not yet died [39] our life can always be seen as fulfilled in the moment in which we attempt to tell our own tale. "How did we get here?" is the primary question we are always answering. If we strive to tell our own tale and the stories that most move us during the passage of Yule, we may well discover more of our own true identity.

As we wake up to the spiritual nature of reality, all of life becomes a story. By telling the tales that move and shake us, we approach the gateways of transformation and awakening. By beginning to reflect on these tales in the light of the Fires of Yule we may well find ourselves better able to approach the turnstiles of deepening self-understanding and radical spiritual empowerment. Such understanding is hidden in the shadows these fires cast upon our earthen landscapes.

Storytelling was a common practice in Celtic society.[40] Everyone engaged in it, more or less, as a common path via which the truth of situations and life itself might come to light. Hearing a variety of stories about a particular event and listening to how they were different as well as to their similarities, Keltelvens believe, helps us better sort out the truth of what has happened. Storytelling is also a basic discipline of Keltelven mysticism. Stories may be used to communicate truths that can not be expressed in mundane, historical, or 'scientific' terms. Today we use fantasy, horror, the *immram* (adventure story) and other genres to unlock the truth of events.

Keltelvens have a bevy of traditional Yuletide stories. These include tales of Saint Deirdre and Lugh-the-Craefty, Brighid and her meeting with the Virgin Mary in the Wildwoods near Avalon, tales of Saint Nicholas and the Elves, and many others. There are also a myriad of tales told about the Druid Jesus coming to mortals as the Mysterious Stranger; — a "madman of Wisdom" who may be met by unsuspecting wayfarers along lonesome roads and out beyond the fields of abandoned farms. As the Mysterious Guest he is also said to come to our doors seeking to bless us with stories and ranns.

Secular and religious culture also is a store of traditional "Christmas" tales. Many of these stories can still be retold vividly today as we approach the Hearth of Wintertide, especially as we re-learn the symbols of Yuletide mysticism. As we devote ourselves to pathing Winter's Solstice, storytelling will re-emerge as a spiritual art simply because to take a journey is to tell a story. For the Celts there was no strict distinction between everyday life and the reality represented by stories. Daily life is as real as the world of stories. As such, these realities interact, impacting each other as we strive after Wisdom.

During the Yule repeat old, familiar tales of the season; ones that have moved us in the past and yet continue to inspire us – as well as attempt the telling of new tales. Though we must remember the old tales, we must never prevent new tales from being told. New stories are often forged out of day to day experiences that suddenly strike us as poignant of life's meaning. They may also be woven from dreams and drawn from the uncertain amalgam of figurative intuitions and more or less concrete hopes that permeate the Yule. New tales tell us where we are *now*, as opposed to where we once were.

Those in our traditions who are the master storytellers, poets and singers we call 'Bards.' The **Hemlock Tree** has been a Bilé (i.e., sacred tree) to all those who engage in the telling of tales – whether in dramatic form, in song or in poetry – as it is an earthen sign of their Mused inspiration. The Hemlock is a stable tree with a straight trunk, soft branches and needles. Its strength is said to reside in its suppleness. Like the Willow it is rarely broken by the wind, and storms do not usually do it much damage. It deflects lightning, and its boughs can survive under heavy burdens of snow or ice.

Owing to its thick foliage and supple branches, the wind blows through the Hemlock's boughs in sometimes eerie and musical ways. This may have resulted in its becoming associated with music. The ancient Bard Taliesin once called it *"the Singing Tree."* As an evergreen, its ability to sing in the wind links it with the creativity necessary to path through the Winter Solstice Season. Hemlocks sing throughout the Winter and may be thought of as the home of both Tree Elves and Angels. Its supple needles drink in the power of the Moon's rays. **Owls** – messengers of the Muse – perch in the boughs of Hemlock trees and keep a watch out for poets passing by. From their seclusion they protect people walking on paths nearby and sometimes inspire mortals with their runic cries. "No one passing the Hemlock in the wood goeth unseen," says the <u>Yuletide Grimoire</u> (1898). Today we might encounter the Muse on moonlit nights near old whispering Hemlocks.

Hemlocks have small, papery cones that have long played a symbolic role in Keltelven storytelling. Since ancient times, a person seeking insight might offer a Hemlock cone to someone known for their story-telling abilities; this person is then obliged to relate the most potent tale they know. Storytelling can be a prophetic act, and to offer a tale upon request can lead either to salvation or doom. To give a Hemlock cone to someone keeping the Thirteen Days of Yule today might still be considered a request for a story or song that will bring illumination. The recipient of the cone might first ask the name of the petitioner. Then, holding the cone in his or her left hand, they should meditate on the request until an appropriate story arises from the Deep Mused Mind. They will then unfold the story, either in prose, poetry or song. The hearer is required to listen reverently.

A Keltelven rune teaches that "**truth is an evergreen**," the branches and trunk of which are always, in part, hidden from us. A "truth" based on clear and certain facts *may* not be as "true" as certain kinds of fiction can be. The compassionate truth branches off from a more intuitive trunk of understanding and deals with how people are related to one another and how they might need to change or grow in order to become more fully human.

Compassionate truth is the object of Yuletide storytelling, which should weave myth, remembrance and symbolism together in the telling of 'what happened' in order to create a sense of living significance. Compassionate truth, when we hear it presented in a story, revives a living hope in the human heart. The compassionate truth of Winter's Solstice stories arises from the realization that things are not always as they should or could be. But the world *can* be changed for the better, if we can find the right path to follow. The stories we tell will hopefully reveal such paths. Life is not static; things change, and there *are* ways in which *we* might change in order to be more human(e). The best stories show us that we *can* choose to live differently. By telling stories that point to the realization of a re-visioned intuition, we plant the evergreen of truth in the soil of our lives.

As you get up on Hemlock Day, get dressed and prepare for the day ahead by reflecting on those Yuletide stories that have moved you most in past years. Which ones have inspired and made you wonder toward visionary realizations? Which stories elevate your imagination to faith in the possibility of a better world? Rehearse one or more of these stories as you go to breakfast and then off to work or school.

Since Nicholas' feast you have been more or less surrounded by stories. Are you aware of them? They include the legend of Santa Claus, the story of Saint Deirdre, the myths of Lugh and Brighid and allusions to Cernunnos. Are there stories in the air that you would like to tell and thereby get a better handle on? The stories we tell on Hemlock Day must work to awaken the sense in us of how things *could be*. Like a good physician, Yule stories should tell us where the ingredients of re-humanizing spiritual sachets, philters and other concoctions may be found in our more or less ordinary environs.

Sometime during the day, meditate on an image of a Hemlock tree. You can usually find such images in a greenhouse or nursery catalog, in an encyclopedia, or in a tree guide. Then dedicate yourself to the tales of Yule and Christmas, saying:

> "Open my heart
> to the light of true tales.
> Open my mind
> to the stories that contain the sparks
> of Wisdom!
> Draw me toward the mystic hearth
> by anecdote, narrative and lyric!"

As on the earlier days of Yule, make a centerpiece for your kitchen table containing a sprig or two of Hemlock. If you can procure the cones of a Hemlock, set a few of these on your Yule Table in a small glass or bowl. During the day, when you want to tell or remember a certain seasonal tale, pick up one of the cones and hold it in your hand and then rehearse the story in your mind as best as you are able.

If you're not much into stories and storytelling, carry a Hemlock cone in a shirt pocket today in order to be reminded of the presence of the stories that are being told all around you. Carrying the cone can also be a sign to **Ceridwen** – the Muse Goddess; i.e., the source of all creative energy – of your desire to be steeped in stories, even if it's not your habit to tell stories or even to read them.

When you go to work or go out for other purposes, endeavor to be aware of how stories fill our daily world, especially during the holiday season. A billboard image may imply a story, though it's usually too crudely commercial to be very edifying. If you pass a holiday display or Santa's Village in a mall or in the foyer of an office building, take a moment to note all the stories implied by this kind of diorama. Does it contain any images or icons of home, family and the hearth? These all imply stories of one kind or another. Are there Elves in it? Is there a "Santa's Workshop" in the front display window of some department store? If so, remember Santa Claus at Tara Lough at the top of the world. If you have time, rummage through used bookstores on Hemlock Day looking for old Christmas tomes. Go and find old Christmas books in libraries. Read a few pages, here and there, until you find a particular story that strikes you. The state of your heart will be revealed by the stories that attract you!

You might want to get together with friends and tell stories on Hemlock Day. This may be done over a meal, though a light buffet with crackers and drinks while you share stories is quite sufficient. Meditate in a circle near the Yule Tree and then let each person tell the story that most inspires him or her. If only one or two stories are shared during your time together, so be it. You will then have less to sort through in order to find the sparks that kindle your own inner hearth. No one who is uncomfortable telling stories in a group should ever be coerced to participate in this ritual. After each story, meditate on it and share your reflections about it.

If you keep this day alone, and if you have a hearth, light it and sit near it, in the evening hours especially, remembering a story or two about the Yule and its mystery. Listen to the crackling of the logs in the hearth! This sound reflects the Yulefire burning in your own internal Hearth as well as the inspiration of the Spirit. Let various images of Yule – stimulated by the stories – pass before your mind. Reflect on those images that move you to a deeper wakefulness to the Season.

If you are by yourself you might want to read a short story or even start reading a longer piece of seasonal fiction on Hemlock Day. Choose a tale that you think will move you or awaken some part of your heart to the coming of Winter's Solstice. Say, as you open the book:

> "Spirit of hearth and heart
> guide my imagination,
> and help me to play a part
> in the tale-telling of Yule!
> Amen."

This rune invites the Muse to inspire you through the stories you read or hear. It also evinces your own willingness to become part of the story, and not just be an interested bystander.

It's important to practice discernment and follow our own intuitions during sacred time. As you go through the day, tending to business, try to be alert to the stories that surround you. Which ones do you accept?

Which ones should be rejected? Why? Not every story that we see an icon of or hear a snippet of during Yule is worthy of participation. We need to focus on the authentic Spirit of Yule and follow Her inspiration when collecting stories.

While you might watch a video or go to the theater to see a new holiday film or play during the evening of Hemlock Day, don't forsake the actual telling of tales. There's a significant difference between watching a film or play and hearing someone you know telling (or reading) a story out loud to an assembled group. Don't be shy. We actually create our own live theaters wherever the Spirit moves us to tell stories. There we witness the continually new incarnation of the age-old "Divine Word" near whatever Hearth and in whatever circle we are gathered.

The experience of storytelling is not something we're used to anymore, though our grandparents' generation no doubt understood it as a more or less routine part of everyday life.[41] Though it may seem alien to you at first – especially if you are of the television or now the computer generation – once you give storytelling a try you may develop a real inclination and love for it, as so many interesting and unusual things can sometimes happen while a good story is being told or acted out! Storytelling is a 'live' situation in which as listeners we participate in a much more active way than when we are watching a pre-recorded story being played back. Epiphanies can occur and the solutions to problems we are having can suddenly get worked out through listening devoutly to a good storyteller.

Storytelling Day is when those who got a slow start in making their journey to Glastonbury Tor often catch up, being grabbed by the Spirit of Yule in and through some story or another. If you tell stories expecting the unexpected, all kinds of things may happen. As you keep the Fires of Yule burning year after year, certain stories will begin to come back to haunt you, again and again. These are the tales by which you will end up recognizing your life's path.

Natural Meditation: Focus on the "Wind in the Hemlock." Imagine a Great Hemlock Tree in you mind or go out and sit near one in a park or in the woods. Listen to the Wind and the song that it sings, and try to imagine what story it's trying to tell you. Before you go to bed, imagine the tree again. Go there in your dreams. In the morning write out an account of any dream you may have had involving a hemlock or related symbols.

Scriptural Meditation: Focus on the Magnificat (Luke 1:46-55) – the song sung by Mary while visiting her cousin Elisabeth – and contemplate what the poem means for our life in Earth and Spirit. The Magnificat is a song of Vision and Inspiration, liberation and rebirth. It prophesies the change in the world that the story of the Gospel (the Wisdom of Jesus) can effect if lived out in devout ways.

5. *Ivy Day (Mother of Hearth Day, 17 December)*

"Brighid is the primary household goddess. Originally an Irish deity, she had been adopted by the Keltelvens by at least the 9th century as their general patron of the Hearth. Along with Nerthus and Coventina she is one of the three goddesses of Yule. ... There are runic tales that tell how she and her Yuletide sisters were befriended by Mary the Mother of Jesus, and that they became divine followers of Christ." (16)

- Cornelius Whitsel
The Keltelven Traditions (1982)

"May the Lady of the Hearth come and vine your Yuletide Heart.
May Brighid en-circle you in spirals of Her Fir.
May the Lady of the Garden of Roses light Fires in your Yuletide Hearth.
Come, Triple Goddess: Brighid—Nerthus—Coventina!" (xxvi)

- Yuletide Grimoire (1898)

As the adventure of Yule unfolds, endeavor to enter ever more deeply into the aura of its symbols, decorations and stories. The themes of Winter's Solstice are pervasive and cannot be confined to the particular days to which they are assigned in this calendar. Once a symbol or theme is introduced, it will come up again and again as the season unfolds and as we path toward our own nativity at the Tor.

The hearth is one of the most persistent symbols of the Yule, recurring almost daily in one form or context or another. Yule is symbolically and spiritually grounded in the immanent presence of the Spirit in the Hearth. The hearth is the oracle of the Fires of Yule, connoting the warmth of life that we receive from its flames. **Brighid –** who is **the Mother of Yulefire** – always has her favored seat beside the hearth. From this seat – usually imaged as an old-style rocking chair – she inspires, exhorts and teaches us new ways to celebrate the Yule and approach the mysteries of Glastonbury Tor.

The 17th of December is a day devoted entirely to becoming aware of the hearth and all of its metaphorical allusions. It's a time during which mortals are visited by the Spirit of Yule under the guise of the goddess Brighid, whose power and love draw us to return to the deepest hearths of authentic dwelling on this day. She is the Mistress of those whose hearts have been gathered to the hearth as the wintry days of December grow darker. She it is who keeps the soul's heart warm throughout the winter months, nurturing the seeds of new birth in our earthen souls.

Brighid is a manifest form of the Earth in the guise of a domestic goddess. Brighid is one of a triad of Yuletide goddesses, her sisters being Nerthus – the Goddess of the Earth in the darkness of Winter's Solstice – and Coventina – the Goddess of spring waters and ice at this cold time of the year. Brighid is the keeper of the flame that blazes in the hearth and which warms and illumines us. When visiting mortals she encourages, uplifts and cultivates positive, humanizing visions of life. She won't stand for any of her children being harmed and she protects anyone who petitions her for refuge. Snakes are sacred to her. She often plays with serpents and keeps them near her as icons of Earthen Wisdom. She patrols the borders of our properties chanting runes against unwanted intruders. She used to appear as a dairymaid in the barn, surprising farmers when they came out to milk the cows before dawn!

Mediaeval grimoires[43] indicate that on this day in the spiral turning of Yule, **Brighid** comes into the place where celebrants are preparing for the Solstice. Keltelvens often speak of her as if she were knitting or praying near the hearth on Ivy Day. She comes to help mortals with their preparations. Her role is that of stoking and protecting the *Fires of Imagination and Compassion* in the hearth of our hearts with spiritual brands and embers, ministering with light, warmth, fire-flicker and the sparks of New Life.

Brighid is imaged as a dark, curvaceous woman of middle age, mature and strong, bearing her own source as a Divine Light within her bosom. She is often dressed in russet red and faded green farming clothes. She bears a basket of nuts and fruit on her left arm. **Ivy** is draped across her shoulders. A chain of small bronze bells hangs around her right ankle. These bells jingle as she walks, driving away evil spirits and negative influences from the place of dwelling.

Brighid's breasts are full of the Milk of Life. On her head is a crown of silver, decorated with red and green jewels. Her eyes are dark blue (seemingly black) in color, and her hair is usually red or iron-brown. Wherever she walks, peace and harmony follow. **Salt** and **milk** are among her primary symbols, along with the **chalice**, which may be filled with beer and raised in her honor at dusk on Ivy Day. To "hoist a pint to Brighid" is to invoke Her presence at the Hearth. She despises drunkenness, however, unless a person is "drunk on her ministrations and loving care." (20, <u>Yuletide</u> <u>Grimoire</u>, 1898)

Keltelven mystics believe that Brighid is one of several ancient deities who encountered Jesus, becoming a friend and servant of the Dream of His Gospel in the divine realms of Paradise. Brighid once met the Virgin Mary at Glastonbury Tor, it is said, near the gates of Avalon, which is where the ancient priestesses lived. They met at a thin place between the worlds where Mary was coming across from Paradise to visit her Son, who was then journeying in Wales, teaching and singing songs of a wise life.

Brighid saw Mary coming across the Sídhe and was awe-struck by her beauty. Brighid approached her, thinking Mary was some great goddess coming out of the Mists of Time. When they met, however, Mary explained that she was just the poor wife of a carpenter from the East. Brighid knew better, and asked her how she came to be so *glorious*. Mary replied, "I've become the Mother of God and now I've followed him to this Green and Blessed Isle. I dwell in Paradise, for I have a seat at the Hero's Table." Brighid was so impressed that she adopted Mary as her sister on the spot, vowing eternal loyalty to the Jewish Mother of God. Together then, Mary & Brighid went to meet Jesus, who was eating and drinking in a house of Welsh Druids who had just begun to dream the Gospel. Once there, Brighid heard the Gospel being sung and discussed, and freely choose to accept Jesus as her divine brother; a Teacher of Wisdom among the gods. Jesus and Brighid now walk together in Paradise.

At dawn on this day, rise and go to the hearth and/or the Yule Table. As a part of your morning meditations, hang a strand of **Ivy** across the mantle above the hearth and/or over the Yule Table. By this sign you acknowledge Brighid's presence in the house. Then say:

"Hail Brighid,
Mother of the Magick of Yule,
grant me compassion
and let me be
a servant of your own good face
and of Mary, ever freely."

Hold an Ivy leaf in your hands (or use a picture of Ivy for this purpose). Ivy leaves tend to get tougher the older they are, and even the young ones are harder to tear than the leaves of other plants. Meditate on the nature of the hearth and the vining of the Spirit through our own dwelling in the Yule.

Ivy has deeply woven symbolic connections with Winter's Solstice. It symbolizes the integrity of the Hearth and the tenacity of the Spirit of Yule. As the Ivy is reluctant to let go of the soil in which it is rooted, so the Spirit of Yule holds onto the earth of our own souls, inviting us toward psychic renewal.

Ivy symbolizes (1) a tenacious love of life, (2) the deep and vine-like connection between all living things, and (3) the motherly compassion of Brighid. Like motherhood, Ivy is difficult to destroy once it gains a foothold. Ivy vines anywhere, climbing buildings and even making its way into fissures and cracks in solid stone, breaking the rock open. As such, Ivy is both a protector and a destroyer. If the house is sound, Ivy tendrils will not harm it; the vines will protect the structure against the effects of weathering and they will help keep a house moist in dry weather. Only if the house is unsound will the Ivy widen cracks and fissures, eventually undermining walls and foundations. The psychic nature of Ivy brings *spiritual cleansing* to a house when it is grown or brought indoors.

Ivy is sacred to women and to motherhood generally, as Holly is sacred to men and to fatherhood (see 20 December). Ivy serves Brighid and Mary both as mothers of Wisdom. Its presence in seasonal decorations makes the role of these powerful feminine archetypes manifest in the human household. Ivy is a symbol of fidelity, and has long been known to bring a tenacity of blessing to soul-friendships, lovers and friends of all genres. Friends and lovers may make vows to one another

91

saying, "Let us be like the Ivy; tenacious, hard to uproot and resistant to the cynicism and mistrust that withers a hard green stem."

Some Ivy plants live to be 500 years old. Their pertinacious, persevering nature connects them spiritually with the ultimate victory of Good over Evil. There is an old saying that, "Ivy wins out!" Ivy vines are symbolic of spiritual soberness and constancy of will. Another old saying indicates that: "The Ivy-hearted attain their goals." Ancient herbalists believed that when an infusion of Ivy leaves was made in wine the resulting elixir was a good preventative for drunkenness. When Brighid enters the house, adorned with Ivy, all vulgar drunkenness evaporates and all willing householders are transported into spiritual reveries and mystical ecstasies. Those who call on Brighid do not become drunk in the flesh; rather, they become intoxicated with her presence.

Ivy is symbolic of the mystery of Spiral Castle in Keltelven mysticism. **Spiral Castle** is a poetic name for the ultimate destination of the spiritual journey. Our mystics believe that the paths we take in this life unfold like spirals, returning us again and again to familiar turnstiles and crosstroads, though at a different stage in our journey each time. The way leading discarnates to Paradise – via their journeys in the next life – is also a spiral path. The traveler in the Otherworld moves through waystations that seem familiar to them from mortal life, though these are actually just epiphenomenal to known material locations or experiences in *this world*. Eventually, this spiraling way leads to the gates of Paradise.

Spiral Castle may also refer to a specific mythic edifice – like a maze – built by divine agency and empowered with *strange magick* (i.e., magick generated by a non-human source). By exploring such a structure, a pilgrim seeks divine guidance in decisions that will concern the direction they undertake in their otherworldly life. When we meditate on Ivy, we trace out ancient allusions to Spiral Castle in its winding stems and branches. Ivy refers to the nature of our earthen journey toward the Inner Hearth.

Ivy Day is a waystation for putting the psychic household in order. Through it we invoke Brighid to aid us in our task. We should meditate throughout this day on the nature of the hearth and its power, asking the Spirit of Yule for an evaluation of the state of our own Heart. Seek out new ways to relieve stress and diminish the anxiety that's either been carried into the Season or created by the busy-ness of the 'holiday season' in our society. Approaching the sacred is never easy, and the road may have some unexpected bumps in it! Brighid's Day is a brief respite; in its embrace everyone may hope to catch his or her breath and then get ready to move on.

Keltelven lore states that on this day the women are to be relieved of all their duties, so that they may prepare themselves for the Solstice. It is to be a day of *otium sanctum* ("holy leisure") in the midst of Yule. On Ivy Day, the men do what they can to free the women from their chores and duties and give them time to themselves. If possible, the women should at least have a morning or an afternoon free to pursue the warmth of Brighid's Fires. (The men will have their chance to be 'care free' on the 20th of December; Hunting Day).

Keltelven women would once have gone out to a local **baunbruiden** (a house where wise-women lived), and spent Ivy Day there engaged in meditation and rituals connected with Yuletide rebirth. They would get together for mutual support and take day-long adventures together. They would seek to awaken one another as the Solstice drew near in gathering darkness. Women keeping the Yule together today might arrange to go to a cabin at a local campground. Spend the day enjoying one another's company and intuiting ways to re-charge your psychic 'batteries' for the rest of Yule.

If you're keeping the Yule in the company of others, offer to liberate the women in your group from as much of their work and responsibilities as possible on Ivy Day. Our schedules, however, do not usually allow for this kind of freedom. Women keeping Yule are often obligated to go to their jobs and as it's the 'holiday season,' are not likely to get this day off. If you can, plan a "personal day" ahead of time and take at least part of the day off from work. For those women who work at home, the men keeping the Yule might take a day off to do the housework, run errands and whatever else needs done.

If you're alone on Brighid's Day, find a place of retreat from your normal routines even if for only two or three hours. If possible, remain near a hearth or the Yule Table during free time. Seek the face of Brighid in the flames or the glow of candlelight. Recall the light and warmth of the hearth while at school or work. If you know of a good restaurant that has a hearty fireplace, go there for lunch or dinner. Call your mother on Brighid's Day and wish her a blessed Solstice Night. If possible, visit female relatives, taking them token gifts. If you have sisters you might contact them and wish them well. If you have a daughter, Brighid's Day is a good time to get together with her and give her a small gift in honor of the Ivy that binds you together in love and kinship.

During the evening, **re-dedicate the hearth** of your place of dwelling. Light a fire with aromatic woods and then meditate on this wondrous icon of the goddess Brighid. Invite the goddess to communicate her blessing to you and your place of dwelling through the aromas given off by the wood you are burning. If you have no hearth, light nine candles on the Yule Table and meditate on the nature of light and the various powers inherent in living flames.

At some point during the day you might execute the ancient "**Egg Spell**." This rite culls together symbols of birth and protection in order to envelop the place of dwelling in an aura of positive psychic force. It utilizes the mystical powers associated with the common egg. Cornelius Whitsel says, in his Table of Sacred Dayes (1992), that:

> "Eggs are symbolic of rebirth and the generative powers inherent in life. The Druids were known to meditate holding an egg-shaped stone called a "Serpent's Egg." The Culdee used similar rocks carved and polished into the shape of an egg as meditation objects. They would hold one of these strange eggs in their hands and chant over it, saying prayers inspired by the Fire of the Divine Presence. During meditation they would utter blessings and benedictions, praying for the spiritual rebirth and awakening of those who had not yet found the Path where the divine ones walk through this life." (163)

At dusk on Ivy Day, take three eggs and boil them until they're hard. Let them cool. Meanwhile, light a fire in the hearth with aromatic woods. Then say:

> "Hail Brighid, Mother of the House
> and devoted Sister
> of Mary, the Mother of Jesus!
> Bless this hearth and the house around it;
> keep it safe from all evil!

> Deliver its boards, stones and pipes
> from wicked influences,
> and keep us holy within it!"

After this, take the three eggs and put them in a small paper bag. Take a hand-bell in the other hand, and go outside. Walk in a circle clockwise around the house carrying the bag of eggs and ringing the bell. Chant sacred names of the Triple Goddess for protection as you do so: "Brighid—Nerthus—Coventina." Bury the bag with the eggs in it at the northwest corner of the house, or else bring them back in, cook and eat them. Throw the bag onto the hearthfire and let it burn while you eat the eggs. If you have no hearth, use the meditation table for this ritual and don't bother to burn the bag.

After the re-dedication, the house will feel psychically refreshed. Imagine that it has been delivered once again from any negative influences. Spirits of disturbance, anxiety or threat have now been loosed from their hiding places and only the good and helpful spirits are allowed to stay. Dance in a circle clockwise before the Yule Tree and at then at the Yule Table to celebrate the house being cleansed.

Celebrate the deliverance of your place of dwelling from negative influences! When this ritual is performed annually over a period of years, it will be difficult *not* to notice the change in the mood of your house or apartment after Ivy Day. You will become aware that Brighid is watching over the house and all who dwell in it! Acknowledging her presence will also make you more aware than you used to be of negative influences that try to get into the house throughout the year and enable you to stave them off.

If you have a statue or icon representing Brighid, set it out on the mantle above the hearth or on the Yule Table after the re-dedication. This icon can be a more or less traditional statue of Mary, as these are easy to find in stores around Christmas time or in religious gift shops. If there is a fantasy craft shop near you, you might visit it to look for figures of a more pagan guise. Whatever statue you choose, use it as a focus for meditation in the evening of Ivy Day. Drape a strand of Ivy around the icon or statue as this enhances the deep psychic connection between yourself and the Hearth.

Before you go to bed tonight, take a small sprig of Ivy and lay it under your pillow. This will bring you peace of mind and tranquility of heart. Those who are troubled should seek the help of Brighid and Mary by sleeping with Ivy in or near their bed. The power of Ivy attracts helpful spirits and sometimes even spirit-guides from the Otherside to you. Imagine them standing over you as you sleep, holding their hands out over the bed and drawing away any negative influences. In the morning you will feel relieved and ready to face whatever trials your day may hold in store for you.

> **Natural Meditation**: Focus on the connection between Ivy, our relationships with others and psychic wholeness. Ivy digs its roots into the Earth and becomes one with the soil. We are similarly planted in the Earth with one another. Ivy can also be uprooted and survive for days without water. We should also be strong enough to be able to be uprooted and still have the perseverance to survive.

> **Scriptural Meditation**: Focus on Joseph's reaction to Mary's pregnancy and the Angel's appearance to him. The Angel first came to Mary (Luke 1:26-38) and only later to Joseph (Matthew 1:18-25). Mary did what she did (allowed herself to become pregnant) without consulting her husband-to-be! Thus she was a true virgin in the Celtic sense. She was a woman of freedom and integrity, in command of her own sexuality, and able to do the right thing without asking a male for advice.

6. *Frankincense Day (Day of Visions and Quests, 18 December)*

"Desiring to receive wisdom and be awakened to the Presence of God, we light spiritual Frankincense in our hearts. We throw it on the Yulefire burning there, and from it the smoke doth rise up out of the chimney of our minds. It ascendeth into Paradise and cometh back to us as spiritual gold. We give away the gold, and receive the myrrh of solace and holy consolation." (82)

- Egbert Whittier
The Thirteen Dayes of Yule (1800)

After the re-gathering of Ivy Day, celebrants of Yule are usually ready for some active pursuits. On this day we go out into the world and down into our own inner hearths looking for signs of the Season, symbols of our destination, and runes of hope. We live this day in anticipation of having some kind of vision of the meaning of the Yule.

A vision may be anything from a sudden *epiphany* through which something of the significance of life becomes clear to us, to a divine gift of prophecy or even a shadow of foresight. A vision usually arises out of the potency of our situation, but it can also come to us like fire to damp logs, when we're least expecting it. A vision may be of either the ordinary or the extraordinary kind. Either way it comes, we hope that it will offer an intuition into the meaning of the Winter Solstice Season!

Our society has lost its ability to "see visions" because it has so down-graded the imagination and the reality of aesthetic experience that it cannot see beyond the "what is" to the "what might be." A vision is an aesthetic phenomenon, often generated by a mix of hope and human(e) ideals.

As Keltelven spirituality affirms the worth of the aesthetic dimensions of experience and as we have hope grounded in Earth & Spirit visions are not an uncommon experience among our practitioners. A vision is aesthetic to the extent to which Spirit works in and through us as the Muse. For Keltelvens, having a vision is not the problem, but rather discerning authentic visions from bogus ones; that is, distinguishing between something that is just a pleasant imaginary scenario on the one hand, and a "seeing through the sight" on the other. A vision is a kind of inner perception through which something is revealed in more or less vivid terms. There are several kinds of authentic vision. By considering these briefly, you will get an idea of what you're looking for on Frankincense Day.

The first kind of vision is sometimes called "double vision" or **"two-fold vision."*** This is what happens when we're looking at the world or some object in it and suddenly see it as a metaphor alluding to something else. A two-fold vision interprets our experience on two levels; the literal level of what's actually there and then on a level where it means something else to us. This second level is the realm of symbol and metaphor, allusion and allegory. The visionary moment is the point at which it becomes a metaphor. We interpret it as meaning other than what it normally means.

The next level – **"three-fold vision"*** – is when we suddenly see something *else* of significance *through* the thing we're actually seeing. That is, we're looking at a particular scene or meditating on some icon, and – as if transported to another place or time – we're now seeing something else in our imagination. What we see is vivid. We sense its meaning, though it may not be directly connected – even metaphorically or as a simile – with the object or scene that gave rise to the visionary experience.

The ultimate level of vision – called **"four-fold vision"*** – happens when we see something in our imagination that wasn't directly caused or even indirectly stimulated by any external or internal event. Suddenly, out of the blue, we may find ourselves in the midst of a reverie of imaginative

---

* Keltelvens seem to have borrowed this terminology of two- three- and four-fold vision from the English poet William Blake (1757-1825), who used such terminology. While Blake never developed a coherent theory of vision, writers such as J. G. Davies' in his The Theology of William Blake (Oxford, 1948; pp. 60-78) and Mildred Young in her book Woolman and Blake: Prophets for Today (Lebanon, PA: Pendlehill Pamphlet, 1970) have attempted to turn Blake's ideas into a theory. These books have influenced my own understanding of Keltelven visionary theory.

seeing. We interpret what this scene means, though we weren't expecting anything to happen prior to the advent of the vision. Nothing obvious is the catapult that launches us into this particular visionary state!

Two- and three-fold visions are more or less empirical, arising out of our experience. A four-fold vision is a psychic gift in that it doesn't arise immediately or even logically out of immediate experience but is somehow 'given' to us. While you cannot create visions or do anything to produce them, you *can* endeavor to put yourself in the best possible milieu for a vision (at least one on the two- or three-fold level.) We can seek out aesthetic vistas and nurture imaginative situations, in which it is possible for our ordinary, physical vision to be augmented into visionary experience.

This is what we hope to do on Frankincense Day! We should live the day seeking out contexts where visionary experiences might best become possible. We can put ourselves in the path of visionary experience in any number of ways. On the eve of 18 December we can perfume our bedchambers with a little Frankincense and go to sleep asking the Spirit for a dream of the meaning of Yule. Dreams are one door through which our normal consciousness gains access to realities on the other side of the veil between the worlds. Keltelven Poets often think of visions as being a higher, mystical manifestation of dreams. "To seek a vision is to learn the meaning of life," the Yuletide Grimoire (1898) declares.

We can also use Frankincense Day to go off on short pilgrimages and mock quests, looking for places where a vision of the meaning of Yule can best arise. Of seeking the Muse who inspires visions and dreams, Gawain Smythe says in his The Way of the Bards (1996) that, "Though She is always at home, we usually have to go out for a walk in order to find Her" (20). Thus on Frankincense Day we should take real and imagined journeys in the hope of opening up the doors of perception.

At dawn, light a few granules of **Frankincense** in a metal or stone incense burner on the Yule Table or throw them on the rush of a newly kindled hearthfire. You might also carry a small incense bowl through the house to disseminate the fragrance. By burning Frankincense you are invoking the help of those spirit-guides who are in the habit of leading mortals to the thresholds of visionary experience. These guides may become known to you or remain unknown. If you have a soul-friend on the Otherside, ask him or her to lead you to a potent place of vision today. As you smell the incense, say:

"Come, (name of guide)
show us the paths
to walk this day.
Teach us which runes to emulate
and give us the intuition
to see where we're going!

We are such plodders,
putting one foot ahead of the other!
Illumine a path that we might follow;
lead us,
O Muse of our own Moon!
So mote it be."

Frankincense has long been associated with visionary experience. The word "Frankincense" comes from the French words *franc* ("pure") and *encens* ("incense"). The raw material of Frankincense is a gum resin exuded as a milky colored liquid from trees belonging to various species of the genus *boswellia*. This white liquid soon solidifies and may be collected in the form of tear-shaped grains that can then be melted down and turned into sticks. It is usually left in its pure state but it may also be mixed with other ingredients. The grains yield a balsam-like fragrance when burned.

Frankincense has been used for at least 4,000 years in embalming, fumigation and in the making of perfume. Ancient Egyptian recipes for mummification (dating to the 3rd millennium BCE) refer to Frankincense. It was used in the ancient world as a perfume – as attested in the Biblical "Song of Songs" (3:6, 4:6, 14) – and was also a key ingredient in the incense burned in the Jerusalem Temple; its fragrance was said to be "pleasing to the Lord." (see the Old Testament "Exodus," 30:34-38).

The Jewish historian Josephus (1st century CE) records that two golden chalices were filled with Frankincense and set beside the Bread of Presence (Leviticus 24:7) in the Holy of Holies; i.e., the most sacred precinct of the temple in Jerusalem. Frankincense was imported into ancient Judah by camel caravan from Sheba (see Isaiah 60:6 and Jeremiah 6:20); a trade arrangement which originated with the Queen of Sheba's visit to see King Solomon (see I Kings 10:10) in Jerusalem in the 10th century BCE.

This highly valued gum resin is sometimes sold in retail stores during the December holidays, as it's a basic ingredient in many common incense recipes. Religious supply stores almost always have it in stock. Therefore, you shouldn't have much trouble finding Frankincense. As it burns, savor its mellifluous fragrance. Imagine all the mystics down across the ages who have smelled this particular aroma while seeking insight and vision. You are now hoping to become one of them! Burning Frankincense we seek to be led to places where we may see signs of deeper significance, even approaching the threshold of Divine Inspiration. During Yule many of our sacred adventures begin to come to fruition. The aroma of Frankincense invites the Muse to illumine our souls and distill our year's experiences. Invoke Her by chanting the names: **"Boann—Brighid—Ceridwen."**

Frankincense was one of the three gifts given to the infant Jesus by the Magi from the East (Matthew 2:11). By offering him this gift they acknowledged that the child would grow up to be a visionary leader of his people. As Pagan wise-men they recognized the divine soul in Mary's child and worshipped him as one of the heroes descended from the twelve astrological signs of the heavens who are sent to Earth to open up the Paths of Wisdom for mortals.

At breakfast, decide how you might best pursue visions & dreams today. A vision is a poetic and imaginative coalescence of insight, experience and hopes. True visions are inspired by the Muse. They may transpire during meditation or else while mortals are out on pilgrimages or while making a quest on Frankincense Day. A **pilgrimage** is a journey to a place of known spiritual significance while a **quest** is a journey in search of wisdom in heretofore unknown locales. As Visions are rarer than diamonds in the dust of existence, though, the day must be enjoyed for its own sake. Don't so *expect* to have a vision that you miss the adventure!

Your task today is to simply open yourself to the Muse and await what comes.

At work or school use any free moments you may have to foster your anticipation of a visionary experience. Meditate during your lunch break and while walking or riding to and from work or school. If the day is free of major obligations or duties, engage in the traditional pilgrimage or quest that aligns our paths with the trajectory of poetic vision. It's best to mix the pursuit of vision with engagement in ordinary activity, however, as most two- and three-fold visions arise out of day to day experiences.

In olden times this was a day for going out into fields and wildwoods, making a trek to dolmens, sacred springs and stone circles. At such places Keltelvens entered into deep communion with the Earth through the mysterious Spirit of Yule. Keltelven mystics are adept at sensing the holy in the natural, and they know how to follow ley-lines (mysterious tracks of earth-energy) to places where potentially arcane experiences may become possible. It's in this hope of fellowship between the human, divine and natural that we journey out from hearth and home seeking encounters with gods & goddesses, spirit-guides, and even the ever-elusive Elves on Frankincense Day.

Today there are any number of things you can do to stimulate visionary insight. You may want to go visit a particular shop in town where old Christmas decorations are bought and sold. You may already know of places that exude an aura of mystery and magic as the Winter Solstice approaches. Consider paying a visit to such places. Shrines of Mary can be visited as also sacred to Brighid. Go to local retreat houses or nature-preserves and walk the trails in solitude. Simply setting out to look for a new place of inspiration – full of anticipation and open to the Spirit of Yule – is often all it takes to open the senses and the imagination to new possibilities of vision. Follow your intuitions and heed whatever hints may be given to you along the way.

I once knew a woman who sat down on a bench in a mall near where a Santa Claus was preparing to meet with hundreds of children who were lined up and impatient to see him. She was exhausted from shopping after a long day at the office. Suddenly, she saw the man in the Santa Claus suit coming toward her and offering her a styrofoam cup of hot chocolate. She accepted it, and while drinking it and watching the crowd of people pass by urgently she began to fall into a state of quiet reverie. She "glimpsed" a truer meaning of the gifts she'd been buying and sensed that life had suddenly undergone a subtle change. That night she had a dream of Santa Claus and vividly remembered things about how Christmas had been celebrated in her own childhood home. This is just one example of a 'visionary' experience emerging out of ordinary circumstances.

While visions can happen anywhere and under almost any circumstances, it can help to go to places where you've had positive experiences in the past. On Frankincense Day we call to mind those places where the Spirit has touched us before. The only problem with making pilgrimages to such places is falling into the trap of *expecting* to experience what was experienced before. When this happens, Frankincense Day gets turned into a sentimental dalliance; an attempt merely to 'recapture' the past. If you always look for strange, *new*, experiences and insights each year, you will avoid this spiritual pitfall. The world is filled with mysteries, most of which have never even been imagined before, much less experienced! Therefore, go out looking for one!

On the morning of 18 December pray for guidance as to where you should go and *with whom* you should go or whether you should go alone. A journey in solitude can be as fruitful as one in company. If possible, go out to the woods and open yourself to the Spirit of Yule, following this path and then that one, trying to get into the groove of the day. Nature is the "Church not made by Hands," as gods & goddesses have always dwelt in Nature without any need of human edifices to 'house' them. There they wait for us to come along and discover them. Look for seasonal signs of the Spirit in Nature's disguise. Pine groves, Holly or Rowan trees growing wild, a Cedar or Hemlock Tree; all these can become turnstiles of our Way to Glastonbury Tor. If you see a deer, think of it as Cernunnos or even Jesus in disguise! If you see rabbits, take care to listen for the voice of Tailtiu or even the Muse in their movements.

Though you might just follow your intuitions out into the woods, there are also more conscious quests that may be taken on Frankincense Day. The first of these is **the Quest for the Cave of the Nativity**, in which you go out seeking the place where the god-child Jesus will be born. Pray, sing quietly or hum a song about wandering and seeking (i.e., "I wonder as I wander" or "We Three Kings") as you go. As you hike along paths and off-trail, follow your best intuitions, allowing the actual landscape to inspire an imaginary one. Hike up and down hills, listening for the voices of insight in the sounds of Nature – flowing water, crows' calls, and the movements of small animals – hoping to hear directions to a mystical destination. Along the way you might find a path that leads you to a cave or rock-shelter or perhaps just into a thicket of pine trees where Wisdom is waiting for you. If you see a deer, follow it, quietly, as far as it will allow! Don't get too close, though, or you may spook it! (Deer *will* defend themselves if they feel threatened.) When you find 'the Cave of the Nativity' you will simply 'recognize' it. There will be no signs or neon lights telling you "this is it!" The site might be an actual cave, rock shelter or thicket, but sometimes it's just a very mysterious spot located way off the well-traveled trails where the Spirit of Yule is just waiting to greet you and inspire hare-raising ideas in your mystery-laden heart. If you see a rabbit, interpret it as a manifest sign that Tailtiu is present.

You might 'prepare' the Cave of the Nativity symbolically for the coming of Joseph & Mary. Clear away fallen leaves and small branches, move small stones out of a central area, and in other ways re-imagine the place as ready for the vigil of Matrum Noctem. While there, build a little model of the Nativity where Jesus will be born – perhaps including a stable, fences and a barn – out of stones and twigs. If you're so inclined, bless the site with water or holy oil. Sprinkle water on the ground at the cardinal points (north, east, south and west), and anoint stones or trees at the border of the site with the sign of the earth-cross (an equal-armed cross). Then invite all holy power to abide there, saying:

> "Cross of Intuition, sign of hale-ness,
> bless this place
> and bring the spirits of good will
> here to help
> every visitor through visioning power!"

If the day isn't already spent by this point, stay at the site awhile, chanting the names of the goddess and perhaps sharing stories of previous quests you've made during Yule before heading home.

The other favorite quest on this day is **"Seeking the Door to Tara Lough."** The operative myth here concerns the Elves who became helpers of Saint Nicholas and their annual Winter Solstice journey across the

Sídhe into the vales of mortal time. The quest for the door to Tara Lough is an attempt to find the 'actual' physical place in *our* world where the mystical sleigh pulled by the Reindeer crosses†over from the Otherworld each year, both on Nicholas Eve and then again on Matrum Noctem.

The door through which Santa and his Elves will pass might best be located – according to the old lore of signs – at the edges of lakes or near the confluence where two streams come together. An isle in the middle of a lake or river is a particularly potent place for a door between the worlds, as is a small pond near a cave or a shrine.

Once you find the place where you believe the door is located, stay there and mediate for a while, imagining the journey of Nicholas from the top of the world *to that door* and *through* it, on his way to visit all of the houses in the region. When you're ready, return home and dream up stories about how Santa Claus has used this particular door over the years. Imagine the antics of the Elves!

If you have to work or go to school today, the evening will be your only time for vision-seeking. If there's no way to get out into the woods by this point – as it may be dark – or if you don't live in a place where going to the woods is really possible, *imagine a quest* out into the wildwood. This can be done individually or in a group. Sit down near the hearth or Yule Table. Center down in meditation and then – with your eyes closed – imagine a snowy, wintry scene. Go snow-booting across ever-pagan hills, searching until you discover a cave in a hillside. Journey up along the banks of a glistening stream to where the Door to Tara Lough opens before you. *See* every step of the journey in your mind and imagine each scene as vividly as you can. An imaginative journey can be just as mystical and ever as satisfying as an actual journey out of doors, on many levels, providing we engage in it playfully and yet seriously as a spiritual discipline.

Children sometimes play out their quest on this day through games of **"Snow Dúns."** This involves constructing a model of a mystical place; perhaps Tara Lough. The snow-dún may be constructed in the backyard and made either out of snow or built with branches and old heavy blankets. Alternately, a snow-dún can be built indoors, using chairs and blankets or sheets. A tent may also be set up, if convenient. Divide the children up into two groups. One group pretends to be elves and goes out to build the Snow Dún. After a while the other group has to go out and 'find' the dún, having imaginary adventures along the way, perhaps that they are passing through strange villages and crossing mysterious hills or journeying down into dark vales. At last they will arrive at the dún where they must address the 'Elves' and seek entrance. The 'Elves' must ask the visitors riddles, which the seekers need to answer before entering. Finally they must be granted access to the dún. Once admitted, a small meal may be staged. The 'Elves' must show their guests all of the hospitality that Yuletide demands.

Another activity requiring snow is the making of "**Snow-Mazes.**" These are simply variously patterned paths through a backyard or field. They may be stomped out in the shapes of Yule Trees, reindeer or other seasonal icons, or they may just meander here and there, created at the whim of the children. Sometimes the more mysterious the pattern of the paths the better. If you want, make a 'labyrinth' pattern in the snow with only one doorway in and one way out! When the snow is deep enough, the paths of the snow-mazes will seem like hallways. If the temperature is right, the walls melt a little during the day and freeze at night, in which case they become excellent for "body sledding," which can be great Yuletide fun!

The kids will usually play tag in the paths – and why shouldn't they? – but they may also use the snow-maze as a pattern in which to path sacred destinations, such as Tara Lough or the Stable of the Nativity in Bethlehem. The best way to encourage kids to participate in the Yule is to get them to play sacred games. This is also one way for adults to intensify their own spiritual anticipation. Walk through the snow mazes with the kids and daydream of holy destinations. See in the snow paths a pattern of your own pilgrimage to Glastonbury Tor.

What is the result of all this activity? Sometimes nothing but a really pleasant experience or an invigorating hike. Sometimes only memories for future Yuletide remembrance are made. Quests do not always turn out successfully and pilgrimages can be misconscrewed from the outset! Participants sometimes return home in the evening – after a whole day of pathing visions – with only vague sensations of having been on the right path, the object of their day's pilgriming having eluded them. This is to be expected, so don't lament too much. Mull over what gains you have made and be satisfied.

Though most quests are never actually consummated, their value is usually found in the going-out and coming-home. We often learn as much from our imaginative travels as we do from actually getting to where we're going — or *think* we're going! The elusiveness of the goal points to the deep mystery of Yule and connotes our sense that we've not yet arrived at our spiritual destination. Journeys should be taken on Frankincense Day, therefore, whether or not they seem to lead anywhere.

There *will* be times when your travels on Frankincense Day will result in a vivid visionary experience of the meaning of Winter's Solstice. Things may happen along the way that are totally unexpected and that will force you to think of your entire Yuletide pilgrimage in quite different terms. Actual visions arise out of ordinary circumstances, time and time again.

When this happens, the mortal imagination leaps to new thresholds and you suddenly see things differently. While the kids are playing at snow-dúns on the living room floor you may well glimpse a sudden rune of insight into the nature of life itself. Expect the unexpected. Remain open to possibilities. Even if you don't experience anything visionary today, your keeping of Frankincense Day may prime the pump of devout imagination, leading ultimately to some ecstasy or glimmer of pure understanding that will come to fruition further on down the road. Our part in the Day of Visions & Quests is simply to put ourselves creatively into the situations where something *could* happen. There's no guarantee that anything *will* happen; but there is equally no guarantee that it won't!

Spend part of the evening meditating and reflecting on the day's experience. Do this near the hearth or at the Yule Table. Light Frankincense and meditate for a while in silence, re-collecting yourself and centering your heart in hope of Illumination. If you're keeping Yule with others you might share stories of the day's experiences that hold relevance for the whole group. If you're keeping the Yule alone, write out an account of the high-points of the day in your journal. Visions sometimes even transpire through this act of recollection and reflection! Before retiring to bed, take a moment to offer thanks for whatever you may have experienced during the day. Be especially thankful if nothing has happened! Nothing is often the doorway to Wisdom.

Natural Meditation: Create a scene in your own heart that reflects Spiral Castle. Choose a site for it and then visualize all of the various details of the place. Next, build the mysterious Castle. See it as constructed of ice and fire. Walk around it. Then walk through its halls and rooms. If you are so led, try drawing this imagined scene or make floor plans for it.

Meditate on the caravan trails along which Frankincense was transported in ancient times. Light Frankincense or hold a few granules of it in your hands and smell their aroma. Connect with the healing and transformative power inherent in this most ancient ingredient for incense.

Scriptural Meditation: Focus on the birth of John the Baptizer and his prophetic role in the Advent of Jesus as a long-expected wisdom-teacher (Luke 1:57-66). John the Baptist was destined to "Prepare the Way of the Lord," and in his wake would come the Messiah, who would make all crooked paths straight. Use Psalm 142 for a chant-prayer. Light Frankincense at verse 2. Meditate on paths and the significance of the path we chose to walk as seekers desiring to participate in the Wisdom of Christ.

7. <u>Mistletoe</u> <u>Day</u> *(A Day in the Quiet, 19 December)*

"The turning of the Season thus far shall be brought into the Inner Hearth of each one's Heart, prayers being said there for the increase of Goode Will, Joy and Merriement. This shall come to pass in the house, by the hearth, and out in the World. Read ye, of holy thinges. Wait upon the Lord. Listen for the Mysterious Visitor, and let Him in if He arrives. He may come as Christ our holy Stag, wandering near windows after dark, scratching upon the panes with His sacred tines, or as a Winter Wind, howling across the mountain or down the street." (60)

- Egbert Whittier
<u>The</u> <u>Thirteen</u> <u>Dayes</u> <u>of</u> <u>Yule</u> (1800)

This day, coming just after the mid-point in the Solstice Season, is dedicated to the disciplines of Silence & Solitude. Those who are keeping the Yule together should anticipate spending a day alone, while those who have already been pathing Glastonbury Tor in solitude, may hope to reap some of the fruit of their journey thus far.

The symbolic herb of the day is **Mistletoe**; a plant known for its potency in healing, it's mystical ability to reconcile opposing forces and its power to mend the emotions during dark, dismal months of Winter. It was considered sacred to Hecate in ancient Greece and in Celtic Britain it was connected with the hero **Bran the Blessed**. Keltelvens later connected it with the basic (re)generative power – called **shunnache**[44] – in the Cosmos. With its glossy ever-green leaves and its white berries it may be thought to embody the potency of the god-force in Nature. Some specimens of Mistletoe assume a rich golden hue when cut and stored in a cool place.

Mistletoe is a parasitic plant that lives by sinking its roots deep into the living wood of a host tree. As such, each Mistletoe plant will be somewhat different, depending on the nature of its host. It often grows far above the ground and is thus only spotted by a keen eye. Thus it was believed to have the power either to reveal itself or hide from those seeking it. Only the wise and kind-hearted can find Mistletoe. If someone were to use Mistletoe as a poison, folklore says, the criminal will be revealed by an act of divination using Mistletoe leaves. Though the berries are poisonous, they may be conjured up in the imagination and eaten as intimations of the wisdom we hope to glean by the 25th of December.

Since prehistoric times Mistletoe has been regarded as a solar symbol. It was used for divination and healing at Alban Arthuan. Its druidical name was *Uchelwydd* and it was popularly known as "All Heal." Herbal lore contends that Mistletoe reveals the inner meaning of things. Its use as a decoration at Winter's Solstice possibly antedates the introduction of pine trees and other evergreens. Many of its earlier Pagan associations were carried over into Christian symbolism.

Understood magically, Mistletoe is thought to catch the rays of the Summer Solstice Sun and then store this power in its white berries as they grow and mature. These berries come ripe in early winter, at which point they may turn yellow, which signifies the solar vigor of Summerwood. Their golden color is also thought to be prophetic of the Sun's rebirth at Winter Solstice. We might interpret this transformation as naturally prefiguring our own rebirth at Alban Arthuan. The White Sun of Winter becomes the Golden Sun of Spring, and as the berries turn from white to gold so we hope to experience renewal, empowerment and transformation in Earth & Spirit.

Mistletoe berries are extremely poisonous if eaten. However, after just the right decoction, they have a medicinal value. Because of its *healing properties*, Mistletoe was linked with *forgiveness* and *reconciliation*. Of the berries Gawain Smythe has said in The Way of the Bards (1996) that:

> "Each berry has four dark marks on it. These four dots surround a dark central spot. The four dots represent the mystic cities of the Sídhe (portals to the Otherworld) from which the Tuatha Dé Danann derived their wisdom and their treasures. The central dot symbolizes the Spiritual Heart, which is called Meath in Bardic spirituality. The four marks around the central dot also symbolize the four extremities of the Cross of Christ." (29)

A branch of the Mistletoe may be hung over a doorway as a sign that "in this house, olde enmitie and neue grievances be now forgiven" (59, Yuletide Grimoire, 1898). According to this grimoire, anyone with a grievance against another could offer the offending party a sprig of Mistletoe. If an offended person found it in their heart to forgive the offender, they were to go to their house and nail the Mistletoe up over their own door. When the offender came out to see who was there, they were to embrace the offended person upon seeing the Mistletoe. This is the origin of our habit of kissing under the Mistletoe! Today we would do well to reclaim the arts of forgiveness beneath the Mistletoe.

Mistletoe Day is a time for personal retreat and keeping to oneself in the company of the Spirit of Yule, whether in- or out-of-doors. Rise early and meditate quietly near the hearth and/or Yule Tree. Watch the lights on the tree blinking or take note of the reflections of the lights in the ornaments. Say to yourself: "I seek the Silent Place of the Heart."

Meditate on the **Druidic World-Cross**, which symbolizes our desire to be spiritually centered. The object of this meditation is to see ourselves coming in from wandering in one or all of the four cardinal directions – where we are normally scattered – thus arriving at the threshold of the Inner Heart. The Spiritual Heart is the center of the world and is called **Meath**. To be at Meath is to be in the omphallos ("world navel") where all magical arts and mystical powers get rejuvenated.

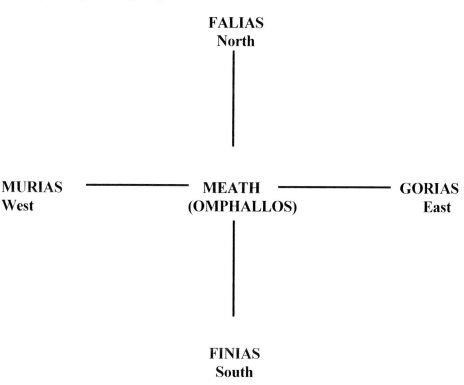

FALIAS
North

MURIAS ——————— **MEATH** ——————— **GORIAS**
West   **(OMPHALLOS)**   **East**

FINIAS
South

Keltelven Druids teach that we are each a navel of the world and that as such shunnache flows through us into the world at large, along crosstroads of the four primary directions. When we are centered in Meath we become the arms and legs, feet and hands, mind and compassion of the gods and goddesses in the world. When we are scattered out toward the Four Winds we dissipate spiritual power. Centered in the omphallos we can be led out in any direction, serving humankind and all of the creatures of the Earth & Spirit wherever we find ourselves.

Before breakfast on this day meditate and ask yourself: "In which direction(s) have I been traveling, of my own accord, and how shall I turn to reach Meath?" Have you been rambling through life more or less without direction? If so, let go of useless activity and return to Meath. There are numerous ways in which we can fritter away our potency in the subtle diversions and seductions of daily life. By meditating on the World-Cross we can come to see ourselves dwelling compassionately and poetically in the Earth. Only when we are centered in Meath do we begin to discern our spiritual 'place' in the larger scheme of things. Once this recognition arises in us we can work toward holy and practical ends, going out in *any* direction from the Center. Residing at the omphallos you are thus preparing yourself to go anywhere and do anything you are called to do. Rest on this day, however, and prepare to go out from Meath tomorrow. The rune of the day says, "Action arises out of the heart of peace."

Arrange sprigs of Mistletoe in a centerpiece on your breakfast table and also on the Yule Table. Be careful of the berries, however, especially if there are children in the house! Meditate on the presence of Mistletoe and reflect on its various properties: healing, forgiveness, reconciliation, and the gleaning of insight. If you're celebrating Yule with others, make plans for the day at breakfast. If it's a work/school day, you'll want to anticipate spending the evening hours in Solitude and Silence. If you're free for the whole day, agree to observe silence, especially at meals. If you're keeping the Yule alone, prepare for a day of deep reflection. Arrange your time so as to have as few distractions as possible.

If you don't have an actual sprig of Mistletoe, use an image of the herb as an icon for meditation. If you're going to work or school, carry this icon with you, perhaps taped to a 3 x 5 index card. As such it will fit conveniently into a shirt pocket or it may be used as a bookmark. Take it out at quiet moments and recollect the nature of Mistletoe, remembering what day it is. As much as possible, abstain from unnecessary talking. Speak when spoken to, of course, but otherwise nurture a mood of stillness in which you can listen with your Heart as well as your ears to what the Spirit may be saying. Learning silence is the best way in which to let go of distracted traveling in the Four Quarters of the World. When we grow quiet we learn what the rune means, "to know without speaking; to do without asking."

Whether at work or at home, the Spirit will lead you into prayer today. Certain people may need a ministry of intercession or perhaps some actual form of help. The Mistletoe will help you to effect healing and change. The Spirit of Yule may draw you into situations today where you will need to surrender yourself in service to others. Never refuse an opportunity for spontaneous and inspired service.

If you've been at odds with someone, this is a good day to cast a spell of reconciliation. If a door opens – one that may lead to forgiveness and a restoration of fellowship or friendship with someone – accept it as a mystic gift in the ambient potency of the Mistletoe. Seek to make things right between yourself and this other person. If you've been in the wrong, apologize. If they were in the wrong, try to forgive them. If you can't forgive them, ask the Spirit of Yule for the inspiration and power to be healed enough to *want* to forgive them, eventually. Sometimes this is all we're capable of, especially if we've been radically broken or damaged by the experience that disrupted a relationship.

On Misteltoe Day, hang a sprig of the herb in one of the doorways of your house or place of business. Every time someone passes through the door, pray for them; for healing and for the mending of their relationships with other people. Do this silently and without pretense. Every time you walk beneath the Mistletoe yourself, imagine all the broken relationships you know of being healed.

If the day's work isn't going to be too strenuous, consider engaging in at least a partial fast. **Fasting** quiets the body and allows it to rest. You might skip lunch and simply have a glass of fruit juice or cold water. If you also skip supper, have a piece of toast or two with a cup of herbal tea or hot chocolate sometime during the evening. If you fast, drink plenty of water (*at least* a large glass at the time of each normal meal).

Fasting is a voluntary discipline. Like practicing a listening silence, fasting is a way of disengaging from our normal routines in order to seek the runes of wisdom. It's not only a healthy practice – when done with simple common sense – but also helps guide us to Meath. If you already know the ropes of fasting and what's healthy for you in this regard, you may fast as radically as you are led. A total 24-hour fast – from dusk on 18 December to dusk on 19 December – is not inappropriate.

If this day falls on a weekend, or if you can arrange to take a personal day off from work, there will be much more lee-way for following the Mistletoe into the Solitude of the Heart. Retreat to your room or go out to a favorite place in the woods after breakfast. You need not be seen again 'til dusk! Pray, meditate and read holy literature in the solitude. Silence is a spiritual place. We find in it the freedom to exist without the crutch of always speaking on our own behalf and filling the voids with useless words. Silence as a spiritual discipline is primarily an act of listening for the heartbeat of the Divine Presence. Mystery's first language is Silence. We only really hear 'Words' of Wisdom to the extent that we grow quiet in heart & mind, body & soul. Meditating by chanting sacred words is fine for beginners, but we should eventually mature into the Heart of Silence.

Solicit Silence, therefore, and engage in personal recollection. You might sit quietly by a window and watch the snow falling. You can also recollect yourself by writing in a journal. When you meditate, see yourself as engaged with Divine Mystery and Listening for the heartbeat of your god or goddess, the TRIBANN or perhaps Mystery itself. By listening for the "heartbeat of the gods" we learn to be immortally still and quiet.

This is definitely a day for **spiritual reading**. Read Celtic myths or perhaps begin a novel that inspires you with Yuletide musings. Read spiritual books and magical literature. Read poetry that opens your mind and heart to healing and reconciliation. Such reading is a way of nourishing the soul and nurturing Devout Mind. Sacred texts speak silently to the Heart in Meath, making it devout while culling our will towards the turnstiles of self-realization and a more total commitment to really living life.

It doesn't matter how little or how much you read today. What does matter is that you read with a desire to be connected with the Spirit of Yule and empowered to continue your journey to the Nativity. Whatever you read it should encourage you to re-collect your energy and seek for Wisdom in the Quiet. Acknowledge others who are observing the Yule with you with a smile or a nod, or even by a handshake or embrace, but without words. No one should speak unless it's an emergency. Talk with people who call you on the phone, but keep the conversation polite and brief, unless there's a real need for it to be longer. This also applies to people who come to the door. It may be useful to tell your friends ahead of time that you will be "away" on 19 December so as to reduce the possibility of visits and calls. You *will* in fact be on a journey – an inward one! – so this ruse is not far from the literal truth.

This is also a day for **quiet walks**. You might walk out to some secreted nemeton in the woods. Go to a favorite Pine Grove, or to a ruined or abandoned site of human dwelling. **Ruins and abandoned places** are perfect places for recollection as they inspire the Heart to remember times past. Entering an old house where no one has lived for years, you will not be able to help wondering who they were and where they are now. Ruins are always waiting for visitors to come and rune out their hidden histories. Confronted with the ruins of human habitation we become aware that things are somehow awry; that something has gone amiss. All human ideals and efforts are ultimately illusory! What we build does not last. People die and cross†over into other worlds, often never to return.

Those who go out to nemetons, groves or ruins should come back to the hearth around dusk. Soon after dark, gather for about half an hour of quiet prayer and meditation. Enjoy wordless fellowship in the glow of the hearthfire and decorative lights. After this, have a quiet supper. Play meditative seasonal music in the background if you want. Those who are fasting may remain near the hearth, continuing in sacred meditation. They might also sing quiet carols, in order to edify the people having supper. During the evening, dwell in the silence or engage in the quiet singing of carols. If you have found Meath today, the evening should be a radiant time. If you've had to work or be at school during the day, the evening will be your primary time for entering into the holy cloisters of Silence and Solitude. Use the time to nurture Silence and Solitude without forcing yourself into pseudo-spiritual states!

Listen in the Silence of Meath for the re-creative Runes of Cernunnos as one of the major revelating presences of Mystery during the Yule. The Runes of Cernunnos may come to you through an image, a feeling or a sound. If you've been reading, the 'Rune' that is 'for you' will perhaps arise as a word or phrase that jumps out of the text. Otherwise, it may come as a quiet insight that reveals something about yourself or the way you are pathing through the Yule.

Learning the language and practice of Silence is a difficult task for most people in our society as we're forever being bombarded with noise, activity and confusion. The first time people try to keep Mistletoe Day they usually can't restrain themselves from talking. By evening, though, most celebrants will have found the key to the Silent Place in their own Heart. If not, there's always next year! Once we find the doorway to Meath, though, being silent on Mistletoe Day will become a joy. Some people will enjoy it so much they may continue to speak less than they normally do for the next few days!

As you keep still, learning how to discover the seeds of Silence in yourself, you will slowly begin discerning the dull meaninglessness of most of the *chatter* we engage in on a day to day basis. We talk when we don't need to, we talk to our pets or the TV when no one else is around, and we may even talk to ourselves, if worse comes to worse. While language is a gift, it's also a primary bane of our existence, as the tongue often goes off on binges, like a willful rudder without anyone to control it.

Once you find a place of Silence, savor it and dedicate it to the Spirit of Mistletoe. Once silent most people are better able to approach the mysteries of sacred seasons, free of the clutter fabricated by endless babbling. Allow the Silence to restore your vital energies. Learning Silence better prepares us for the advent of Wisdom's revelation in the midst of life as it frees us from compulsive self-expression. If you keep Mistletoe Day well you should be prepared to approach the Manger of Rebirth on Matrum Noctem free of all of the baggage you normally haul around with you. Traveling in the Silence of Meath should enable you to experience your own Rebirth more or less free of distraction by the time you get to Glastonbury Tor on the morning of 25 December.

Natural Meditation: Focus on the eternal flame of the Sun as captured in the berries of the Mistletoe. Procure a sprig of Mistletoe – preferably with the berries intact – from a local florist or greenhouse or get a good color picture from a guide to herbs or an encyclopedia. Meditate on this as an icon, and seek out the ley-lines of reconciliation for yourself and others with whom you may be at odds.

Scriptural Meditation: Focus on the Benedictus (Luke 1:67-78); the song sung by Zechariah, the father of John the Baptist. Reflect on its implications for our life together and for our witness to the World. Concentrate on how Jesus entered his world alone, having left his Father and Mother (the Holy Spirit) in Paradise, and how alone Mary and Joseph must have felt, knowing what they had been told by the Angel Gabriel about their child.

8. <u>Holly</u> <u>Day</u> *(The Day of Hunting Fire, 20 December)*

> "Ignite the Holly of the Heart! The Stag flies to us, and
> now we discover the hoof-prints of supernal Reindeer in
> the mud! Now we come hither, to the frost upon the hide,
> and hear the Spirit whispering from the Othersidhe: Yule is
> here, and the Stags of Hope are full of goodly cheer!" (60)

- Egbert Whittier
The <u>Thirteen</u> <u>Dayes</u> <u>of</u> <u>Yule</u> (1800)

After the quiet and solitude of Mistletoe Day you should be rested and ready for another round of more out-going activities. On this last day before the Winter Solstice, we devote ourselves to **the ancient mysticism of hunting**!

Hunting has been a key element of human spirituality for countless generations. Anthropologists have shown that human beings have practiced hunting as part of their mode of subsistence since earliest times. While the primary sustenance of pre-historic human groups consisted of what could be gathered from the land – fruits, nuts and berries, roots and vegetables – hunting provided necessary proteins. By about 50,000 BCE a division of labor had emerged in which women did most of the primary gathering, providing most of the food for the group, while men went out on hunting forays, returning with whatever meat they could procure.

This experience of hunting is deeply engrained in the human consciousness. As such, it gives us a clue as to why hunting remains so strong today, even in areas where the number of hunters sometimes seems to outnumber the animals hunted! The hunt became a factor in subsistence but also evolved into a paradigmatic quest as well. Hunting drew participants into mystical encounters with other animal species who dwell with-us in the Earth. It also brought men & women into contact with their gods & goddesses.

While out on a hunt, tracking down an animal, unsuspecting hunters were sometimes led over into mysterious tracks of divine quarry by benevolent spirits who were moving and shifting the track of the animals being hunted. Along these altered tracks hunters followed animals that became like the representatives of gods or goddesses. The wild Boar might be seen on these hunts as a manifestation of the great Earth Goddess while the Stag was an incarnate form of the god Cernunnos.

Over time, hunters began to go out on purpose to look for manifest forms of their deities. This became the **mystical hunt**, around which a complex mythology evolved over the millennia and about which a great wealth of stories was eventually told. What does it mean to encounter your god or goddess in the wildwood? What will happen? Will you ever get home again, or will you be taken back to the Otherside to live in a Divine Dún or Faery Ráth for all eternity, as a friend of the god or goddess? How should a mortal act when encountered by such a divine animal?

The hunt for the divine Stag became one symbolic manifestation of the Celtic desire to know the gods of the Wildwood more intimately. Those who sought Cernunnos in the depths of primeval forests came back with stories and tales to tell that would in turn guide later hunters in their quests. Cernunnos is no ordinary deer, though the deer may lead us to Cernunnos. We can recognize him as he has a third antler on his forehead shaped like a cross. His eyes are supposed to be blue instead of black, and his hooves are coated with a thin skin of pure black gold.

The Stag eventually became symbolic of the human Heart as well. The Heart in which the Goddess has revealed her Wisdom to us is like a wounded Stag searching for the one who has wounded it. The Heart in love with Wisdom is like a person seeking his or her Stag-Lover. Thus the heart of the hunter becomes a compass, drawing him or her out onto the path of the Stag. As such, the Stag-Hunt became a metaphor for higher journeys of the soul into union with the Goddess. The urge to go out on a mystical hunt is called **Hunting Fire** by Keltelven mystics.

In olden times both men and women were called out on mystical hunts, en-fired by the spirit of Cernunnos or perhaps by some other animal god. The hunters tracked their prey by means of images, symbols and inner promptings. These hunts could be as short as a day, but often lasted longer. Ancient hunters packed well for their expeditions and spent weeks at their camps tracking one mystical manifestation of their god after another. They usually returned home as exhausted as they were empowered or disillusioned by their experiences in the woods. Over the following days or weeks, they retold their stories of the chase, the waiting, and the long nights of anticipation.

Stories are also told of early Celtic followers of Christ who looked out of their oratory or monastery window and suddenly saw Christ-the-Stag standing near the edge of the farm fields! When this happened, the saint would get up from whatever he or she was doing and follow the animal off into the woods. Inspired by Hunting Fire, these men and women often went their wild ways along paths where only their God had gone before! They hoped to track Christ-the-Stag to a Pine Grove, where He would stop and allow the pilgrim to approach, always in a state of true and self-revealing worship. Tracking the Stag as a manifest form of God was considered to be a great boon to one's faith, enabling saints to overcome sins and be healed of old psychic wounds. Upon their return, these men and women would be empowered to undertake their ministry with more gusto and devotion than before. Many, however, never returned from these forays into the wilds and were considered "Lost in God."

The Great Stag, when finally "cornered," was described as having shining sapphire colored eyes, glistening brown fur splotched with black markings (like runes), and a long white tail. His rack may have had 7, 12 or 24 points, and he would be often strewn with vines, especially Ivy, in which pieces of Holly and Mistletoe were snared. As the mysticism of the Hunt evolved, Holly became symbolic of the life-force inherent in the Stag-hunter.

Hunters who meditate on Holly during the Yule see the piercing power of Earth's eternal life-force in the spiny leaves, the nourishing power of the Muse in the berries and the mysterious psychic web that connects everything in the Cosmos with everything else (called "Manred") in the twisty woody parts. Holly is rooted in Earthy darkness and thus symbolizes the Mystery that is beyond knowing. Because the Great Stag has Holly draped across its antlers, the Day of Hunting Fire also became known as Holly Day.

Holly is an herb with masculine powers. It represents paternity and fatherhood. It is usually linked in mystical symbolism with the Ivy and Mistletoe as one of the "divine family" of herbs. **Holly** is the Father-force, *Ivy* is the Mother-force, and *Mistletoe* is the potent energy of youth. Holly manifests the god-force inherent in Nature just as the Ivy emanates the goddess-force. Because it bears its berries at the onset of Winter it has long been connected with Alban Arthuan.

Holly guards against lightning, poison and evil spirits. Planted around the home it protects the house and its inhabitants from negative and mischievous influences. It was once believed that when thrown at wild animals Holly made them lie down and leave you alone. Holly water (infused or distilled) was once sprinkled on newborn babies to protect them from negative psychic energies. Holly is related to the essence of life. The green leaves with their pin-like tines are symbolic of the fecundity of the flesh, while the red berries, which are brightest near the Winter Solstice, symbolize blood and its inherent life-force.

When you get up on the 20th of December, be ready to break silence and come out of solitude. Go to the Yule Table and set up an icon of a Stag or at least some picture of a deer. Meditate on this icon, and say the following invocation:

> "Hail Cernunnos, Stag of the Woods_
> Come to us, we pray you!
> Inspire our hearts with Earthen Faith
> and an adventurous love of life;
> Lead us and we will follow You_
> through the Wildwoods, to the Heaths_
> where the haunted ones of Wisdom's Light
> await the darkest Night
> of Mystery's Embrace! Amen."

After this, light a candle scented with **Hollyberry**. Place a Holly bough on the breakfast table. Tell hunting stories, recollecting the ways in which the Day of Hunting Fire has been observed in years past, or perhaps how it might be kept (if this is your first Yule). After breakfast, move the Hollyberry candle to the Yule Table.

On this day, engage in a symbolic hunt for the Great Stag. It is the complement of Ivy Day, and is thus a time for the men to get away by themselves and prepare for the Solstice and Glastonbury Thorn Day. Thus the women should do all they can to liberate the men from their obligations and responsibilities on this day. The preparations we make should aim at one of three possible adventures: (1) an imaginative hunt, (2) an actual foray out into the woods with a camera, hoping to catch an image of the Great Stag on film, or even (3) a real hunt with the intention of slaying a deer.

If this is not a work or school day, the Hunt may last from dawn until after dusk or even all night and 'til dawn the next day! If you are not free for the whole day, enact the hunt during the morning, afternoon or evening hours. No matter which 'hunt' you engage in, depart from the hearth with a small ceremony. As in Olden Dayes, stand before the hearth with your 'gear' on, and say:

> "Stag of Grace; Deer of Time,
> let us glimpse you in good mime!
> We will path You, here and there,
> falling neither into fear nor snare!
>
> May we track you with our hearts
> to places where Wisdom starts us
> with its itinerary of rejuvenation!
> So mote it be."

Then shout: "Amen! Shemmash!! Hurrahya!!!" This may be followed by loud shrieking, stomping on the floor and also a few growls and snorts imitating the wildness of the prey you are seeking. Then go out, leaving the house with high hopes, perhaps chanting the holy names of the query: **"Jesus—Cernunnos—Dumas—Oisín!"** – over and over again.

The men may gather together in a room by themselves or out at a cabin in the woods in order to engage in their imagined hunt. Sit in a circle. Discuss the nature of hunting. If anyone in the circle has actually hunted with a bow and arrow or perhaps a gun and brought down a deer let them describe their experience in 'real time' terms. Having done this, meditate and begin to *imagine yourselves* as if out on a hunt. Stomp your feet, walk in a circle and make like you are climbing trees to get up into a deer blind, and in other ways act and talk out your imagined experiences.

The turning point of the hunt comes when someone says, "Is that a deer over there?" If it is, follow it in a playful way, but if not, keep hunting or watching. If you're near a hearth, light a fire as if you have come to a campsite. Remember that imaginative hunts – like actual ones – don't often go as planned. You might not see a Stag for a long time, or you may not all agree on what you see. If you have trouble getting to an imaginative place where the Stag Hunt can begin, revert to storytelling and the recollection of prior hunts.

This kind of imaginative waiting and tracking can go on for hours 'til you finally get on the trail of the Great Stag. You may not be able to sustain an imaginative scenario like this for very long the first time you try it but with practice you'll be able to 'hunt' almost indefinitely, breaking only for meals and sleep. It is important to nurture vivid scenes in your mind and agree on the scenery you are seeing.

During the Hunt imagine yourselves being able to run as fast as the deer you see! When you finally encounter the Stag, follow it even deeper into the wildwood. It will eventually stop, usually in a thicket or near a mysterious pond or lake. There, you will have the chance to adore the Stag in your imagination. Once this encounter is consummated, you will usually find yourselves alone. The Stag will have gone and you will then have to discern the way back home.

There may then arise a real sense that that you are *lost*, as imaginative hunts – like the real thing – are often wild and unmapped chases, undertaken without taking much account of which paths were taken. If so, you may have to ask the Stag for a magical mode of getting home! Don't just say, "Oh, we forgot our way, so we'll just call the game off." You must try to *imagine* finding a way home, even if it's only a matter of asking Cernunnos or some Elves for a 'magick carpet ride.'

As you are venturing home in your imaginations it may be difficult to talk about what happened. If so, wait until your journey is over and then break for refreshment (Beer and bread? Wine and cheese sandwiches? Coffee and blackberry pie?). As you eat together discuss the hunt and what happened along the way. Describe the different scenes you saw in your imagination in detail and reflect on the prey. What did the Stag look like? What did he *do*? What happened to you in his presence?

If you can make an actual foray out into the woods on this day, go hoping to spot a deer or two, and take your camera with you. Go stealthily. It takes at least as much skill in the woods to shoot a deer with a camera as it does to bring one down with a rifle. For this adventure you must the learn the arts of hunting, becoming familiar with camouflage, the use of tracking techniques and the craefts of stealth. You may stay out in the woods all day and never even see a deer, though, much less a Stag. Be thankful, therefore, no matter what the outcome. As on Frankincense Day, the journey is what matters most.

If it's "deer season" in your area and if you have experience with fire arms and have procured a license, you might choose to go out on an actual hunt – preferably with a bow and arrows – hoping not only to see the Great Stag but to bring down a deer. If you're successful, you will have to butcher the animal. You will then have venison for Alban Arthuan.

If you have a fortunate hunt, make some sacrifice to the animal's kin-spirit for the taking of the life. Take a bag of good apples or several ears of corn with you. Whether or not you kill a deer, leave the apples or the corn in a place that deer seem to frequent. We cannot take life without giving up something of our own. There is a sacred balance at stake! Hunting the Stag is about more than 'male-bonding' and 'exercise.' An encounter with the Stag is a potentially transforming experience. Even to glimpse the Stag is to become aware of the Spirit haunting us in the Earth!

Those who don't go out on the hunt should take part in any last minute preparations for Alban Arthuan. This usually involves procuring food, baking, and setting up the place where you will keep the celebration. Many of the traditional foods for the Winter Solstice are still customary around Christmas time. These include cranberry sauces, apple cakes, blackberry and minced-eat pies, plum puddings and small cakes of various kinds and flavors. Home-baked food is always better than store-bought, as it symbolizes the surplus of our own cupboards and fruit cellars. In as many ways as possible, make the place where the Solstice will be kept seem like 'another world,' richly decorated and scented with candles, the aroma of food being prepared and the icons of the Season all arranged in ways that create a mystic ambiance. There should be "no lack of anything" on Alban Arthuan.

> **Natural Meditation**: Focus on the connection between Mistletoe and the Great Stag. It is Cernunnos, as much as the Dark Earth Goddess Nerthus, who brings us into and through the crucible of transformation at Winter Solsticetide. The Stag is decorated with Mistletoe because

he reconciles us with the Spirit of Life and heals our brokenness. Meditate on the various aspects of the Stag; – his horns, the tines of his antler, his blue eyes & golden hooves.

Scriptural Meditation: Focus on the journey of Mary and Joseph to Bethlehem. They are seeking the meaning of what has happened to them as they go. Thus they are on a quest akin to that of hunters on Holly Day. Mary carries the god-child in her womb, but she must still quest the meaning of its mysterious conception. They are journeying out from the hearth of their home in Nazareth to Bethlehem, which means "House of Bread" in Hebrew.

A Winter Solstice Log (20 December)

Down in the Dell, the Olde People were speaking.
"Walloby_ Walloby_ Everything is changing!"

Howling into the Wintry spaces_
gathering ancient Yuletide traces
we all came out to play
upon the lawns and with the Fawns
of Christmass Ghosts and Tales.   1

As down in the Dell the Olde Folk were saying:
"Walloby_ Walloby_ all sin is straying!"

Sleighbells tinker along a road
upon which souls are traveling_
coming to Solstice Festivals, Unalone!
They come with Holly, Bells ringing_
to sit upon the old Hearthstone!   2

As Over the Vale, Olde People are singing:
"Walloby_ Walloby_ Yule bells are ringing!"

Coming to the Gate they tarry
where stars are falling, all frozen!
Admitted to the Heart of Dwelling
they ramble in merry costumes,
sharing tales runed by the dozen!   3

And then the Olde People come caroling:
"Walloby_ Walloby_ GOD is cajoling us!"

Souls hung near the Solstice Hearth
throw logs upon the fire_
And with their Hearts unfurled,
the ghosts of children cry out:
"Christmass! Christmass! HURRAH!!"   4

Until the Olde Folk take up the tune:
"Walloby_ Walloby_ Sings the Solstice Log!"

Crisps and cringles _it sings,
sparking life in home-gathered hearts!
Hail the Solstice Log now glowing;
within the Heart of Yuletide Showings –
we listen for its Magical Tune!   5

Ancient Ones now all gathering, sing:
"Walloby_ Wallalloby_ the Solstice Runes us!"

Olde Souls come toasting the living,
as Elves dance 'round the room!
Evermore the Spirit blazes
and with open Hearts She razes –
all resistance to Love & Joy!   6

And then the Olde Folk Toast the revelers:
"Walloby_ Walloby_ the Saints live again!"

Amen.

9. <u>*Alban*</u> <u>*Arthuan*</u> *(The Winter Solstice, 21 December)*

[Natural icons: Bay leaves, Juniper & Pine Groves]

"At Winter's Solstice we have reached the darkest passage of our mortal existence in the Earth. The longest night. On the canvas of this night ancient peoples painted their dreams of a better world and lived out their fears. Are we still frightened of the dark? Do we still long to be reborn in the light? On this night, journey out away from the lights of town and city and perhaps you will get a taste for what our ancestors went through as they waited for sunrise on the morning after the Solstice." (196)

- Robert Werner
<u>The Way of the Poet</u> (1971)

"NERTHUS—BRIGHID—COVENTINA is the chant of the Winter Solstice."

- <u>A Yuletide Grimoire</u> (1898)

"On the eve of the Solstice collect Juniper and Bay Leaves, bringing them into the kitchen for use in preparations. This is a day for concoctions of many kinds. As the Sun dies and as we wait for it to be reborn, practitioners create salves, ointments, poultices and remedies which have to do with birth and rejuvenation." (133)

- Cornelius Whitsel
<u>The Keltelven Grimoire</u> (1993)

The Solstice arrives, and now we're closer to our destination than ever before. In the symbolism of Alban Arthuan we come to the last crosstroads of Yule, where our journey of rebirth and rejuvenation reaches the primary cauldron of change. Our desires for transformation are now acted out in Nature in the dying and rebirth of the Sun. Following the Sun we hope to disappear into a spiritual sleep tonight and then awaken – tomorrow morning – with a renewed sense of life.

Winter's Solstice is a night to let down our hair, party and enjoy the darkness. We have arrived at our primary destination, and everything after tonight will simply be reaping the fruit of Solstice Night. Celebrating Alban Arthuan is a magical passage steeped in ancient symbolism and mythic themes. The meaning of Winter's Solstice is interpreted through the acting out of mythic events that – while probably older than civilization itself – unfold annually in the lives of those keeping the Yule. The symbols and rituals for Alban Arthuan will help us realize our goal and experience the results. Get up on the morning of 21 December with a sense of anticipation. No strict discipline needs to be observed during the day. We can do almost anything until dusk, provided we don't stray away from spiritual authenticity.

There are three primary symbols connected with Alban Arthuan: **Bay Leaves** (Bay Laurel), **Juniper** (Gin Berry) and the **Pine Grove**. These natural icons represent the mystical nature of Winter's Solstice. To intuit their place in our festivities is to touch upon the meaning of Alban Arthuan.

Bay leaves symbolize strength, victory, and integrity. They were attributed with many herbal and religious uses in the ancient world. They were used in spells of protection and purification. They were employed in rites of divination as they were thought to enhance clairvoyance. They were decocted in oil and put on salads, as a way of blessing a guest with a taste of courage and honor. Bay leaves were laid near the places where heroes were born.

Bay leaves are connected with the cycles of the Sun in general and especially with the Winter Solstice as a time of death & rebirth. They are associated with rejuvenation in Keltelven lore and are said to be found by magicians in the Cedar chest where the goddess Sul (Mistress of Sunlight) keeps her solar firebrands. Sul gives these brands to Cernunnos at dusk on 21 December. He then brings them to us as we enter the darkness of Solstice Night. We see these solar brands glowing in his black eyes during the night as he wanders through the wildwoods of the Otherworld and comes to our hearths to inspire us.

Bay leaves later came to symbolize the birth of Jesus the Carpenter-God, whom his followers believe is born again symbolically each year on

Glastonbury Thorn Day. Myths relate how Brighid visited Bethlehem at the time of Jesus' birth. There she laid Bay leaves in the manger as a symbol of the divinity and heroic destiny of the god-child Jesus. Bay leaves are thus used to decorate the Nativity scene, which is set up before dusk on 21 December.

Juniper is an evergreen whose efficacy makes a house 'secure.' Hung over the hearth, Juniper invokes the greening power of the Spirit that blesses the occupants of the house. It works to further the welfare of occupants, provided they are living hospitably, practicing charity and kindness toward strangers and animals. When hung by doors it was a hex against thieves. To wear Juniper as an amulet on a chain hung about your neck symbolizes the security of your heart against malediction. Cernunnos is often imaged on the Winter Solstice standing in a grove of seven (a solar number) Juniper trees.

In Mediaeval times, English Keltelvens carried sprigs of Juniper out to nearby **Pine Groves**. This act probably remembered the earlier practice of offering evergreens to the dying Sun on Solstice Day before dusk. These sprigs of Juniper were thought to prime the grove for the arrival of the New Sun's Light, which would become manifest at mid-night on Solstice Night. Later these sprigs were thrown on the bonfire of Matrum Noctem, as Keltelvens danced and celebrated. Juniper was thought to attract angels and saints as well as deer and crows to the circle of a Grove.

On Solstice morning, *fill a chalice with pure water* and set it on the Yule Table. This symbolizes the cosmic waters through which the Sun will be reborn. Pray for discernment and wakefulness, saying:

> "Hail, Waters of Life,
> make us alert
> and free us from strife.
> Envision in us the coming of the New Sun,
> and let us dance
> free and hopeful,
> 'til we get another chance
> to renew our hearts!"

Then stir the water in the chalice with a knife or spoon, while throwing three pinches of salt into it. Cast the salt into the water in the names of

Brighid, Nerthus and Coventina. This represents the effect we are supposed to have on the world around us. It also indicates our desire to be reborn with the Sun during the course of the Solstice Night passage.

Whereas in olden times the Winter Solstice was the Thirteenth Day of Yule, today it comes four days before Glastonbury Thorn Day. As such it's now a 'first threshold' of the rebirth we are expecting as we pilgrim through the Season. Though tonight will be the natural earthen turnstile of light's rebirth, after which the days will begin to get longer, we will continue to path the nativity for three more days.

Use twigs of Juniper and Bay Laurel leaves to decorate the breakfast table. Also place these sacred woods on the Yule Table. Use a branch of Juniper to sprinkle the doors of the house with water. This purifies against evil influences. During the day, be in a festive mood. Make any last minute preparations for the Solstice Night festivities, and then go out and have some fun.

Though Alban Arthuan used to be kept in Pine Groves in the wildwood, today it's generally celebrated either in someone's backyard or else indoors, in a cellar or a spacious attic. A secluded yard will do for Solstice festivities, if weather permits and if neighbors aren't either going to be disturbed or disturb you, but the festival may just as effectively be held indoors.

If you're going to celebrate outdoors, create a fire-pit in the middle of the yard or field and leave a wide girth around it for circle dancing. If you think it's going to be warm enough to cook outside, set up a grill off to one side of the field or near a porch or patio. Also set up a table for buffet-style eating, as it may later get too cold to sit down for too long, as this *is* a winter festival. Trim at least one of the trees growing in the yard or field, either evergreen or deciduous, with festive lights. If a hedge or fence surrounds the yard you might also trim it with lights and greenery. Having "prepared the sacred grounds" in this way, you're now ready for Solstice Night.

If the festivities are to be held indoors, choose the largest room in your house or apartment – perhaps the basement or attic – and set up a small round table in the middle of it around which people can dance. Set up Yuletide icons on this table and cover it with Pine, Juniper, Bay and Holly. Then set up four candles, aligned to the four cardinal directions – North, East, South, and West– on the floor around the table. You may also add miniature colored lights to the table if you like. The table should be festive and small enough so as to leave more than ample room for people to move around it. If no table is available, use a round hassock and cover it with a sturdy piece of glass or wood. Also set up a table for the Solstice buffet. Having done all of this, you're ready for an indoor celebration.

The circle is a symbol of our earthen horizons. Stand in one place and raise your hand toward the North Pole. Then, turn around 360° and watch as your hand points to the horizon in every direction, forming a circle around you. The horizon of the human world where we live is always a circle. To sit in a circle and meditate is a way of finding ourselves at the omphallos of the cosmos (remember the Druidic World-Cross?) To dance in a circle is to 'travel' through the Earth, offering praise, thanksgiving and worship to the Spirit of All. This is the basic impetus for circle-dancing at Winter's Solstice.

A **Nativity Scene** – depicting the birth of Jesus of Nazareth and, by extension, our own desires for rebirth – may also be set up on Solstice Day. This diorama should be erected on or near the Yule Table. If the meditation table takes the place of a hearth in your place of dwelling, set up the Nativity somewhere near it, rather than on it. Carefully plan how to stage the story of the Nativity in the scene as you set it up. The figures of the holy family, the animals and the shepherds, for instance, should not be set out all at once. On Solstice Day the stage is merely set for this imaginative drama.

For the next three days you'll want to reflect on the empty manger in the Nativity and prepare yourself for Matrum Noctem through the 'appearance' of the various Nativity characters. Set out the figures of Mary & Joseph on 22 December, lay the infant Jesus in his manger at mid-night on 24 December, followed by the shepherds at dawn on either the 25th or 26th of December. The Magi get added last, at dusk on 6 January. As the events of the Nativity myth did not happen all at once, we must reflect this in our Nativity drama. Treat the Nativity as a living story. It is *not* a decoration. Rather, it's an image of what's hopefully happening in the heart of each person; psychic and spiritual rebirth.

If you have a hearth, and if there's a large enough tile or brick skirt around it, you might participate in the ritual of the **Yule Log**. Sometime on Solstice Day, bring a large log into the house and thrust it into the hearth. If you want, 'dress' the Yule Log before lighting it. As Egbert Whittier (1800) said long ago:

> "Decorate the log with Juniper, Bay Leaves and Holly. Anoint it with Bay Wax. Then, everyone shall lay hands on the log and bless it, before laying it on the grate! It shall scent thy house as the scent of the pine tree begins to fade away." (89, <u>Thirteen Dayes of Yule</u>)

Light the log soon enough before dusk so that it will be blazing before the Sun goes down. The Yule Log symbolizes the year that is passing as well as the Old Sun as it is consumed by the natal darkness.

Alban Arthuan begins officially at dusk on 21 December. As the Old Sun goes down, ring bells of mourning. This sound initiates the night's festivities, inviting everyone to come to where the Solstice is being kept. The night is known as the **Vigil of the Sun** as through it celebrants will await the rebirth of solar power. Experience the Sun's setting as your own descent into a night of sleep beyond the Sídhe!

Just after dusk, enact **the Death & Rebirth of the Sun**. This informal drama begins with an older man lamenting the facts of age, perhaps hobbling around the circle where you are keeping the Solstice, complaining of aches and pains. A woman – who is playing the part of **Nerthus** – then comes out to invite Old Sun into Her cave, where he can rest. Three times She bids him and he refuses. Finally, as "the day is growing dark," Old Sun relents and enters into the Cave of the Goddess.

Those who aren't acting watch Old Sun lay down. They then listen as Nerthus tells the story of how Old Sun was her son, and how he has been at his job all year long. She laments his yearlong age, after which she leaves the stage for a minute or two. The actress then returns with a pillow stuffed up under her dress, symbolizing the fact that Nerthus is pregnant. She speaks of the wonders of childbirth and then comforts Old Sun as he falls asleep. Once he is sleeping he dies (usually signified by loud snores which stop abruptly), after which Nerthus assures her audience that a bright new Sun will be coming into the world by dawn. At this point the play ends, following which the night's festivities begin.

Alban Arthuan prefigures the return of vital power to our lives. This drama of Nerthus and Old Sun anticipates our shift from the quest for

Illumination to our pilgrimage into Enlightenment as Matrum Noctem approaches. We begin the festivities by lighting the **Solstice Bonfire**, which must be kindled just after dark with wood from seven different sacred trees. There are specific trees designated for this purpose, such as Oak, Cherry, Hawthorne, Rowan, Birch, Dogwood and Apple. However, if you can't find these, other more common woods may be substituted. If you have no hearth or fire pit, place small twigs from seven sacred trees on the Yule Table and bless them, sprinkling them with salty water from the chalice. You might arrange them to look like a campfire, or so that they spell out a sacred word.

After the fire has been lit, hold the **Solstice Feast**. At this meal all the traditional holiday dishes – cranberry sauce, turkey and filling, ham candied yams, minced meat pies and other delights – may be served. The feast is dedicated to Nerthus as the Lady of Solstice Night and to the Great Stag Cernunnos who in Keltelven myths is seen as the son of the Sun and the Earth Goddess. Sanctify the food to the coming rebirth of the Sun and to Jesus, whose festival will soon be observed. Let everyone pray:

> "Mother Nerthus, Sister of Mary
> Bless this table,
> and all who sit around it.
> Lord Cernunnos, Christ our Stag (or "The Stag our Christ"),
> come to us and let us be
> frolicsome and filled with compassion
> this night, and be forever free!"

Play recorded music in the background that's both joyous and that has a good danceable rhythm. Instrumental CD's of Irish reels and jigs are good for getting everyone going as Solstice Night begins. Olde tunes light the way for visiting spirits and even facilitate getting your ancestors into the mood for the sometimes exhausting but always enchanted passage through Solstice Night.

After the feast there should be ample time for fellowship, and then, once people's stomachs have settled a bit, "a crier shall stand by the hearth and hearken all ye to the night's rounds of dancing and merrie games! Let him say: 'Yule is for Yuling! 'Tis time to go a'Yulin'!'" (88, Yuletide Grimoire).

If you're keeping Solstice Night somewhere other than where the feast is held, everyone now leaves the feasting area and goes, either walking or riding, to the sacred grounds. This procession may be no more elaborate than a walk from the kitchen down to the cellar or up to the attic, yet it should be made to seem like a mysterious and arcane trek. Imagine being accompanied by Elves, Faery and other folk from the Otherside as you go. Once you get where you are going, address the Spirit of Yule, saying:

> "Old Sun is dying,
>   and New Sun is trying
>   to come into the world and be born!
>   Ho! Ho! Ho!
>   Let us bid farewell to Old White Sun.
>   Hey! Hey! Hey!
>   Let us greet New Gold Sun
>   with Faith and Faery Horn –
>   for his year-long sway!"

Once you arrive, illumine the place where you're going to spend the night by lighting candles and turning on electric holiday lights. Let a man and a woman – who represent Joseph and Mary on their way to Bethlehem – walk around the circle with joined hands, perhaps singing a verse of the old carol "We wonder as we wander," as they go. Then let everyone address the Sun, saying:

> "Hail, Light of the World,
>   we will keep you in our hearts
>   'til the New Sun is born
>   on the morrow!
>   Blessed be Bright New Sun,
>   and blessed be Cernunnos,
>   who shines the Light into our hearts!"

At this point begin to play music, either performed or recorded. If there are no live musicians among you, it's useful to record your own collections of songs with tempos that facilitate dancing. The music should be seasonal and yet not just the usual carols or holiday tunes you hear all the time. As the dancing begins, Joseph and Mary both leave the circle, continuing their journey to Bethlehem.

Imagine dances in which you move in a circle around a bonfire. If you have a small table or tree at the center of your 'sacred grounds,' light all of the lights and candles on it, and dance around it, careful not to knock over anything with an open flame in it. Dance in concentric rings, holding hands or not as you choose. Some may dance around the perimeter of the circle, keeping time to the tempo of the music, while others dance in their own free-form styles within the circle.

The general flow of the dance must move *widdershins* (counter-clockwise) until mid-night and then *deosil* (clockwise) from mid-night until dawn. This symbolizes the descent of the Sun in to the Waters of the Night and then the rising of the New Sun from the Womb of Goddess. Traditional square dances and their round cousins are appropriate to the night's festivities. If you and your group know how to do them, doe-see-doe and have some fun 'til everyone is too limber-legged to go on!

Fragrant-burning substances, including herbs, sachets and aromatic incense, may be thrown on the bonfire as the dancing continues. These are intended as offerings to both the Old and the New Sun. They are meant to invoke the rising of the New Sun out of the death of the old year.

If you have no open fire, light fragrant smelling candles, scented with Frankincense, Bayberry, Hollyberry and Balsam Pine. Smoke from incense lit on the Yule Table or thrown onto the bonfire signifies the holy intentions of the Solsticers. The smoke attracts the attention of Nerthus & Cernunnos, who watch over our festivals from their Holly & Pine encircled Grove in the Otherworld.

During the night, Nerthus & Cernunnos will visit the party! **Nerthus** should be dressed in faded green & russet colored clothing. She may have a crown of gold or silver on her head. **Cernunnos** should be dressed in brown leathers or denim and may have a horned hat on his head. In Olden times, he would have worn a helmet with the antlers of a deer mounted on it.

The woman playing the part of Nerthus makes her entrance around 9 or 10 PM, after which she should dance around the circle for a while, either alone or with willing partners. She then goes and sits off to one side of the festal grounds, adjourning to a quieter place where celebrants can ask for her advice. The person playing this role must be compassionate

135

and wise. She not only gives advice, she should also be willing to pray with people and lay her hands on those who desire some healing or transformation. Nerthus heals us during the dark dancing, and as a result we'll be more 'whole' once the New Sun rises. Her magick is strongest at Winter's Solstice.

The man playing the role of **Cernunnos** should don his antlers with a bawdy sense of good fun! He shall "arrive secretly" and then walk around the Solstice grounds encouraging everyone to celebrate with earthy enthusiasm. He gets sad people laughing and encourages the timid to dance. He also keeps those who really don't want to dance from being teased or shunned by those who are all too ready to carry-on. He may cheer those who aren't inclined to dance with games of chance. Card playing tables and board games may be set-up off to one side of the Solstice grounds.

Alban Arthuan is a night of revelry, fun & games; a time to blow off tensions that may have been accruing during the Yule. No matter what our personal temperament, we all need a good party now and then, just as we all need to learn to experience the Silence and dwell in authentic Solitude from time to time. Whereas reflective, introverted personalities will better appreciate Mistletoe Day, outgoing, extroverted personalities will feel much more "in their element" on Solstice Night. However, those of a quieter nature should make every effort to participate in the Solstice, just as people of a more boisterous and outgoing character need to find the "Quiet Place" on 19 December. Only by doing so will we expand personal horizons, overcome our individual limitations, and achieve soul-equilibrium.

Let everyone celebrate in his or her own manner. Encourage the reflective people to stay at the Solstice party, even if they sit quietly and talk with one or two other people. Likewise, encourage the more outgoing types to remain sober and not hurt anyone (or themselves!). **Brighid** is present as the Solstice sister of Nerthus, and she despises drunkenness! Cernunnos, however, is also here, and he likes to be rowdy and play pranks! Therefore, let everyone strive for *balance*, respecting the ways in which others keep the festival. If this little rule is kept, "a good and lively time shall be had by all." (130, Yuletide Grimoire, 1898)

As the festivities may last the whole night through you will need to pace yourself so as not to become totally exhausted before dawn! The place of the Solstice festival becomes a tapestry of repose and activity, therefore, different groups engaging in a variety of activities and pastimes as mid-night approaches. At mid-night, the person playing the role of Cernunnos should venture to the eastern edge of the Solstice grounds (or to an east window, if the festival is held indoors). Looking to where the New Sun will rise, he should declare: "The Sun has been reborn out of the Cauldron of the Night!" At his cry, a new round of wine or beer may be poured and the coming of New Sun cheered with a toast! Those who abstain from alcohol for spiritual reasons or on account of their health may toast the New Sun with tasty apple cider, holy grape juice or a wanton mug of hot chocolate.

After the re-birth of the Sun is announced, let the partying continue with renewed gusto and a revived hope. Some participants will want to go to bed after the announcement, in order to get some rest before going to work or school in the morning. "Messengers of the Sun" will be sent to get these people up again just before dawn, though, so they can witness dawn's first light.

Cernunnos & Nerthus may stay until the wee hours of the morning, dancing and counseling. As they are the parents of the New Sun, however, they should leave the Solstice shortly before dawn. Keltelven lore says that they retire to their cave-nemeton in the wildwoods of Paradise where a goddess of springs and sacred waters named **Coventina** acts as mid-wife in the birth of the New Sun. Coventina carries a water-lily in one hand and a pitcher in the other. As a goddess of gushing springs she represents the waters of new birth. Once the New Sun rises, Coventina is praised for her services.

About half an hour before the Sun comes up on 22 December let everyone gather at a place where they can see the Sunrise. Traditionally this has been on the top of a heath (a treeless hill overlooking the surrounding countryside), but you might just as well go to the roof of your apartment building or to the parking lot of a mall located higher than the surrounding countryside, preferably out away from town. As you witness the rebirth of the Sun, cheer and cry out, rejoicing in New Sun's Light. Sing and toast the Sun's good health.

This is the high-point of Solstice Night. All of the feasting and dancing has been in anticipation of this moment when the Sun is seen rising over the eastern horizon. After experiencing this dawn, allow the Fires of Yule to burn more brightly than ever in your Heart. In the rising of this New Sun we experience an awakening to the process of rebirth in our own souls. After the sun has risen above the horizon, pray for the coming of Light into the world – i.e., for the awakening of all mortals to the Presence of Mystery – and then go to bed, if there's time, before your day begins.

> **Natural Meditation**: Meditate on the death and rebirth of the Sun by reflecting on the symbolism of Bay Leaves, Juniper and the Pine Grove as symbolic touchstones of this great event. If we're going to be reborn, we must participate imaginatively in the death and rebirth of the Sun. Hold Bay Leaves in your hand and meditate on spiritual integrity. Hold Juniper in your hands and pray for the security of your house and the blessing of everyone in it. Imagine sitting in a Pine Grove with Cernunnos nearby, watching you with benevolent sun-lit eyes just beyond the circle of trees.

> **Scriptural Meditation** is again focused upon Mary and Joseph's trek to Bethlehem, and on the hospitality they were shown upon the way.

> Keltelven lore tells that the holy couple met three Druids along the road who were "wandering the world." Like the Magi, these three Druids recognized Mary as carrying a god-child in her womb and uttered prophecies, just as Anna & Simeon would later do in the temple in Jerusalem (Luke 2:20-39). Meditate on this encounter.

> Other traditions say that – on the way to Bethlehem – Mary got hungry and wanted Joseph to fetch her down some apples from a tall, spindly tree. When Joseph could not reach the apples, the tree – recognizing the divine child

in Mary's womb – reached down her limbs to allow Mary to pick three golden apples. The apples represent Wisdom as well as the solar power with which the child in her womb was infused. Use this story in your meditations on Alban Arthuan and reflect on the state of your own journey to Bethlehem/Glastonbury Tor.

A Yuletide Song (21 December)

Hail, hail _to Winter's Solstice,
Coming round from far and near!
In its frocks of white and dazzle
the Windy City of the Sídhe we hear!   1

Dolmens of Christmass sing aloud_
in Faery strains of forgotten harmonies!
Fly we now upon the ungilded Cloud_
with Fire & Eros for Yuletide!   2

Sung and Merry_ the Solstice Elves,
who take the ribbons from the shelves_
jingle along in olden harmonies,
shaking bells strung out upon the trees!   3

Hark! _the heralding Ghosts come near;
for renewed prophecies they wait to hear!
Shimmered in their frosted frocks,
we take them out for early morning walks!   4

"To the Stones! To the Stones!" we cry,
   to re-awaken our Earthen destiny!
"Come with tokens of the Grove & sing
   with Dasher prancing in the wind!"
Druids waken from their AEON of sleep
   un-binding the mundane shackles,
keeping troth with beggars for the Dream –

139

"Here we come! Here we come!
    _With full hearts we joyfully scream!"   5

Stranded upon the blinded towers,
consumers of the world fall dumb –
down upon dull concrete & broken glass
they collapse into sleep, and wallow!
The World is dying_ but GOD is flying
        upon Her ever-salvific broom!
Come and sail, GODDESS, we pray –
into the light of a New Solstice Day!   6

Hail the Solstice! Hail the Dream!
Come to the Scented Fires and let us sing_
of dew-drops on souls of the lost,
with our breath warming the faded frost!
Conjure bliss out of cracks
in the world's sidewalks, and relax_
SHE WHO IS shall *waeccan* us all _at last!   7

Skirts of snowy glory come gliding
along Ancient Avenues from Avalon!
Winter's Solstice Light gleams up heathen hills,
betwixt cruel stones and cold fire-Styx!   8

And in our Hearts GOD's Inspiration perches,
rendering joy into ecstatic myth-fits!
Hail the Christ in a Merrie Olde Yule
and pray we'll find New Life_ once upon a time!
Here we come_ to warm our merry cockles
upon the fires of an Olde Mystic Way!   9

"Covet Nothing_ Here Comes a New Day!"

10. <u>Yew</u> <u>Day</u> *(Spirits of the Hearth Day, 22 December)*

"As the Sun dies and is reborn at Winter's Solstice, so may we die and be born again in this life, and then again in the next. As the Sun rises on the day after *Alban Arthuan*, spirits come flocking to the hearth of devout Pagans, bringing cheer and new insight in their pouches" (199)

- Cornelius Whitsel
<u>Table</u> <u>of</u> <u>the</u> <u>Sacred</u> <u>Dayes</u> (1990)

"Now the spirits of the hearth come near, bringing laughter, song and good cheer!" (93)

- Egbert Whittier
<u>The</u> <u>Thirteen</u> <u>Dayes</u> <u>of</u> <u>Yule</u> (1800)

Most of those who keep the Solstice will need to go to bed for a few hours today in order to recover from the all-night birthday party for the Sun. If you don't need to get up for work or school, stay in bed until about noon and then, when you rise, acknowledge the birth of New Sun, saying:

"Powers of Light,
Fires of the New Sun's Face,
bless me as I rise this day
and grant me Wisdom's Grace."

Go to a place in the house where you can see the New Sun, or – if it's a cloudy or snowy day – honor its unseen presence. Those who keep the Winter Solstice in a more or less rowdy way, year after year, tend to relish Yew Day as a time for rest, recovery and an intense savoring of the Season's turning.

The New Sun infuses the hearths of Yule with renewed energy. Light a fire in the hearth today with Birch & Apple sticks as kindling wood. Birch & Apple are both connected with renewal and birth. **Birch** gives its name to the first month of the Keltelven year (November) and stands for the power to make a new start, the cleansing of the soul that enables us to

141

put the past behind us, and the empowering fire of new ideas, feelings, and inspirations. "Take a birch stick and thwack it against the hearth three times for luck," Egbert Whittier says (94, Thirteen Dayes). **Apples** foster choice, and Apple wood attracts the spirits of Wisdom that will enable you to embody your new choices in day to day life. "The ideals of Apples are all of equal beauty." (Yuletide Grimoire, 1898). Eat an apple at breakfast or after dinner to symbolize your participation in the Sun's renewed powers.

As this newly kindled fire in the hearth blazes up, meditate on the Fires of Yule that are now burning in your Heart, fueled as they are with a desire for earthen and mystical enlightenment! Recite this rann as you gaze into the hearthlight:

> "Hearth of light, fire of Brighid,
>   burn in my heart
>   from night to night.
>   Kindle the embers of my own Hearth's fire
>   and let my life be
>   a beacon of Wisdom and Love to others."

As the warmth of the hearthfire suffuses the room and the house so will solar powers infuse your place of dwelling. You are now turning from the quest for Illumination toward the pathing of Enlightenment.

If you don't have a functional hearth, place Birch or Apple twigs – perhaps tied into crosses – on the Yule table. Replace the stubs of tapers and other candles on the table with fresh ones. Light these new lights and, while meditating on the rebirth of the Sun, speak the following prayer:

> "Fire of Life, Fire of Love
>   rid us of dissension,
> as a New Sun's reign is begun!
> Come, Hearty New Sun,
>   indwell these flames
>   and be our light
> for a wheel of months to come!"

After the prayer, sing an appropriate carol. "The Christmas Song" (i.e., "Chestnuts roasting on an open fire") has become an 'old standard' on Spirits of the Hearth Day. As you sing the last verse, get up and go to breakfast. If you have a few Horse Chestnuts, lay them out on the breakfast table, perhaps as part of the centerpiece. Later arrange them on the Yule Table, as symbols of natural rebirth.

This is a day for acknowledging the "spirits of the hearth." The rising New Sun re-charges a variety of spirits in Nature, empowering them to come near the hearths of human dwelling. Imagine that there are earth gnomes and water nymphs, pixies of the air and fire gremlins living in the Earth. Though these spirits normally sleep between the early days of November and the first days of Spring, they awaken after Alban Arthuan and amble about for a day or two before returning to their caves, lairs, nests and holes. As the day unfolds, nurture an awareness of such spirits.

Elemental energies are not the only 'spirits' that walk abroad on the day after Solstice Night! The birth of the New Sun energizes all of the paths that connect one world with another, making it easier for souls of the dead to find their way across the Sídhe. Once on this side of the veil they often come home to the hearths they were familiar with when they were alive. The light of the newborn Sun becomes a beacon that the departed souls of ancestors, loved ones and friends may follow back to this mortal vale, seeking hearths where they can be warmed by memories of the lives they once lived.

On Yew Day, therefore, strive to be open to any of these spirits and souls that may be about and receive them as guests at your hearth. Keltelvens tend to believe that souls of the departed can sense when their presence is desired in the vales of mortal time, and that they will come for visits in response to invitations, if they are free to respond (i.e., if they are not otherwise engaged in some quest or adventure in the Otherworld, or if they have not become involved in the mentoring of an incarnate soul-friend).

One way to invite a discarnate soul to visit our hearth is to make a **Soul-Cross**. Take one Apple stick and one Birch stick (each about ¼ inch in diameter and 9 inches long) and tie them together at right angles. Then, take a supple shoot of Yew and wind it up and down around the arms of this cross. Secure the Yew to the cross with red or green twine. If the Yew has red berries on it, so much the better. Finally, sprinkle the Soul-

Cross with water that has been infused with salt. Lay the cross on the hearthstones or on the Yule Table. It is said that when souls see this Yew Cross they will acknowledge the welcome it proffers by touching the cross and turning it around a few degrees on the table.

At the first meal today invite any spirits that may be visiting your house to abide with you near the hearth. Places may be set for them at the table. No incarnate person should sit in these seats during Yew Day. Place a sprig of Yew on the plate. As you eat or sit at the table during the day, be aware of the empty seat. Remain open to the possibility that it may not be quite as empty as it seems!

As a day connected with the mysticism of crossing†over and returning, 22 December is ruled by the powers of Yew. The myths concerning this strange and efficacious evergreen speak to the reality of death as well as the proximity of the Otherworld to our own mortal vale.

Yew (*Ioho* in the Celtic tree alphabet) is a mysterious evergreen often found in graveyards. Yews are gateways to the Otherworld and as such they are symbolic of our survival beyond the event of death and our ability to return to the mortal world. These trees may live for many centuries, though not in the usual way; the Yew renews itself and is born again from its own death. When its branches touch the soil they grab hold, sprouting new roots and becoming new trees. An elder Yew is thus going to be an intricate complex of older and younger individuals all grown together with the older ones eventually dying off and providing – through their decay – fertile soil in which the younger trees can be nourished.

As such, the Yew symbolizes regeneration & reincarnation. There is an unbroken continuity in the growth of any Yew, the present tree being a distant descendant of the original parent tree. Because of this unique way of propagating itself, Yews also have a tendency to migrate, inch by inch and foot by foot, from where the original tree was planted!

It is believed that the spirits of the dead pass back and forth between the worlds through the branches and roots of ancient Yews. In Pagan times people often buried their dead near consecrated trees and in Northern Europe there was no more hallowed place for interment than near an old and gnarly Yew. Over the centuries, Yew Groves became Christian graveyards. To walk in some of the older cemeteries in England and Europe is to be in a place where people have been buried for upwards of 2,500 years. The Yews surrounding these graveyards may be at least as old as the oldest burials. Keltelvens have long planted Yews near nemetons,[44] groves[45] and dolmens.

The Yew is energized by a deep-running psychic power. Touching the tree may connect an incarnate mortal with the soul of a loved one who has recently crossed+over. If you have lost loved ones, friends or relatives in the past year – since the previous Yule – make a journey to a cemetery on Yew Day to visit their graves. If a Yew is growing anywhere near the grave, touch it. A connection is thereby established between the living and the dead that may help the departed person find their way home for Matrum Noctem. If you cut off a small sprig from a Yew near the grave of a loved one or ancestor and plant it by your house, this will act as a beacon to guide the souls of these beloved dead to your home.

Yule is a season when all of our ancestors, friends and lovers may come together for reunions, both those living in *this world* and those on the Otherside. Though we see death as a profound and often tragic reality, it does not ultimately or permanently separate those who have died from fellowship with the living. A similar truth lies behind the Catholic teaching on the "Communion of all Saints." The dead are not lying around in their coffins waiting for some future resurrection of the dead. Rather, the resurrection of the dead happens to each mortal person soon after the event of death and the discarnation of the soul. They awaken on the Otherside and there they experience a "judgment."

If a person has lived a "good life" – that is, one in which their main object was to seek Wisdom and live life accordingly – they will wake up in the afterlife full of energy and ready to continue their quest. If a person frittered *this* life away, however – never seeking or, worse yet, resisting the highest or best possible goals – they will wake up more slowly on the Otherside. It takes these people some time before their psychic energy is revitalized. Those who lived "evil" lives (i.e., in ways destructive of the fragile goodness of life, acting to obscure wisdom and amass the 'good things' of life only for themselves), often simply 'fall asleep' at the moment of death and *never* wake up.

If a person was well treated in their lifetime, they might return eagerly to familiar hearths at the Winter's Solstice. However, if a person was mistreated in life, they may well return with a bag full of tricks that they will unleash on the living until some recompense is made or offered. This old understanding of the afterlife may be behind much of the popularity of 'Christmas ghost' stories.

If someone close to you has died during the year, hang a small paper ornament on the Yule Tree with his or her name written on it. Do this at dusk on Yew Day. Spirits haunting the hearth will see the ornament and seek out the person named on it. Then imagine being visited by this person. What would they say? What would *you* say? You may also hang a memorial ornament on the tree containing the names of ancestors who died long ago. Every hut of dwelling has at least one ancestor who is always close by, who hears the pleas and complaints and praises offered by those living in the house. These ancestors are the guardians of Heart & Hearth.

To meditate on the rarefied powers of the Yew is to connect with the nearness of the Otherworld, which exists in the same spacetime as we do though in a different 'dimension' (for lack of a better word). The Yew can also become a doorway into Paradise (the Celtic equivalent of "Heaven"). Yet people in our materialistic culture are forgetting about the Otherworld. They are finding it difficult if not impossible to believe that we survive the death of our bodies. This is one of the clearest signs that a culture is losing its spiritual moorings and has become shallow and vain. The Rebirth of the Sun at Winter's Solstice is an earthen intimation that life does not end in the dolmen of death.

The Solstice is also a sobering symbol of the profound role that death plays in our existence. Those who experience the Winter Solstice in poetic and spiritual ways cannot remain ignorant of death. Those who celebrate the Yule are reminded of the fact that spiritual rebirth does not save us from physical death! The denial of death in our culture is as much a sign of spiritual breakdown as is the failure to believe that life might continue beyond death. Be careful, therefore, not to let the remembrance of the dead become a denial of the reality of death. We all die, but we also continue to live on in another 'place' after death. Belief in the afterlife is neither a sugarcoated placebo for alleviating our mortal grief nor a fantasy that allows us to avoid dealing with death; if it becomes this, we are in denial!

Winter's Solstice prefigures Matrum Noctem in natural ways. The Rebirth of the Sun prepares us for the rebirth of our selves as foretold in the legends of the birth of Jesus of Nazareth who is seen as a solar god-child in Keltelven myth. After the Solstice we are drawn into the sway of the renewal that is unfolding in us. As Matrum Noctem approaches, Spirit prepares each of us to become like the Yew, dooring between the worlds. Through our Yewness a new vision of life becomes possible.

The Jesus of Keltelven legend seeks to awaken those of us who long to give up the world's superficial adornments and become like the Yew. Our minds then become doorways through which Pagan Wisdom can address us in hearty words. On Yew Day Keltelvens ask: "How might I become a Yew, through which the gods & goddesses can become manifest in the World?" This question guides the course Keltelven mystics take along the wildwood paths in the days following Alban Arthuan.

During the evening, as you imagine entertaining the spirits of the hearth who have come to visit, hang up your **Yule Stocking**. The tradition of the stocking is connected with the legend of Saint Nicholas, who sometimes left gifts for unfortunate children in ordinary stockings that were hung up by a window or the hearth to dry. Though today we make elaborate symbolic stockings out of green, red & white felt and other materials, try to remember that such stockings were originally very ordinary.

Stockings may be large or small, and either elaborately decorated or left plain. They may be kept from one year to the next, and if so, not much preparation needs to go into getting them ready to be hung up. Once the stockings are prepared, hang them along the mantle over the hearth or perhaps along the front of your Yule Table, if you have no hearth.

The Yule Stocking stands for more than a child's expectation of gifts from Santa Claus. Rather, hanging up a stocking is a way of asking the Spirit for whatever gifts you may be able to receive this year on Matrum Noctem. We rarely if ever put anything in these ritual stockings. Rather, they are left empty of material reward, in order to symbolize our hope that they will overflow with gifts of an invisible, spiritual kind, by the morning of Glastonbury Thorn Day.

Another practice associated with Yew Day is the setting up of a **Yuletide Train**. This has obviously become a 'tradition' only in the 20th century. However, it has quite quickly put down deep roots in the Christmas psyche. It is often connected with our attempt to visualize Santa Claus' mode of transportation on Matrum Noctem, intimating that he can now use more modern vehicles rather than just a reindeer-drawn sleigh to get around the world. The Yuletide Train is still a "spiritual carriage," however, and as such is also one of the "spirits" of Yew Day.

As the day passes, set up a small toy train near the hearth or the Yule Tree. It may be a wooden model of a train or one that actually moves under electrical power. This icon signifies that the train of the Spirit's Wisdom is traveling all around the world, encircling it with compassion and possibilities. If you have kids in the house or if you're a railroad enthusiast, you might want to set up a full-fledged model train set, either under the tree or on a train-table.

There's something enchanting about watching a model train running along its track in the days just before Matrum Noctem. The electric train may symbolize the mysterious ways in which Spirit moves in and throughout the natural world during the Yule. Its engine and cars may have seasonal decals painted on them to identify the train with the Spirit of Yule. Those who like to paint models may procure car-kits and paint them seasonal colors. If a train-board is set up, it should depict a wintry scene relating to Winter's Solstice. Let the kids play "Yuletide Delivery Trains," imagining that the boxcars and flatcars are loaded with clothing and food for the needy, and then – later on – gifts from Santa Claus.

As the Sun goes down, enact the **"Invitation to the Dead."** This ritual involves calling out to those who have died in the previous twelve months and making them welcome near the hearth, where they may join in our festivities, even if vicariously. Ghosts empowered by the New Sun may come and visit loved ones and walk among the living for a few days, lingering near the hearth until dusk on 26 December. (Some linger longer, but most depart with the Gifting Stag on the 26th of December.)

For many ancient cultures – including the Celts – ghosts were believed to visit the living in the darkness of the Winter months. This belief is still evident in the popularity of ghost stories at 'Christmas.' As we come to the end of this day, we should bless the spirits who have been attracted to the light of our hearth. Use the following dialogue as a preamble to the Invitation to the Dead:

"We call on the Fire in the Hearth to inspire the spirits known to us!"

"We invoke the Fire in the Hearth to welcome those souls unknown to us!"

"We call upon Brighid as Mistress of the Hearth to protect us from any spirits who may come
without welcome and who mean to harm us."
"Lady Brighid! Protect us from the malevolent hordes, yet do no harm to those who have
already been wounded, oppressed or shut-out!"

"Come, silent kin from the depth of memory! May you find our hearthlight wholesome!"
"Name yourselves and we shall hear you! Come and revel in the warmth of our hearth's fire!"
"Come, kin and friends, lovers and acquaintances from the Otherside; be welcome here."

Write the names of deceased friends, relatives, spouses and ancestors on slips of paper, and then put these in an envelope with a holiday card. Seal the card as if you are going to mail it and set it on the mantle or on the meditation table. Then say the following Invitation, joining hands as you do so:

"Come dwell here,
all who have passed from this hearth.
We welcome you, with open arms,
and receive you with Hearts aglow with New Solar Fire.
Abide with us for a spell,
and depart again in peace: (<u>names</u>)"

Pause between the recitation of each of the names. Each participant in this ritual may say each name aloud or to themselves. You might then read the following words from <u>The Yuletide Grimoire</u> (1898) as a benediction to any spirit or soul that has come to lay claim to your mortal hospitality:

"Everywhere we turn in the tides of Winter, whether stormy or mild, we will sense you; the host of those who have crossed-over and who now bless us with your presence! We shall not ignore any plea for fellowship, from either the living or the dead, in this holy season!" (117)

This can be a very emotional time, especially if there has been a recent death. The ritual should therefore be approached reverently. Care should be taken to mention names in a considerate way, being attentive to those among you who may be most effected by each remembrance.

If you have free time in the evening, spend some of it near the hearth or Yule Table watching the flickering flames. This is usually a good time to tell stories about those named at the Invitation. It's not uncommon for a shiver to be felt as the possible presence of a disembodied soul is suggested. The more we get used to the idea that the dead are not far from us, however, and that there are elemental spirits and energies suffusing the world around us, the more at ease we will be with such stories.

Keltelvens feel no need to keep the dead at a distance and thus we welcome visitations from the Otherside. Only those who have mistreated the dead in this life need to fear them in the next life. 'Ghosts' are not to be seen simply as unfortunate souls who are 'stuck' here and who need to be shoved away into 'the Light,' as so much contemporary pop-spiritualism keeps telling us. Rather, they often *enjoy* returning home and should be welcomed when they do grace our places of dwelling with a visit!

This day provides mortals with a time for positive and even joyful remembrance of the dead. As such, it's a good time to pass on family stories about relatives and ancestors to children. If they've not yet experienced the death of a person they've been close to, they may have experienced grief as the result of the death of a pet. The names of all such animals may be included in the Invitation.

"Do individual animals visit our hearths?" Yes! Each animal species has a kin-spirit into which the life of each animal returns when it dies. However, when an animal develops a personality of its own, it *can* survive death in its own right. These animals – especially those that have had a powerful connection with human beings – often return 'home' and may be encountered near their former nests, stalls or cages. Therefore you can reassure children that their favorite pet *is* probably in the Otherworld. Allow them to call their deceased pets back to the hearth once a year on Yew Day.

Yew Day should end quietly. As you go off to bed, offer anyone still near the hearth – whether in the flesh or discarnate – a blessing. Common benedictions include: "May the Solstice Sun live in your soul," and "Solstice is past, the Tor is now before us!" As you drop off to sleep, ask the Spirit of Yule to allow you to dream of someone you know who is now beyond the Sídhe and living in the Otherworld. At the very least suggest to yourself that from now until 25 December, "No one shall be alone who ventures into the glow of our hearth's spectral light." (90, <u>Thirteen</u> <u>Dayes</u>). This wish encompasses the 'dead' (so-called) as well as the living (i.e., the "incarnates" among whom we live). As such, Yew Day extends our Yuletide hospitality beyond the realm of the incarnate to include *all* those who wish to dwell together in peace.

> **Natural Meditation**: Focus on the meaning of the rebirth of the Sun. Imagine the New Sun's strength, its potential power, and its destiny (at high summer), when it will bless the crops, making all life fertile and vibrant. Then connect this meditation with the fire in the hearth. Meditate on the Yew and its powers as a door between the worlds. We are at a new junction in life, once again.

> **Scriptural Meditation**: Now we move on to Bethlehem and seek out the Inn where comfortable guests are being housed. Reflect on the hearth at the Inn and then turn to the stable out behind this public-house where Mary & Joseph are forced to take up residence, as the guestrooms are all taken. Meditate on the virtues of dwelling together in unity (Psalm 133).

11. <u>Silver *Fir* Day</u> *(Nemeton and Heath Day, 23 December)*

"Follow the sacred animals of Yule – rabbits, deer and crows – for they have felt the Sun's magick and will lead you to nemetons and to heaths where Goddess will bless. The tines of time are turning us toward the Tor, and we must now quickly learn to enter into the passageways of mysterious cairns and barrows, in order to break free from our old selves." (197)

- Cornelius Whitsel
<u>Table of the Sacred Dayes</u> (1990)

Long ago it was believed that, on the morning of 22 December, the New Sun's light shone down with renewed mystical as well as natural vigor, touching every living thing and the dead. This occurred whether or not the day was cloudy or clear. Keltelvens teach that the Sun's rays fall to Earth in threes on the day after the Winter Solstice, blessing fields and wildwoods, renewing the Land's Fertility, and falling benevolently on the roofs of ráths, barns and houses, stoking the warmth of human dwelling.

The beams of the New Sun's light bathe the heaths where the ancient gods & goddesses still walk in the shadows of our lives. The Sun rekindles the powers that are often resting latent in these sacred hills. This power is known in Keltelven mysticism as **shunnache**; a name for the original, proto-physical energy of the universe which now hums in the background of all existence. This energy can be tapped and used by magicians, diviners, healers and shamans who need to recharge their psychic 'batteries.' We go out to heaths on the second day of the new solar year in order to commune with the New Sun's Light, which the sacred hills have absorbed by 23 December. There we drink in the shunnache!

The New Sun's Rays also descend into the sacred space of **nemetons** located deep in the woods, where deer & rabbits gather and frolic throughout the year and especially before dusk on this second day after Winter's Solstice. The innate power of nemetons becomes dormant on the eve of Solstice Night. Their geomantic dynamism then remains inactive until the sun rises on the first day after Alban Arthuan. We wait for a day or so, and then we go out to nemetons to glean some of this new power from the twigs, branches, stones and leaves we find there. At nemetons on the 23rd of December practitioners of the Yule may meet the spirits of the ancient saints of Christ, who also meditate in sacred places on Silver Fir Day. If we listen well, they may whisper runes of Enlightenment in our ears.

On this day we go to heaths exposed to the Sun's light, there to bask in the presence of New Light. We journey down to nemetons in the winterwood – secluded by brush, thickets, fallen trees and undergrowth – in order to harvest the prescient and penetrating power of the New Sun. Visiting such places we seek runes of our own renewal, which is to be found in the process of enlightenment unfolding between Solstice and Matrum Noctem.

Silver Fir (*Ailim*, in the druidical tree calendar) is an evergreen with curious antique connections with the Moon and thus with death & rebirth. As such it symbolizes the mysteries of 23 December. We plant Silver Firs around Groves and at Dolmens where we celebrate both New Moon Days & Full Moon Nights during the wintry months. We also plant Silver Firs at the nemetons where we will go to enact the drama of the Nativity on Matrum Noctem. Silver Firs sing the song of the birth of Jesus and thus of our rebirth as the wind blows through their boughs. They drink-in the power of New Sun's light and become 'batteries' of mystic Solar energy.

Silver Fir is also connected with the reality of the Otherworld. It was once a custom to carry a candlestick, the holder of which was decorated with a sprig of Silver Fir, around the bed where a woman was holding her newborn child lay. The *anam* ('soul') of the Silver Fir drew the memory of the newborn child into this world, thus permitting it to forget the world it had left in order to be born again in the flesh. Keltelven folklore suggests that one reason why babies cry is because of the innate sense they have of what has been left behind – in the Otherworld or in Paradise – in their coming back to this world.

Silver Fir is masculine like the Holly, invoking strength and spiritual healing. It also invites those who are languishing back to life. It is thought of as 'far-sighted,' as it grows upwards of 100 feet. Those who climb a Silver Fir in their dreams achieve an unobstructed vision that may enable them to better glimpse the future. When found growing on a heath or mountaintop, the tree gathers prophetic powers in its needles. Holding the needles allows one to prognosticate events that may be evolving out of present situations. If the present choices men & women and their gods or saints are making don't change, certain ends will come to pass.

Standing near a Silver Fir, face east in order to foresee futures implied by the present moment and its configurations. We can never *predict* the future, as it has not yet happened, but we can *anticipate* it intuitively by glimpsing the implications of the present state of things. The future is largely dependent upon the present we have made for ourselves. We can intuit the fruition of our actions. If we can alter the present and thus the near future, the eventual futures implied by this particular present will also have to be altered in some way, though not always predictably.

If you face west you are looking toward the fountainstones of present events. We cannot change the past, but it can be recollected and re-understood. By understanding where we have come from, we may gain insight into why the present is the way it is. The old aphorism that "those who do not know history are condemned to repeat it" is a cliché because it is all too often true.

Silver – the symbolic color of 23 December – connects us with the Moon, magick and intuition. To remember the past or anticipate the future, we must be actively intuitive. Intuition is one of the primary foundations of magick, prophecy and authentic spirituality, for these are all imaginative modes. An active Intuition breeds a fecund Imagination. By intuitively listening for runes of the Spirit we will grow clear-sighted and may eventually be able to re-imagine the world in new ways. The Spirit cannot inspire us to live our dreams if we have no ability to imagine things as ever being any different than they are today. The Silver Fir facilitates the development of intuitive imagining as a spiritual discipline.

Initiate this day by adorning the breakfast table with a sprig of Silver Fir and something silver. Occasionally you will find silver-coated candles in the stores during December. You might purchase a few of these and keep them to set out on tables and mantles today. As you plan your activities, meditate on how to incorporate the tradition of **going out to a nemeton and a heath**. You might reflect initially on the basic pattern of pilgrimage (i.e., "there and back again"), since getting to a nemeton or a heath implies a journey. If you don't make an actual trek to one of these sacred places you might want to meditate on an image of a nemeton or a heath, and *imagine* journeying out to it. However you engage in "Nemeton and Heath Day," seek to be connected with the New Sun's radiant power in Earth *and* Spirit.

A **heath** is a bare hilltop from which you can see the horizons in every direction. It doesn't have to be the highest point in the surrounding countryside, but the higher the better. If you know of a good heath, go there either with others or by yourself, and take in the panorama of the horizons. Heaths are haunted places of the Spirit. They are natural 'altars' where we may 'sacrifice ourselves' to our true selves and gain insight in the form of 'clear seeing' and 'clear knowing.' To climb a hill is to enact a spiritual parable. The Keltelven life requires endurance and perseverance. Only those who climb the heath of life with enthusiasm and dedication will finally hear the runes of Wisdom.

If you journey out to a heath, take binoculars and perhaps a camera along, as the panorama may be impressive. While surveying the horizons, you will also come to realize that you are 'exposed.' Not only can you see for great distances from a heath, but you can also be *seen*. Heaths are places where mortals become open and vulnerable. Going to a heath is an act of surrender, therefore, as much as an attempt to path to a place where we can drink in the Sun's mystical rays. While there, meditate on the ways in which a heath 'absorbs' the power of the New Sun and then imagine how this is different from the way in which a valley absorbs solar power.

A **nemeton** is a site in the woods where earth-energy becomes unusually manifest. It may be created by a tree or two falling to create a clearing or it might be a place where a spring of fresh water burbles out of a hillside. Like heaths, nemetons gather solar energy and store up shunnache. Nemetons tend to be down in valleys, nestled in the folds of the land and hidden from ordinary eyes. They might also be located in the cleft of rocky mountainsides or else located on an uninhabited isle in a lake.

Journeying to a nemeton, seek to be aware of how sunlight makes its way down through the trees and landscape to it. Look for traces of animals (and possibly saints & ghosts) who have visited the nemeton since Yew Day. Interpret these signs as alluding to the ways in which you may be visited by the emissaries of rebirth and transformation before Matrum Noctem. Once at a nemeton, it's nearly impossible to get away, at least quickly. Whatever shows up, you must stay and encounter it! Therefore, going to a nemeton, like climbing a heath, is an act of surrender.

Be on the lookout for traces of the advent of the New Sun at either heath or nemeton. Look for signs of your own approaching rebirth. This requires a devout and unassuming imagination! If you can't get out to an actual heath or nemeton (either because of weather, work or geography), you might treat the Yule Table as your nemeton, or go to a window in the highest storey of a building and regard a large window or the rooftop as your heath. I've known people who have gone to a restaurant in a high-rise office building on Silver Fir Day, eaten lunch there and afterwards used binoculars to look out toward the horizons. If you live in an apartment building, go up to the roof and try to see beyond your own neighborhood. If you live in a city or town where they decorate for the 'holidays,' this will be a good prospect from which to observe the trimmings all over town. Any magical or mystical place can serve as a nemeton or a heath if only you can imagine it as such.

Shared experience often plays a profound role in personal growth. Therefore you may want to set a rendezvous time in the evening when people can gather to share the fruit of their day's journeys. Whoever hosts the get-together should serve hot cider and some kind of light snack, to accompany the telling of your Nemeton and Heath Day tales. As evening approaches, seek to discern what stories you will share with others and which ones should be kept for your own private edification.

Ask questions of one another in the hopes of stimulating a revealing conversation. "So, what has happened to us as we wandered around today?" "What stories have you brought for us to mull over?" "Has anyone seen the Stag?" "Who sensed a presence near them?" "Where did you go?" "Have the dead haunted anyone?" If strange and interesting things have been happening during the day, you might end up spending an hour or two just narrating events and interpreting them in the light of the hearth and the glow of the electric Christmas decorations.

Many practitioners of the Yule begin to experience the first fruits of their journey on Silver Fir Day. As you share what's gone on during the day don't be surprised if enigmatic narratives begin to take shape, framing spiritual insights into your own self and one another. Telling stories of "there and back again" tends to illumine the nature of your own personal journey through the Season.

156

Harvest all of these experiences and intuitions, and then, as you are able, prepare yourself for tomorrow; the last day before Matrum Noctem! Spend the rest of the evening in the subdued glow of candle & hearth-light. Leave only the tree-lights on and the fire in the hearth (or a few candles on the Yule Table) burning. Then, in almost total darkness, sing or listen to carols and other quiet, seasonal music. This is the iconic mode for the transition we are about to undergo.

We now enter into the darkness and mystery of rebirth and transformation. Tomorrow is the day! Tomorrow night is the culmination of our long seasonal journey! Two days from tonight you will be able to look back on the Yule and reflect on the journey you've taken, and discern whether or not it was well charted.

Pray for a final awakening to the presence of Mystery in your Heart. Pray that Brighid, Cernunnos and Nerthus will all work through you to bring about inspired changes in the world in which you live. Before you go to sleep, say the following rann:

> "Blissed of snow shining silvery white,
>   the eyes of the saints see far –
>   Out across Heaths now Fire-lit,
>   We espy the yellow-eyed Cernunnos!
>
>   Out of the Darkness, the Stag He comes –
>   with Runes of Winterwood
>   we succumb
>   to his Wise Love!
>   May He now embrace us, as we sleep,
>   guiding our Hearts
>   to the Hearths of Authenticity!
>   Nema."

Natural Meditation: Focus on images of heaths and nemetons that are conducive to the belief that we have been visited by divine beings, spirits and ghosts. Image scenes that evince the presence of the New Sun that has risen to

157

bless the Earth with its warmth and light. Meditate on the mysteries of both natural and divine visitations.

Scriptural Meditation: Focus on the Magi from the East and their trek to find the one over whose manger the Star was hovering (Matthew 2:1-2). This was a journey to a nemeton and a heath all in one. Their being 'astrologers' from a far away land is a biblical type and foreshadowing of our own Pagan journey to the Nativity of Jesus of Nazareth.

12. <u>Bayberry</u> <u>Day</u> *(Hearth of the Heart Day, 24 December)*

[Bayberry Day lasts from dawn until sundown]
"Bayberry Tallow has many properties. Its tasty wax contains a power to return us to the locality of our birth, either in dreamed visions or imaginative travels. It also makes possible a deepening of mystic transformation; aiding our journey into god- or goddess-hood. When we burn Bayberry candles on *Matrum Noctem* we invoke our own psychic rebirth, experiencing a pagan transfiguration in holy earthen paths. ... It is necessary to burn Bayberry on the day before we reach the Tor, as an spiritual incentive stirring up the soul to the desires of perfection." (107)

- Cornelius Whitsel
<u>Mythbook</u> <u>of</u> <u>the</u> <u>Balefire</u> (1990)

This is a day of final transition, in the course of which we hope to come to the precipice of our soul's final Yuletide awakening. The spirits of the hearth, souls of spirit-guides from the Otherside and helpful ancestors are all near the hearth this day, inviting us to enter ever more fully into the new life that has been prophesied by the mystical runes of Yule. We have a tendency to fall asleep and forget that the cosmos is suffused with mysteries and that Divine Mystery is evident all around us. Bayberry Day is a last reminder that the Fires of Yule are burning nearby. Wake up!

As we walk through this life, we all too often wander without direction through the four-directions of the World-Cross. Therefore, as we approach Matrum Noctem at last, we must meditate on the Druid Cross (as described in the section on Mistletoe Day) and return to Meath (i.e., the spiritual Heart), seeking to reside in the omphallos of the cosmos as our mystic journey comes to its consummation. We must begin – on the morning of Bayberry Day – to imagine what it will be like to finally *arrive* at the turnstiles of the transformation that we have been longing for. Today we resolve ourselves to the fact that our destination is just over the next hill, or just around the next bend. We can taste the joy and empowerment that will more than likely be ours by mid-night tonight!

As you get up on the 24th of December, say: "Holy Cernunnos, come and lead me into the Tor today, so that I might arrive at the manger of my own rebirth tonight." Expect the Stag to appear to you in a vivid daydream sometime today. You might have impressions of His Shagginess as you go to work or go about household chores. If you live near woods, keep your eyes open for deer coming near.

Bayberry Day lasts until dusk on 24 December and is generally a joyous if busy time. There's usually a lot of last minute gift-wrapping and baking, phone calls to friends and relatives, and a general euphoria that lasts all day. Many people spend this day waiting for family members to arrive home. If it's a work/school day, start off with a good breakfast, but if the day falls on a weekend or if you have the day off from work, you might consider fasting until dusk. If you fast, drink plenty of liquids.

To engage in at least a partial fast on Bayberry Day is a long-standing Keltelven tradition. It symbolizes a willingness to give up natural sustenance in anticipation of receiving the mystical victuals that will soon be offered to us from the Divine Country of Meath. If you fast, remember that you are not trying to lose weight. You are anticipating being drawn closer to the hearth of Divine Mystery.

On the morning of the 24th all other scented candles should be put away until after Matrum Noctem and **Bayberry** candles set out in their place. Put them on the kitchen table, the Yule Table and also near the Hearth. These candles have a very distinctive odor, which Keltelvens understand as symbolizing spiritual awakening and psychic rebirth. The aroma of Bayberry is a stimulus to our last-minute devotion before the consummation of our pilgrimage. It enhances our poetic as well as psychic well-being on this Twelfth Day of Yule. Therefore, burn Bayberry candles today, wherever you are.

Bayberry is one popular name for the **Myrtle Wax tree**. Myrtle Wax is an evergreen shrub that grows to about 3 to 10 meters high, putting out fragrant stems and branches. Its berries are covered with a pungent green or yellow substance, which is called Bay Wax, Candleberry Wax or Bay Tallow. This 'wax' is actually an edible botanical fat. It has been harvested in North America since early colonial times. Native Americans recognized its herbal properties and used the bark of the Myrtle Wax tree in folk teas and also as an aid in certain internal healings. It has long been used in the making of scented candles, a bushel of berries yielding about four to five pounds of wax.

As the Myrtle Wax tree grows primarily in North America its use during Yule must be of a more recent origin than many of the herbs we have discussed so far. The ancient Celts never burned Bayberry candles, of course, unless Saint Nicholas or one of his Elves brought it to them from across the ocean!

If you have access to a Myrtle Wax tree, bring a small branch of it into the house and put it in water. This twig can be looked upon as an icon of spiritual rebirth during the day. Meditate on the healing properties of the tree and the symbolism inherent in its berries. Consider them as fragrant intimations of the fruit of your journey to Glastonbury Tor. Smelling the scent of Bayberry, reflect on the spiritual experiences you have had since Nicholas Eve and then say:

> "Bayberry is our liquor,
> bright and tingly;
> through its aroma let us now pass
> into the Heart of Mystery
> together and all but singly!
> Merrily, merrily,
> we cut and wax the mysterious Bayberry!"

If you have leftover wax from Bayberry candles, don't let it go to waste. The remainders can be melted down and turned into wax icons, as Bayberry wax will remain fragrant for several years. Heat the wax slightly in a pan until it melts. (Do not overheat it!) You may then pour the liquid wax into metal molds of a seasonal design. Use the resulting wax figures as icons and ornaments. If you make pentacles (five-pointed stars representing protection and also the 'five stages' of life; birth-growth-consummation-death-rebirth) out of the wax, these may be stashed away in secreted places around the house after Glastonbury Thorn Day. When found during the year, they will remind you of the Fires of Yule.

The function of scenting the house with Bayberry is to prepare participants for the Night of Rebirth. Though we never become fully whole in this life, the Yuletide journey draws us ever closer to self-realization from year to year. We shouldn't necessarily expect colossal changes to come over us during Matrum Noctem, as personal growth is a life-long process. However, those who observe the Yule with devotion each year will come ever closer to total spiritual transformation.

Meditate on the scent of Bayberry. Allow that this aroma will help to make you aware of the spiritual reality in which we all live, seeking Wisdom's boughs. The fragrance of Bayberry penetrates everything. The aroma of the wax will attract even more beneficent spirits to your hearth, all of whom come to help us prepare for the next 24-hour period, empowering us to experience it productively.

During your morning meditations, reflect on the state of your heart. Address any problems you are experiencing or have had in your life recently, and turn these over to Brighid at the hearth. Note any reluctance or fear that might be preventing you from awakening more fully to the presence of Mystery in your life and surrender this to Brighid as well. Brighid is our Yuletide Physician. She carries a staff of Yew and wears Holly garlands around her neck on Bayberry Day. She is the Lady of Healing and Inspiration. To turn to her is to seek the firelight of inspiration and thus be warmed for the last night of our journey and the days of reflection and consummation that follow.

An old rann says, "On this day your heart will become like a child's, as only a child can touch the thorns of the Glastonbury Tree and live" (Yuletide Grimoire, 1898; p 119). By causing us to focus our spiritual energies on getting to Glastonbury Tor, the praxis of Yule simplifies our desires and aspirations and in that process we find ourselves empowered to reclaim something like the heart of a child. This is not an excuse for child-ish-ness but a summons to child-like-ness. It's an invitation to the willing openness to life that we experienced as children but that we've all too often lost in the process of becoming adults. The Yuletide practices of Keltelvens have the effect of helping us reclaim glimmers of our child-like-ness. As adults we must be mature and accept the trials that life metes out to us, yet we must also reclaim, year after year, the childlike heart that will keep our souls grounded and vital. To be childlike is to approach the **Cauldron of Transformation** and take a spoonful of the broth it contains.

Cernunnos is the keeper of this Cauldron[46] of Transformation during Yule. He keeps it bubbling and seething at the entrance to the Cave of the

162

Nativity in the side of Glastonbury Tor. As we track the Stag to the Tor today, hoping to find the Glastonbury Thorn and the Cave, imagine the smell of what the Stag God has cooking in the cauldron drawing us on toward our goal! On the way, pray, saying:

> "Cernunnos our Stag, let us today
> find the entrance to the cave
> of your own Heart and ours!
> Lead us now to Meath
> where we are already waiting
> to be transfigured.
> Nema!"

Meath is – in this context – not just the name of our own Internal Hearth but the name of the mystical Cave where the Nativity will unfold tonight, during Matrum Noctem. The Cave of the Nativity – located near the Glastonbury Thorn in the side of the Tor, *is* also – in a way – the Cauldron of Transformation.

The destination that we are approaching involves three distinct guiding images. First, there is **Glastonbury Tor**; the poetic dún of psychic transformation. Glastonbury Tor – while corresponding to an actual geographical site in England – is also understood to be a mystical 'place' in the Aether[47] where spiritual self-revelations become possible for devout pilgrims in the last swags of the Yuletide journey. It is also a 'place' where the runes of our soul's transfiguration become open to deep interpretation.

Near Glastonbury Tor we hope to find the **Glastonbury Thorn**; the mysterious tree descended of the original Thorn planted by Joseph of Arimathea and which intimates the renewal of life in Winter's grip. The Thorn is located near the Tor – or even on its terraced slopes – but you will never find it in the same place twice. To follow our guide Cernunnos to the Tor is to discover the spiral path leading to the Thorn. Once you find the Thorn, you'll see the entrance to the Cave of the Nativity.

This brings us to the third distinct guiding image: **The Cave of the Nativity**. Once it is located near the Glastonbury Thorn, this where you will find the mysterious **manger** in which the god-child Jesus is born each year again at mid-night on Matrum Noctem. From dusk on 24 December until mid-night we path the Stag to the Tor, the Thorn and the Cave. Upon arrival we enter the Cave and then make a devout journey down into its inner sanctum. There we come to the spectral City of Bethlehem; a mystical or "Faery" icon of the city where Jesus was born 2,000 years ago. The rest of the night is then spent in meditation and celebration, communing with Divine Mystery and experiencing our own rebirth.

Taken together, these guiding images should help us focus on what we're preparing to do – in mystical-poetic terms – as Bayberry Day unfolds and we make last-minute preparations for Matrum Noctem. As we approach Glastonbury Tor and the Nativity, we must willingly anticipate wondrous possibilities. The journey we have made through the Yule will be deemed worthwhile or not depending on how deeply we are participating in the realities of Glastonbury Tor by dawn on 25 December.

Whenever you feel it's time to begin making formal preparations for Matrum Noctem, approach the Hearth/Yule Table and meditate there for a few minutes. Create an image of a Hearth in your soul. Imagine a warm, brilliant fire burning in the hearth and allow yourself to be warmed by the energy of this spiritual flame. Once this passionate fire is burning in your Heart, pray:

"Cernunnos our Stag, kindle today
the fire of Wisdom's Love
in our inner Hearth.
Lead us, Staggering One,
to places where our powers are needed.
Amen."

Meditate for a while at your Inner Hearth on the sparks that have been kindled during your journey since Nicholas Eve. Are you ready to make the final passage to Glastonbury Tor? Are you willing to claim the fruition of your journey to the Nativity?

By dusk you should be imagining yourself dwelling in Meath, meditating there on the fire of transfiguration. As the last light fades from the western sky, pause for a moment and pray:

"Cernunnos, our light and our torch,
burning ever bright,

> let us come with you to the manger
> in the middle of the coming Night."

As we dwell in Meath – deep in meditation and prayer – we are drawn toward the illumination of Yule-Light, which shines as a beacon guiding us to the Cave of the Nativity.

The rays of Yule-Light that begin to shine as the sun goes down radiate out from the Hearth of Paradise, where Brighid, Nerthus and Cernunnos are sitting – three-fold to the Three Rays[48] – chanting with the intention of drawing us into the mystery of Matrum Noctem as a night of death and rebirth. Jesus is coming as the son of Wisdom, and his mother Mary – who is also on her way to the Cave of the Nativity in Glastonbury Tor – is already sensing that her birth-throes are upon her. So now is the moment of spiritual reckoning! Everything you've done during the Yule has helped to prepare you for this moment. As Bayberry Day comes to a close, it's time to take stock of yourself and your environs, asking, "Do I have everything I need to get me through the night?"

As dusk approaches, go to where a Bayberry candle is burning. If you're at work or somewhere else, stop for a moment and conjure an image of the Bayberry candle in your inner vision. Kneel there, thanking all the powers and spirits that have watched over you during the Season for anything they may want to accomplish in you. If you haven't experienced much in the way of spiritual awakening this year, don't be discouraged. Whatever you need, it will ultimately be given to you. Sometimes, if we wait for a long time without making much headway, we reach points where we advance quickly in a short time. Spiritual progress can never be measured in a straight line, however; it's always more like a spiral.

Spiritual awakening is often only discovered in the very smallest glimmers of Wisdom. Therefore, be thankful for whatever you receive this year, no matter how insignificant it seems. If you haven't yet experienced much benefit from your journey through the Winter Solstice Season, cast the runes of guidance[49] and remain patient! Perhaps the Fires of Yule hold something in store for you that you haven't yet fathomed.

Re-decorate the Yule Table as the sun goes down and as the world moves into the sublime Darkness of Matrum Noctem. Set up fresh candles and put greenery on it. If the Yule Table functions as your hearth, light some of these candles at dusk but save the rest and light them at midnight when the moment of rebirth will be announced. Are you now ready for "the Night of the Mother?" When the bell is rung at dusk to announce the beginning of Matrum Noctem you will know! After this, the world of those immersed in the Spirit of Yule shifts toward quiet devotion and holy expectation. Nerthus is waiting for us in the Cave of the Nativity, and though we are in labor we need not fear, for Mary and the goddess Coventina will be our midwives, keeping watch with us through the night. Amen.

> **Natural Meditation**: Focus on the nature of birth & rebirth as symbolized in the Bayberry candle. Imagine yourself sitting beneath a Myrtle Wax Tree on a foggy hillside, where deer are wandering nearby. Reflect on your own spiritual hopes for the future.

> **Scriptural Meditation**: Dwell on Joseph and Mary in Bethlehem. Imagine them reflecting on their frustrated attempts to find a decent room for Mary to give birth. By evening turn to meditating on the "stable" – located in the entrance of a cave – and its environs, in preparation for the mid-night re-enactment of Christ's birth.

Vigils Prayer (24 December 1996)

I saw the aura of GOD going
Will-o'-the-Wisping through the forest
all wintered down.
Sleek with sleet She was flowing freely,
Electricity sparking embers beneath Her feet_
Saint Elmo firing!
Past frosted Sentinels of Oak and Pine_
It was a scripture's Earthen tine!   1

"In Vigiling prayers I rune Your Way!"

White wizened, Solar Light was streaming down,
visiting hillsides
       sled-ridden
         gleaming
        where Footprints in the snow gave way
to teetering glints of a Newer Day!
Soft fantastic faces there met me
      where She was Playing!
I photographed them between tall drifts
while Elves were cantering in shifts!   2

Soft-crystal pure Her skirts came gliding,
snowflakes skittering & colliding –
   I fell down frozen in Holy Love!
But then_
   She caught me up in HER Gemmed Embrace,
torches firing near;
     His sapphire eyes
        shining on GOD's verdant Heath!
Past Midnight's Watch I yet remained –
of Vigiling Prayer was I sustained!   3

She drew me up at His distant Voice,
catching Snow in the laced silk fringes
      of Winter's Faery Gown!
I remained on ice;
     Faith's Ballerina –
souls caroling Spiral-Chapel tunes,
awaiting His Advent!
I felt flaked Light fall from Her smile
   and I gaped_
Sequined across our Moonlit Nightscape!   4

She cusped me 'cross my Heart's own nape_
where Grace alone could lift my velvet drape;
Invisible He came!
Traversing Paths Owled & Willowed 'round,

Stomping_ Hoofing_ Hollowing_ Freeing_
Christ came
Glistened of Snow's own Fire
into Clearings of Yuletide Loving –
melting_ singeing_ swooning_ raging!   5

_I once saw the aura of Christ coming
Adventing pure as the driven snow_
Eyes Fired of Love's own Glow!
Heathen rhymes Stormed us a Trinity
out of Friendship's Beauteous Infinity!
Tines tuned WISDOM-SOPHIA's drumming
accompanying God's Seasonal sapphiric strumming!
Into our Hearths the Savior He Comes!   6

It'was a Night of Moonlight Faring,
when GOD was expanding horizons of caring
that – a Father's own Winter Brilliance
Made All Mortal Flesh Keep Silence!   7
Amen!

Matrum Noctem (Night of the Great Mother)

(Dusk on the 24th through dawn on the 25th of December)

"Over the hill and not so far away, Cernunnos leads us into the mysterious landscape of Glastonbury Tor. Tonight we will find the treasures of the Tuatha Dé Danann, if we're not careful! The Thorn Tree of Joseph of Arimathea is guarding the mouth of the cave of our own rebirth. Watch with eyes open! Listen with well attuned ears! The music of the Elves of Nicholas will be our beacon and guide!" (126)

- Cornelius Whitsel
The Table of the Sacred Dayes (1990)

"Gathering runes of ancient tunes
the Elves come out to play_
with mortal friends who are unsure
of Wisdom's wistful Word[.]"

- Yuletide Grimoire (1898)

"The magic of the Season comes down to this: when the sun sets on Christmas Eve, the Sleigh of Wonder and Hope is on its way, and we find ourselves knee deep in mythical snow surrounded by savvy Elves who must be kept under raps til we go to bed! What a night!" (297)

- Hildegard Whittier
The Elf Plot (1992)

As darkness envelops us, we ring a crisp-sounding bell to clear the air. At this point we shift between two worlds. This happens subtly and poetically, as if someone has suddenly shifted the meter of the cosmic verses in which we've been living. Those who aren't devoted to the pilgrimage of Matrum Noctem rarely notice this shift, though divine encounters and miracles now become much more possible for those who are enspirited. All the waiting we've done now comes to fruition!

Our journey is nearly over. If all has gone well, Cernunnos has by now led us into the locale of Glastonbury Tor and the sacred Thorn that marks the entrance to the mysterious Cave of the Nativity. We must now equip ourselves for the events of the next twelve hours. We are nearing our destination! The goal is attainable, but we've not yet completed our quest. All of the magical symbols of this long anticipated night now begin to come alive by Elven Magick and by the Spirit's infusion. Most quests falter in the last few steps, so be careful how you keep tonight in its solemnity! Light the fires of your Imagination with all of the poetic kindling you've gathered since 6 December, and proceed.

Matrum Noctem means "Night of the Mother," a name alluding to the powers of natural as well as spiritual birth and rejuvenation. Life gives birth to life. *This life* will end in death, but the soul lives on, ready to embark upon other adventures and eventually it may be born again into a mortal coích anama ("soul house;" the body). Therefore we should meditate often on the processes of birth & rebirth. Tonight we shall apply the symbols of nativity to our mortal situation. The first half of the night is called the **Vigil of Expectant Repose**. This watchfulness will last until mid-night, when our own rebirth in the Cave of the Nativity will be announced, after which the **Vigil of the Nativity** will begin. This second watch lasts until dawn. Those who stay up all night will enter into what is called "the Great Silence."

Ideally no one should leave the house or apartment once Matrum Noctem begins. We are all willing captives of Spirit and Wonder, awaiting our liberation. When the bell rings at dusk, gather together – with spirits and other human celebrants – near the hearth. Once there, recite this invocation:

> "Come, all who are hopeful,
> heed the bell of this holy eventide!
> Give up your false aspirations,
> and accept the Season's holy tide!

Come, all who are Wisdom's friends,
worn down upon the quest –
Come and wait at New Life's Manger;
Having changed your rags to meet the Guest.

Come, all who are unfaithful,
　long-burdened and un-true!
Shed your wings of false glory,
kneeling down on straw in the night-dew!

Come, wayfarers of Yule,
　with all your trials in hand –
Brighid this night shall heal your souls
in her cauldron of restoration!"

After this invocation, meditate for a few minutes in soul-stilling silence. In your hearts, invite the living realities of the Yule to make themselves known. You may find that, after your long journey, you will more or less *fall* into this Silence. The disciplines of Yule have prepared you – more or less well – for this moment, so if you are comfortable, remain in the silence and savor it.

You need not do anything else for an hour or so if you don't want to. Then, once the Silence has quieted your Heart, illuminate the **Nativity Scene** as a sign that Matrum Noctem has begun. Some people lay a line or two of clear electric twinklers in the cedar chips around the diorama, while others prefer to set up small lamps or even miniature spot lights that will shine down on the holy scene of rebirth. If there are flammable materials around the scene – such as straw or Cedar chips – it's best not to illumine the Nativity with candles! However you light it up, though, you should be able to *see* the scene even with all the other lights – both the regular house lights and the electric holiday lights – turned out. After mid-night, in the wee hours of the morning, only the lights of the Nativity scene, Yule tree and hearth will be left burning for those staying up to keep the Vigil of the Nativity.

The Nativity diorama will be the central focus of the night and will remain at the heart of your celebrations throughout Glastonbury Thorn Day. All the other symbols of the Thirteen Dayes of Yule now come to

171

fruition *in* and through the Nativity. If you haven't yet done so, set the manger into the scene and place the figures of Mary & Joseph near it. Meditate on the presence of the parents of Jesus in the stable-cave and imagine what it must have been like for them, staying in a strange town all by themselves, waiting for a government-enforced census to be taken.

The Nativity is your final mystic destination of the Season. It is located poetically/psychically in the Cave in the side of the Tor. Therefore, after you illumine the Nativity scene, you should go off to some far corner of the house to prepare to enact the final leg of your journey. If you live in just a couple of rooms, go outside; even down the street a ways. There, meditate on your Yuletide journey thus far. You are close to the Tor; you can *sense it*. Imagine yourself in a thinning wood filled with bushes and smaller trees – like Crabapple, Plum and Holly – that are partially obscuring your view. You can smell the marshy land beyond this wood, though, and your intuition tells you that you are close to Glastonbury Tor. Then start and make a 'journey' of walking back to where the Nativity Scene is illuminated. *See yourself* walking along damp paths, *smell* the scent of the now decaying apples that have fallen from the trees around you during the Autumn, and *listen* for the night-sounds of stags, birds and wild cats.

As you wind through the halls and rooms of your house or apartment building, imagine that you get a glimpse – through a copse of bushes, perhaps – of the Tor standing out on the plain beyond this wood. Walk (or fly) toward it! Imagine each room or hallway of your place of residence as part of a maze of paths leading to the Nativity. Then you see him: Cernunnos! He leaps out of the bushes near you, bounding through thickets and holy touchwoods out onto the wide-open marshy expanse between you and the Tor! Follow him! Cut through the bushes and thickets and come out onto the marshland. You get out of the wood just in time to see in what direction Cernunnos has gone ahead of you in the moonlight. The Moon (which is always imaged as 'full' at Matrum Noctem) comes out from behind a cloud and thus you can now *see* the Tor. It looms up from the watery land around it, seeming to be reaching out to touch the Moon in the sky overhead! There are no trees on the Tor that you can see, through some dark silhouettes do grace its terraced slopes and there's a small light at the top of the Tor, which you intuit is from a light in the window of a small tower-like structure.

Cernunnos stands in front of the Tor, beckoning to you. You see him in the moonlight and you begin to go after him! It takes from five to ten minutes to cross the swampy land around the Tor, depending on how good you are at staying on the paths through the reeds, grasses and brambles. No path ever goes directly to the Tor. They wind this way and that, taking you now toward the hill and now away. The Tor looms like a mysterious beacon of Wisdom's gloaming over the marshland.

You lose sight of Cernunnos during your circuit but then – as you come to the head of one of the many maze-like foot-trails that lead pilgrims up the side of the Tor – you see him again. He's up ahead of you, beckoning! You now begin your own ascent. You have left the ordinary landscapes of every day life and entered a mystical geography where *anything* might happen. Cernunnos leads you up the side of the Tor, along winding, rocky paths that have been traversed by pilgrims – both Pagan and Christian – for thousands of years. As you ascend, the cliffs along which the little foot-trails snake get steeper. The beauty of the ascent takes your breath away! You seem to circuit the Tor about three times in this ascent before anything significant happens. And then_

Rounding a turn against a steep cliff wall you look and see that the path has leveled out here, and that it has widened. Up ahead of you – only about nine yards away – Cernunnos is standing. As the Moon is behind a cloud, the Stag-god is but a silhouette. Then, however, the Moon comes out to illumine the scene and you see – beside where Cernunnos is standing – a huge and straggly Thorn tree! This is the **Glastonbury Thorn;** a tree whose ancestor was planted by Joseph of Arimathea in Glastonbury.

Joseph was a leader of the Jewish Sanhedrin (a council of elders) at the time of Jesus of Nazareth. Legends say that he brought the cup – used at the Last Supper (the meal eaten before Jesus was crucified) – from Judea to Britain and established the first mystical community of Christ's followers on that Isle near Glastonbury Tor. The "cup" he brought to Britain was later known as the Grail. The Thorn he planted had been brought from Judea. When he stuck it in the ground near Glastonbury Tor, it sprouted. This was the divine sign to Joseph that he was at his final destination. Keltelvens have long believed that the Thorn of Joseph of Arimathea marks the place in the side of the Tor where the Cave of the Nativity may be found each year during the vigils of Matrum Noctem.

Thus, when you see Cernunnos standing beside the Thorn in the Moonlight, be aware that your destination is very close by, hidden perhaps only by a gorse bush or a straggle of Rowan bracken!

Cernunnos then leaps behind the Thorn_ and vanishes! You walk up to the Thorn (the Yule Tree in your place of dwelling) and look around it, scanning the terrain for the mouth of a magical Cave. Then you see it! You climb up to it and, just as you reach the entrance, the clouds above you reveal a brilliant Star just above the entrance to the Cave.

Stop and ponder this **Star** for a few minutes before going on. You have followed this Star since Nicholas Eve and now you know you must be *very* close to where you need to be! This Cave is the place where the Nativity of earthen Rebirth is still a living reality. Address the star, saying:

> "Light of Night, gift of guidance,
> lead me/us into this Mystery,
> perchance to find New Life."

Now, enter the cave. Go down the dark passageway until the Moonlight from outside is fading away. The passageway grows darker still, and then, just as you are about to run out of light, the tunnel ahead of you begins to be illuminated from a source deep down in the Earth. Descend prayerfully. As you draw closer to the source of the light you realize that you are nearing the edge of a town. This is ancient Bethlehem; the town where Jesus of Nazareth was born and where *you* will experience whatever degree of psychic and spiritual rebirth you are prepared for!

When you come to the edge of the mystical "town in the cave," imagine that you can smell all the rustic odors that would have been in the air in those days. The smell of camels, hay and straw, the scent of human habitation and of exotic Nature all fill the air. As you walk onto the first street, imagine being travelers from a distant land. You need to find the Inn where Joseph & Mary have sought refuge for the night. It will take prayerful discernment to find the right house, not to mention the stable behind it where the holy couple is now put up for the night, owing to a lack of room at the "inn."

As you finish your pilgrimage to the Nativity, imagine arriving at the inn and being led by the inn-keeper to Joseph & Mary in the stable behind it. Come to the stable respectfully. *Of course* Mary & Joseph will welcome you! The ancient Jews were as keen on hospitality as were the ancient Celts. Can you imagine what that first meeting with the holy couple would be like? This Jewish couple would seem very ordinary in most respects, even in the fact that the woman – Mary – is heavy with child and is already beginning to feel the stirrings of birth in her pelvis and belly. Having been welcomed to the stable in the cave, it is time to wait and keep the vigil of rebirth with these rustic parents.

In 'real time-space' you have now completed your journey from where you started – at some distant corner of the house or out on the street – and you should now be sitting or kneeling near the Nativity Scene. The Yule Tree has become a symbol of the Glastonbury Thorn and you should continue to think of it as such for the next day or two. As you prepare for the vigils of the night, get a hot seasonal drink and get situated for the vigil. Begin by singing a song or two that will help you to center down in meditative anticipation. Avoid singing songs about Jesus' birth, as this event is still a few hours away.

Now take stock of where you are in your imagined nemeton – the stable behind the inn in Bethlehem, in the Cave of the Nativity in Glastonbury Tor – and try to visualize the surroundings. What do you see in the cave-stable? It is a fairly cold night. The Star that you have been following is shining overhead and there are animals all around you. Try to imagine a mule, a couple of horses (these belong to guests at the Inn) a cow and perhaps some chickens. People of a Celtic inclination might also envision a Stag and a couple of geese along with a wolf, several rabbits and even a wild boar prowling around the scene or even resting *in* the stable-yard. The Stag is Cernunnos, the wolf represents Lugh, the rabbits represent the triple goddess (ANU—DANU—TAILTIU), while the boar represents the Divine Presence.

Once you have visualized the scene, it is time to enter into **the Vigil of Expectant Repose**. It's a *vigil* because you're waiting for the birth of the god-child Jesus to take place. You wait in "expectant repose" because you expect your own transformation to be fostered in this place. We are all pregnant with a god or goddess this night. 'Jesus' is one mythological touchstone of our own divinization. The journey of the human soul is one of ever-increasing divinization achieved through pursuing wisdom and remembering who we are – given our parents, our personality, gifts and

175

character – as well as who we were in past lives. We awaken to our true self all along the way, yet Matrum Noctem is an especially potent time of the year, for the New Sun's powers now begin to really increase. Begin the vigil by praying:

> "Come, Keeper of the Light,
> invigorate our spirits!
> Come to this manger we have prepared as a place for you,
> and startle us!
> Let us be awakened in Your presence,
> illumined by your Wisdom's Song."

The manger set up in the Nativity Scene is the symbolic locus of our own rebirth. Meditate on this icon throughout the night. This is the longest period of generative darkness in the entire ritual year. The outward manger, of course, points to the **Manger of the Heart** at the center of our being, where we are constantly being reborn into a more divinely human image. Our own Heart is now the Bethlehem of the Spirit. We are here with Mary & Joseph, awaiting whatever may be in store for us before dawn!

This is a night of natural beauty and symbolic consummation. All the trimmings are up, some of the greenery has been replaced with fresh boughs and sprigs, and all the candles are lit. It's a warm and fruitful atmosphere in which to rediscover our best selves and cast off the dross of worldliness that clings to us like the liquor of decay. Luxuriate in the colorful glow of the lights illuminating your place of dwelling! It's in this atmosphere that all things now become possible. Our prayers and our magick this night will stir the Cauldron of Inspiration and enable us to reap the rewards of our pilgrimage.

The Vigil is inaugurated by the singing of a carol of anticipation, such as "O Come, O Come Immanuel." After this, you might sing other carols that evoke a sense of anticipation. Try retelling the story of Mary & Joseph in Pagan terms as the evening unfolds, recollecting their journey to Bethlehem and everything that has happened to them along the way.[50] As you reflect on the mythic themes embodied in this tale from the Christian scriptures, relate your own experiences over the last couple of weeks to that of the biblical characters. Read each section and share your poetic responses to it.

Instead of just reading the biblical text or recounting it from memory, try enacting a **Nativity Pageant**. If you're keeping Matrum Noctem with other people, this will be easy enough. Even a couple of people can play out the story, changing roles as one scene leads to another, walking through the various actions of the plot. The biblical texts containing the tales of the mysterious conception and birth of Jesus are broken up into a series of more or less discrete vignettes that lend themselves well to episodic retelling or dramatic enactment. Compare these tales with Celtic myths of divine birth.[51]

Depending on how much of the evening you want to devote to 'house theatre,' you can relate either more or less of the Nativity myth. If you want to go through the whole tale, start at Nazareth, with the Angel who announced to Mary that she was pregnant by God. Enact the story of how Joseph almost decided to break off his engagement with her and then how he was approached by an Angel who reassured him of Mary's integrity. Imagine what Mary & Joseph must have felt after this experience! If you don't have much time to spend on the pageant, however, begin with the journey to Bethlehem and bring the couple to the stable in three or four 'scenes.'

Adapt these stories to your own Pagan intuitions. Try to relate them to your own spiritual tale as the pageant unfolds and even make up your own script while keeping as close as possible to the original tale. However you re-enact it, the presentation should end with Joseph & Mary resting in the stable in Bethlehem – right where you are this night – knowing that Mary will soon give birth. The play should end on a note of wonder! "What will be the meaning of this birth?" "What will this child be like?" These questions are asked about Jesus as a character in the myth, yet they are also reflexive, being asked about us as well. Remember that theater was originally a religious performance in which devout people acted out the most powerful stories of their mythology. Though it might be entertaining, sacred theater has a much more profound function, in that it brings myths to life before people's very eyes.

At the end of the pageant the actors and actresses may pose as a living Nativity scene for a while. If the players are really into their parts, let them entertain questions from the 'audience' while still in character. During this interview they might try to express how they *feel* and what they *think* after everything they've gone through. Ask them what it was like to encounter an Angel! Do they *believe* what the angels said, and if so, why? Ask them – as the characters they are acting – to describe their experiences of doubt and faith in non-exclusive, Pagan terms.

Once you have enacted or retold the story of Mary & Joseph there are a number of things you can do as you wait in expectant repose for mid-night. Those who know how may pray a Pagan version of the Rosary as they wait with Mary for her child to be born in us (this involves using a cord with nine knots or beads on it to represent the nine months of pregnancy leading up to birth or the nine traditional nights of psychic rebirth. The practitioner prays a short and meditative chant at each bead or knot, thus hoping to center themselves in Meath and go deep in the Spirit).   Others might pass the evening by caroling while seated or kneeling near the hearth, Yule Tree or Nativity scene. The singing should be quiet and meditative, harmonizing the mood of the evening. Music has long been known as a vehicle for psychic and spiritual transformation. If you're not into singing, play recorded music appropriate to the mood. Sing along or just meditate on the words. As you wait for the birth of Christ in your heart, relax and watch the decorative lights blinking, gaze meditatively into the fire in the hearth, or even engage in spiritual reading. Those who want may watch a Christmas video. On this night of all nights, however, tune out the commercialism of the world by turning off the radio, the TV and the PC!

At the moment of the middle of the Night, ring a bell to announce the hour. Mid-night, however, is *not* 12:00 AM! It is that point exactly halfway between dusk and the following dawn. As during Solstice Night you will have to *calculate* the exact time of mid-night each year by getting a calendar that lists sunsets and sunrises and figure out how many hours and minutes there are between dusk on 24 December and dawn on 25 December. Divide this quantity of time in half, and then add it onto the time for dusk on Bayberry Day. Thus you will discover the true mid-night.

At Mid-Night, sing the old carol "*It came Upon a Midnight Clear*" or else some other equally appropriate Pagan song. During this song the figure of the infant Jesus is brought in to where the Nativity scene is set up and laid in the manger. This may be done with more or less ceremony.

178

Next, you might sing "*Away in a Manger.*" The appearance of the newborn baby Jesus symbolizes the birth we have all been expectantly awaiting. After this ritual advent, meditate on meaning of the Nativity Scene, pray near it and sing carols, including "*The First Noel,*" "*Joy to the World,*" and others.[52]

If the Yule has been well kept, someone may be moved to speak. It's not unknown for prophetic utterances or inspired 'speeches' to be heard in the course of Matrum Noctem. Whatever is said must be offered in a spirit of earthy humility and with some caution, as it's easy to get carried away at this mountaintop of the holy season. We sometimes say more than needs said. If you're going to speak, share only what you think comes from the Spirit and is for everyone's edification, not just your own. When the Word has subsided you might want to sing "*Silent Night*" or some other appropriate song.

After the singing, extinguish all the house lights and snuff out the candles. The tree lights are usually left on all night, though other electric Christmas lights should be turned off. In this way the Nativity – backed up by light from the hearth & the Yule Tree – becomes the primary focus of attention. Now the **Vigil of the Nativity** begins; it is time for the Great Silence. No one should speak until the bell is rung at dawn. Participants may either stay up all night, remaining near the Nativity, or go off to bed. Children usually go to bed at this point, after setting out a snack for Santa Claus. Once they are in bed, presents may be put under the tree.

Those who leave these presents should think of themselves as the servants of Saint Nicholas. If we participate in the myths we tell our children they will have more meaning. Go to where the gifts are hidden and bring them out as though Santa Claus and his Elves have deputized you. Imagine that you have been inspired at the Hearth of Tara Lough – Santa's Workshop at the Top of the World – to give the gifts you have chosen and wrapped.

Some people find that wrapping presents between mid-night and dawn on Matrum Noctem is a good way to pass the Vigil of the Nativity. If this is the case, let these people set up a table or go to the kitchen and – in the light of red and green candles and twinkling lights – wrap the Yule gifts in solemn silence. As this is going on, those who are staying up to keep the Vigil of the Nativity need to center down near the Nativity scene and engage in quiet chanting or prayer. Appropriate music may be played – at a *very low* volume – in the background, if this will enhance the solemnity of the night. Gregorian chants are good for this vigil of transformation and self-realization, as they calm the soul and help to center all our energies in Earth & Spirit.

Having experienced the Vigil of Expectant Repose and then the drama of the Nativity, we find that – at least as the years pass and our experience of the mysticism of Yule grows deeper – that this second vigil of Matrum Noctem becomes extremely profound. Once those who are going to bed have departed, meditate on the passage you made earlier this evening toward Glastonbury Tor, up to the Thorn and then into the Cave. Once again imagine yourself as a visitant at the spectral town of Bethlehem and then bring all of these experiences to a focus in attending to the newborn infant in the manger.

This infant is a god, incarnate among us. Though among Christians the incarnation is unique, among Pagans this is a *common* mythic theme. In the icon of this birth we find many runes of spiritual Pagan truth. Jesus represents the intersection of divine and human realms. His birth signifies the rebirth that mortals undergo – often more than once – in the course of their life's pilgrimage through Earth & Spirit. The newborn infant Jesus is the affirmation of the possibility of rebirth. As Jesus is born in the manger, so may we be reborn in the midst of life, becoming more and more "Children of Wisdom."

Meditating on the icon of the infant in the manger, pray that your own spirit will experience a rebirth in the next few hours, before dawn of Glastonbury Thorn Day. Focus on the manger and the newborn child in it, and reflect on everything this child signifies. Then pray:

"Holy Child, come from Divine Realms,
come and be born in me this night!
I name the City where the Tribes
of the Ancients
all receive their just rewards tonight!
Christ-mass! Christ-mass!
Let us be reborn in Bethlehem
in the runes of holy light! Amen."

As the night passes, chant to yourself the names of the god: "**Lugh—Cernunnos—Jesus—Bran**." If you see the Star above the manger in the sky, chant: *"Star of Light, Star of Delight, lead us through Wisdom's gate, this holy night!"* If your attention turns to the Moon as it descends toward the western horizon as the holy night passes, chant: "**Ceridwen—Brighid—Boann**" over and over again until her light becomes a reality in the Hearth of your Inner Heart.

The Vigil of the Nativity begins in wonder at the birth of Jesus of Nazareth in the manger and ends in the experience of our own renewal, in whatever degree this is realized before dawn and in the aftermath of keeping this night's vigils. Though we aren't usually 'reborn' all at once, what we experience each year during the Yule and in the passage of our souls through Alban Arthuan and then Matrum Noctem will help bring us by stages into the umbra of transfiguration.

The manger and the stable in which it is located are both instances of the Cauldron of Transformation. This Cauldron takes many different forms during the year, but always contains the inebriating Mead of Wisdom. As dawn approaches, imagine that you are offered a taste of this mead and be thankful for whatever transformation you may reap this year during the Yule. As the dawn lights up the eastern sky, the mystical world of Matrum Noctem begins to fade. It is time to move on.

Light Candles to the Light –
Cernunnos sings Wise Runes in Yule's Night!
Bless Stable and the Manger where the Wise Ones meet –
for here Mary birthed a Divine Son. Amen.

13. <u>Glastonbury</u> <u>Thorn</u> <u>Day</u> *(White Poplar Day, 25 December)*

[Alternate Name: "Apple Day"]
"Dawn comes to the heart in a number of ways, caroling us toward the moment we've all been awaiting – Christmas morning! The rich poetic ambiance of this event is difficult to express in mere prose. However, it sounds like the ringing of silver bells and it tastes like succulent holiday sauces and powdered sugar desserts!" (156)

- Robert Werner
<u>Wintering</u> Upon <u>the</u> <u>Way</u> (1970)

"We arise today as pilgrims having finished our rounds. Here in the Cave of the Nativity we reside in a God-Haunted place where our own intuitions are finally full-filled with the shining wisdom of the Yule's Invitation. The Spiral of our journey is complete, for we are back where we were last year, yet we're at a 'new place.'" (132)

- Mabel Hester
<u>The</u> <u>Veil</u> <u>in</u> <u>the</u> <u>Well</u> (1993)

"The Aspen was once sacred to the mystics of Cernunnos. These men and women roamed the forests of yore, pathing their wildwood lord and foraging for spiritual sustenance in hidden thickets and Aspen groves. Later, Aspen became sacred to Christ's followers, who thought of it as a tree through which intuition and psychic renewal were communicated to the devout friend of God." (56)

- Cornelius Whitsel
<u>Mythbook</u> <u>of</u> <u>the</u> <u>Balefire</u> (1991)

Dawn on Glastonbury Thorn Day has long been experienced as a magical moment full of deeper mystical potential. As you wake up (or

182

else break your vigil as the sun rises) meditate on the **three Virtues of Rebirth** – *Love, Hope and Joy* – symbolized by *Myrrh, Frankincense and Gold* respectively. These are the three gifts that will be brought by the Astrologers from the East to the infant Jesus in the manger on 6 January. As we make our way toward Epiphany in the Light of the Nativity, these three herbs become icons of our journey.

Myrrh is sacred to the Moon in Keltelven herbalism and is believed to attract true lovers to one another. Those gifted in herbal mysticism teach that Myrrh also represents our love tryst with the Spirit. **Frankincense** is an herb of vision and as such is connected with hope, vision being necessary if we're going to see that things can be better than they are now. **Gold** has the spiritual property of inspiring laughter and joy. It's a solar mineral and as such is used to rune out the joy we experience on the morning that symbolizes our own rebirth after spending the night in the Cave of the Nativity.

Love is nurtured near the hearth by many things: the glow of the lights of the tree, the smiles of children and by fostering the memories we have that humanize our hearts in the aura of the Fires of Yule. Anoint the hearthstones with myrrh oil at dawn today, using two fingers of one hand, signing three small crosses on the stones. If you have no hearth, anoint the Yule Table with myrrh oil in its stead.

Hope is kindled once again each year at Winter's Solstice. The announcement of the birth of Jesus in the Cave of the Nativity at mid-night during the vigils of Matrum Noctem then ignites the embers of renewed Hope. Light Frankincense incense near the Nativity at dawn on this day.

Joy arises out of the encounter we have had with our own true self in the icon of "the child-god in the manger" during Matrum Noctem. Then at dawn we become living witnesses to our own rebirth in the wake of Alban Arthuan! As the Divine Son en-lightens the world, joy breaks forth as spiritual satisfaction, en-firing us with dreams of a better world. To symbolize this, use a few gold-colored decorations on the breakfast table this morning.

If you've celebrated Yule with others, someone should go through the house playing Santa Claus at first light. This person walks up and down the halls past rooms where people are sleeping. The one playing this part should dress in an appropriate costume so as not to be recognized by the children, should they try to get a look at their mythic benefactor! One or two others might wander the halls dressed as elves, whispering about the gifts that have been left. Even if there are no children in the house, this can be a playful way of engaging in the day's magick.

Someone should then ring a hand-bell at dawn. This audio rune announces the end of our pilgrimage to the Nativity. The vigil is now over, and our satisfaction in the divine birth begins to be realized. We have come to the Nativity of the Heart! Hurrahya! The mystery that was enacted during the night has turned out to be the enervation we need to continue in the ongoing spiritual journey that is life itself. The sun has arisen on our experiences, en-lighten-ing in us the meaning of the Spirit's presence in the Earth. If we've kept Yule well, we will see this truth a bit better than we did before. The way this becomes manifest, however, may differ from person to person and from year to year.

Some people find that pathing their own mysterious rebirth through the Yule brings them to a deeper state of inner peace, year after year. Others find it harrowing or exhausting to be a pilgrim to the Cave of the Nativity. A few will always find it perplexing; these few see the contradiction between what's going on around them in the Thirteen Dayes and what normally goes on in the world! How are these to be reconciled? The ideal vision of life represented in the drama of Matrum Noctem is always a paradox, yet to live in and through this and other paradoxes of existence is to transcend what 'merely is.'

Regardless of our state of mind, dawn comes on 25 December. When it does, celebrate with what vigor you have left, keeping this last day of Yule as the brightest day of the year. All the Fires of Yule are now burning with an empowering glow, and all we need do is warm ourselves in their aura. Hearthfire, candlelight and the illumination of the spirits of Yule all function to draw us ever more deeply into the sublime intimacies of mystical love, hope and joy.

After you get up, pray for an awareness of the Presence of the Spirit of Yule in the house and in the world. Before you get dressed, address yourself to Mystery in these terms:

> Awaken me, Cernunnos, and I shall see You_
> peel the shadows from my eyes!
> Speak to me, Brighid, and let me hear You_
> fill my Heart with the Light of your Word!

Come to me, Jesus, and we shall be friends_
inspire me to states of mystical attention!
Let us be fellow travelers in the Spirit of Yule,
for I long for True Freedom's Simplicity!

Tear down the walls of resistance, avoidance
and refusal _and let me see You;
        Divine Hunter of my Heart! Amen.

After this prayer, begin bringing the house to life by lighting candles, putting sacred music on the stereo and rekindling the hearth. If you're keeping the Yule with others, lay out a buffet breakfast in the kitchen. Arrange a variety of symbolic evergreens on the kitchen table and light Bayberry scented candles around the house. Let the place of dwelling be suffused with this potent aroma. Then lay out a similar arrangement of evergreens and candles on the Yule Table.

Before breaking your night's fast, go to the Yule Table, the Yule Tree and the hearth in turn, taking in the scene and savoring it in your Heart. Remember your journey to Glastonbury Tor! Meditate on the way the trimmings, the lights and the gifts transform ordinary reality into something mysterious and wonderful. As you approach the place where gifts are laid out, reflect on the nature of giving. What does it mean to give and to receive a gift? Ask, "What have I given?" and "What might I receive?"

Next, recite the simple words of the 15th century Druid Cathbad, as recorded in the <u>Yuletide Grimoire</u> (1898): "May we give without gloating, and receive graciously!" Nurture the deep recognition that everything in life is ultimately a gift. We deserve nothing. It's only the mores and customs of our particular culture that convinces us that we 'deserve' what we have or what we lack. These rules are ultimately chimerical! Therefore, even what we work for in life we should try to receive as a gift. Be grateful for jobs, for possessions and those we are fortunate enough to work with at our jobs. Be especially grateful, then, for gifts that we haven't 'earned' in *any* way. The gifts we exchange and give during Yule are always a wonder, no matter how many or how few we receive! Accept what's gifted to you, in the Spirit of the Season, and be glad!

The best gifts we receive on 25 December are always intangible. Before entering into the usual rituals of unwrapping and feasting, stop and reflect on the immaterial dimensions of what's happening all around you. Reflect on life itself as a wondrous gift, regardless of your circumstances. Remember parents, without whom we would not exist. Be thankful for your natal family. If you have siblings, call to mind experiences you have had with them. If you are married, be thankful for your spouse and for any children that have graced your union. At their best, children show us what we've forgotten about life and Mystery. Consider friends; those who are now in your life's circle as well as those who have taken other paths, breaking the bonds that once existed between you. Meditate on the gift that we are to one another. Thank the Spirit for your livelihood, your talents and abilities.

By following the runes of the Yule we have come to a wondrous place. We have created the Nativity in our place of dwelling. Thank the Spirit of Yule for creativity, intuition and hope.

What if you're alone in the world? Do you have anyone with whom to exchange a gift? Perhaps not, but you can give anonymous gifts to others! Even if there are no gifts under the Yule Tree for *us*, we still have many things for which to be thankful. We can express our gratitude by giving unexpected gifts to people in need. It's best to give these gifts without letting the receiver know who you are, as then you will not 'oblige' them to return the favor in any way. It's better to give to those in need (psychic, emotional or economic) than to give to those who already 'have enough' of what life has to offer. There's too much poverty, abuse and neglect in our world to be isolating ourselves in our own cocoons, all but unconscious of the needs of people in the world at large!

Perhaps (when we become wiser?) we will ask Nicholas and his Elves for peace on earth, goodwill between people and their governments, for the reconciliation of all races, including the resolution of wars and conflicts that arise from thinking 'our way' is the only way. Perhaps we will ask for an abundance of justice for all human beings everywhere. Perhaps we will stop believing that to receive a pile of trinkets and perishable goods will make us – or anyone else – happy. Perhaps we will someday stop asking for hoards of things and come to see the virtue & simplicity of asking for gifts of the Spirit. Then, perhaps, we will discover an innate mystical ability to give others what they really need.

The culmination of the Keltelven Yule has long been connected with two sacred trees: the **White Poplar** (called *Eadha* in Druidical symbolism) and the **Glastonbury Thorn**. These two trees contain arcane runes of the deep understanding Keltelvens have gleaned from the Winter Solstice Season. At the end of our Yuletide journey we should see ourselves as coming to these two trees, at which we may glimpse what we have experienced so far and see what may be in store for us after 25 December.

White Poplar is deeply connected with remembrance and memory, rebirth and psychic renewal in Keltelven mysticism. Around the time of Winter's Solstice Druids were once wont to go out to a White Poplar and meditate. There they would call to mind certain powerful ancestors and seek a visitation by one of their spirit guides.[53] Through this act of remembrance and via this encounter their psychic 'batteries' would be recharged for whatever psychic or magical work needed done.

White Poplar – also called **Aspen** – may be seen as a natural storehouse of ancient memory. This includes personal remembrance but also the general collective memory. By practicing a form of devout meditation – called *bilé deccad* – near this tree, a person can link into the collective memory of their tuath (i.e., tribe; the word is used today to refer to a Keltelven community) and discover one's place in it. Meditating at a White Poplar – whether in the external world or in the internal world of the Imagination – on Glastonbury Thorn Day enables those who seek wisdom to gain insight into the mysteries of birth and rebirth. Its wood was once used to make shields, so that it is also a symbol of physical as well as divine protection.

While Glastonbury Thorn Day is lived in present time, year after year, it is also a time of deep **remembrance**. We create new memories every time we approach the Hearth in the wayfaring of Yule, yet we also recollect old memories. Down across the centuries, men & women have had so many deep and varied spiritual experiences on or about 25 December that the day has become a virtual database of human memories. White Poplar is the mythical 'CPU' through which all of these memories can be stored and accessed by those who seek to live in ever-wisening ways. Going to a White Poplar tree on 25 December is therefore a way of seeking out your best memories of the past.

As we remember the Hearths of Yule from our own and past generations, we may begin to recollect images and assorted memories of family & friends who have died and crossed†over to the Otherworld. Every living soul included in the compass of our love may be brought to mind and invited to partake in the celebration of White Poplar Day. This includes loved ones, friends and even animals we have known. The spirits who joined us on Yew Day are also still with us. The memory of the dead – not to mention their actual presence – must not be neglected.

We might also recall, on this potentially wonder-filled morning, the memory of anyone with whom we may have been at odds. It's easy to invite a loved one back across the Sídhe but it takes a certain degree of Slán (wholeness) to invite someone back with whom you were at odds. If you're not at peace with someone – whether living *or* dead – pray for his or her wellbeing on White Poplar Day.

We all know people who rub us the wrong way. On 25 December – as we sit near the hearth – ask the Spirit for the patience necessary to deal with such people. The god-child Jesus is an icon of reconciliation, and at his manger we might hope for a world in which the broken are healed and those at odds are reconciled. This hope may well have the tendency, over the years, to disarm our hates and loathing, kindling a fire of compassion in the place of these more negative emotions. If you fan this fire with the alchemy of restitution, compensation for wrongs, and forgiveness, great things become possible!

White Poplar is a touchwood of the kind of spiritual strength that is sourced in the depths of human consciousness. This strength enables us to forgive, nurture a kind endurance toward others and discover the direction in which we must now path in order to arrive at Wisdom's Hut. Yuling awakens us poetically and enables us to better discern the paths leading to Wisdom's threshold. One old way to 'invoke' or 'realize' this discernment is to use a small branch of White Poplar as a kind of 'divining rod.'

Keltelvens often exchange small twigs or branches of White Poplar on the 25th of December for this divinatory purpose. The recipient should take this stick and sharpen one end of it. The stick is then laid in a bowl or pool of water and the water is stirred. You then wait to see in which direction it will point. Once the stick aligns itself to a particular direction, the diviner knows in which direction to path out from the back door of

White Poplar Day in order to discover wisdom in the coming year. If you perform this divination today, meditate on the symbolic aspects of the direction you are shown:

North	East
Earth	Air
Falias (Guardian of Wisdom)	Gorias (Guardian of Wisdom)
Emerald	Topaz
Bear	Eagle
Ash	Aspen

South	West
Fire	Water
Finias (Guardian of Wisdom)	Murias (Guardian of Wisdom)
Rubies & Garnets	Sapphires
Stags	Salmon
Oak	Willow

All of these associations have deep mythic resonances that can still be tapped into by those who are living in and through ancient poetic paradigms. Each direction's associations represent things on which you can concentrate during the year. By using this oracle, you will be led on – by mysterious powers – toward Wisdom's doors. Research the meaning of each of the associations of the particular direction in which you are to move and interpret these meanings in light of your Yuletide experiences.

Receiving White Poplar as a gift is also an omen of revitalized psychic powers as well as the spiritual stamina necessary for undertaking the tasks and chores of one's daily life. White Poplar is a tree of both spiritual & practical encouragement. Part of White Poplar's role in the mythos of Winter's Solstice is to remind us of the realities we must face in day to day life, now that Yule is almost past. The spirit of White Poplar invites us to leave the Hearth where we have kept our vigils, feasts and celebrations, and return to life's ordinary rounds and routines. Tomorrow the Yule will be past. Over the next twelve days you will leave the Hearth of Yule and the Cave of the Nativity behind once more. When you do, how will you live? You will have made some progress this year as you kept the days of Yule. This progress must be incorporated into your normal lifestyle.

White Poplar runes out the Spirit's being with-us and assures us that we are now more able to draw near to the mysteries of life's meaning than ever before. White Poplar symbolizes the mysterious poetic powers we tapped-into during the vigils of Matrum Noctem. The wind whispers through the branches of the Aspen, rendering the voice of the Spirit audible to *waeccan* (see endnote 34) souls.

Keltelvens believe that every year on White Poplar Day the fruit of the Season's journey may be expressed in potentially **prophetic utterance**, as White Poplar is also an oracular tree. Listen for words on Glastonbury Thorn Day that may well be prophetic of the future direction of your life. You might hear something significant said in the context of a meal or while spending time with children. Something you read might awaken you to a new possibility or an aspect of your life that you had not previously noticed. Often the action of opening gifts inspires a sense of wonder in us, and this, too, can lead to prophetic words. The experiences of the Yule now distill themselves into insight!

Prophecy is a matter of revealing the nature of reality; it cannot predict an unalterable future, as the future is not yet 'made.' However, we *can* see into the marrow of today's reality and intuit how tomorrow will be shaped by the present, provided we don't alter our course of action. White Poplar is an icon of this prophetic insight, which often comes to fruition as we complete our Yuletide journey to the Thorn Tree on Glastonbury Tor and then emerge from the Cave of the Nativity on the 25th of December.

The Thirteenth Day of Yule is also connected with the **Glastonbury Thorn**. Today we engage in meditations focusing on the nature of the Thorn. We reflect on how we found this Bilé (sacred tree) the previous night, and how it marked the entrance to the Cave of the Nativity for us. Emerging from the Cave at dawn today, look back at the Thorn as a mystical marker of potential self-transformation. The Tree and the Tor on which it stands will be an icon for our meditation in the afterglow of Yule all the way to Epiphany. Remember the journey you made across the marshlands to the Tor, and reflect on where you found the Thorn Tree *this* year, as next year it probably won't be in the same place!

Some practitioners of the Yule like to go out and bring a few small branches of a local tree that has thorns on its branches and boughs – such as the Thorn Apple or the Crab Apple – into the house. These may be set out near the hearth or Yule Table in a vase or perhaps just laid on the table or hearthstones. They are left bare (not decorated in any way) as this symbolizes the naked potency of the Thorn Tree in winter. Though denuded of its leaves, its wisdom can pierce our flesh with its power.

The Yule Tree may also serve as the symbolic and living presence of the Spirit of the Glastonbury Thorn in our midst. At some point in the morning on 25 December, address the Yule Tree, saying:

> "Hail, Thorn of Life!
> unveil to us your Wisdom this day
> and sharpen our wit's knife.
> Mingle your thorns with our experience
> and weave our fears into tapestries
> of new insight!
> Hail, Thorn of New Birth_
> naked bearer of truth and worth,
> insight resides in your spines!

From this moment on the room wherein the Yule Tree stands *is* once again the terraced slope of Glastonbury Tor where the Thorn grows. This scene runes out the truth of White Thorn Day. As you pass by the Yule Tree during the day, allow your mind to leap imaginatively to this 'other' place.

The Glastonbury Thorn has become an emblem of the intermingling of Celtic & Christ-centered wisdom that began about 1600 years ago. It symbolizes how the Jewish teaching of Jesus of Nazareth – as interpreted through the perceptions of his often Hellenic disciples – can be planted and become a Living Tree in other cultural contexts. It represents the potential for Pagan-Christian ecumenism. As Glastonbury Thorn Day, 25 December is thus seen as a time for the tolerant embrace of other people's cultural, mystical and religious traditions as well as the exuberant affirmation of our own. There are many ways to celebrate the Yule, the Solstice and Christmas. The Winter Solstice is observed under a wide variety of names around the world. The Glastonbury Thorn gives us leave to accept Wisdom's runes wherever we find them, even in traditions that have at times been horrendously exclusive and even violent toward Pagans and their Earthen Wisdom.

Whereas most people fear pluralism – usually because they think it threatens the truth of what they believe – in reality pluralism only threatens the falsehoods that arise from thinking our way is the 'only' or even the 'best' way. When people – in any tradition, whether cultural, religious or political – begin to think of their understanding of Wisdom and their approach to life as 'absolutely better' than other ways, our integrity as human beings becoming human is threatened. While some particular traditions and rituals, practices and beliefs may in fact be more humane than others, and while we certainly want to follow a path that is more rather than less humanizing, it takes a deep draught from the ever-seething Cauldron of Wisdom to understand what does and does not humanize.

Keltelven spirituality is and has always been an ecumenical, inclusive path. We understand Truth as a Goddess who can wear many different styles of clothing and who can adorn Herself in such a way that only by a depth of perception can Her real identity be realized. The Glastonbury Thorn is the Keltelven symbol of the intersecting and often overlapping roads leading to Wisdom's Thresholds.

Keltelvens have a profound faith in life and in the reality of the Presence of Mystery. So long as we keep our hearts focused on the icon of the Glastonbury Tor we can find Wisdom in the teachings of non-Pagans – such as Jesus or the Buddha – without losing sight of how this Wisdom has been obscured and even denied by those who sully the ideals of their own traditions. We can look at Jesus from a Pagan Heath while allowing that other people might believe something different than we do about him. From this vantagepoint we can share our fascination with Jesus or Mohammed or the Upanishads without any 'evangelical' desire to 'force' our enthusiasm on anyone else!

The Glastonbury Thorn – with its longevity, inner strength and its sharp thorns – represents the potency of particular truth in the context of reality as a whole. It allows us to accept the truth we believe we possess without being antagonistic toward those who espouse a different vision of what is true, wise and beautiful. It enables us to live our lives according to the truths we have discovered – as well as those that have been 'handed down to us' in the Tradition we follow – without feeling insecure about what we believe. What we believe is what *we know* to be *true*, and yet our particular truth represents just one way of approaching the larger Truth

192

that's being aimed at by other seekers. A spiritual form of beauty emerges when every path to Wisdom is being expressed in non-alienating ways, open to the truth of other paths.

Meditating on the Glastonbury Thorn in our pluralistic context on 25 December we hope to find ever better ways of honoring the Spirit of Yule, both through an openness to share our traditions with others and toleration toward the wisdom others espouse. Be conscious today of all of the different ways in which people in your family and elsewhere in the world approach Wisdom and express Truth. We each have our own style and as a result we each get something a bit different out of Yule. By cultivating this awareness, you become able to celebrate the day without stepping on other people's mystical toes!

The truth of the Thirteen Dayes of Yule is 'true' even if there are other ways of understanding it and the season this calendar celebrates. As you move from breakfast to the opening of gifts and then to the activities that follow, be open to the vastness of Truth, which only becomes available through the concrete particularity of our own experiences and through the traditions in which we participate.

Glastonbury Thorn Day is also sometimes called "**Apple Day**." This is due to a story told by the Gwrach (Keltelven wise-women) about the first one of their order to meet Joseph of Arimathea back at the end of the 1st century CE. It is said that, while crossing†out of the mists between Avalon and Glastonbury Tor she saw the foreigner encamped at the water's edge with his family and his followers. She walked up to him under a cloak of invisibility and was surprised by his wise appearance. Becoming visible to him she offered to rune out for him the wisdom he held in his heart. Joseph – as startled by the Gwrach as she was by him – agreed to this divination. As she told him what she saw and felt in his presence, Joseph offered her an apple in return for every true rann she spoke about him and his friendship with Jesus the Crucified and Risen Child of God.

By the time they had finished their conversation, she had been able to dream an entire story of the Gospel and capture some of its teaching in the hem of her walking cloak. She and Joseph became friends, and as they got to know one another she became a friend of the Christ as well. She understood the similarities between the wisdom of her own people – the

Celts – and the wisdom of the stories Joseph told about his carpenter-god. Over time she grafted the Wisdom of Jesus onto her own Bilé of Truth.

Though both the Gwrach and Joseph went their separate ways after this encounter, they got spiraled around in life's paths to meet at the site of their original meeting on the very same day of their original meeting for the next nine and twenty years. By the end of their lives, nine apple trees had sprung up on this site. As they had first met on the afternoon of the Winter Solstice (at that time, 25 December), White Thorn Day has always been dedicated to rekindling the spirit of their meeting.

If you have apples in the house, set a few of them out in a bowl on the morning of Glastonbury Thorn Day. By evening these apples should be eaten by those who have kept the Yule together. If you are celebrating the Yule alone, give the apples away as gifts or bake them into a pie or dumplings and gift this dish to someone who will appreciate it. Apples are symbols of wisdom. They are the fruit of those who cross†over and back between this world and the Aether. They represent the spiritual food found in Paradise. As such, they also exemplify the spiritual bounty we have gleaned from the Yule.

As the world outside is usually quiet on 25 December, some people find a morning walk in this silence to be a necessary reprieve from the intensity of Yule. If in town, walk around the block. If you live out in the country, go for a small hike around a field or into a wood for a little while during the early morning, taking in the silence of the day. If the weather isn't cooperative, remain indoors and stay near the hearth, talking and partaking of seasonal drinks such as eggnog and various kinds of wassail.

At mid-day or perhaps in the middle of the afternoon, hold the **Feast of Commonweal**. This meal is an occasion for more than just stuffing ourselves with all of the traditional holiday foods! It's a stage for acting-out ideals of friendship, hospitality and equality among the gathered, as well as love for the stranger. 'Commonweal' implies that one's wealth is to be shared in common with others. A 'commonwealth' is a country where everyone is given access to the wealth that is deemed to be the rightful property of every citizen. No one is poor in a true commonwealth. There is no impoverished class in a real political commonwealth!

Though not egalitarian, ancient Celtic societies where often practical 'commonwealths' in that there was very little difference – in economic terms – between the chieftains and warriors at the 'top' of the socioeconomic ladder and the farmers at the 'bottom.' Though there was a difference in 'wealth,' when compared with the societies in which we live today, the various Celtic tribes seem to have had very little socioeconomic stratification. Those who had 'more' were not 'rich' (by our standards) and those who had 'less' were not impoverished. While people did get into debt and while criminals and those who could not manage their own resources well enough were often left without the means of support, the Celtic ideal insisted that the unfortunate and inept be taken care of and that the criminal who is willing to act out restitution or pay compensation for damages done be re-integrated into society.

The general Celtic social ideal involved taking care of one's neighbors, being hospitable toward the stranger and the traveler, and helping anyone who desired aid. There was a sense in which all those who were members of the tribe suffered or excelled together. The Keltelven traditions have inherited this ideal, and it is this ideal that we seek to enact at the Feast of Commonweal.

If you know of someone who is alone, invite him or her to your table on White Poplar Day. If you live in an apartment building, you might arrange to get together with other tenants who may be alone unwillingly or who may not be away visiting relatives for one reason or another and who would like company. Work together with those with whom you have kept the Yule to create a situation of harmonious unity. Look on everyone who gathers at your table as equals in this life.

By equality is not meant some arbitrary or dogmatic dumbing down of everyone to the same lowest common level. Keltelven philosophy has always acknowledged the differences between people in terms of abilities, innate gifts and experience. We cannot deny the differences that accrue between people in the living out of this mortal life, yet we can see to it that nothing that would contribute to a person's humanity is denied them. This is what we mean by 'equality.' No one at our table – and by extension, no one in the communities in which we live – should be deprived of any resource or experience that would maintain, enhance or fulfill their humanity.

If a person is blind or if they are not talented enough to hold down a certain kind of job, we do not therefore deny them access to the resources that allow them to be humanized. If a person is super-intelligent we do not expect them to do work that will bore or frustrate them, unless they chose to. Each person should be allowed and encouraged to do what they are capable of doing, and no one should either be held back or thrust into situations in which they will not be able to function with competence. This is what Keltelvens mean by 'equality.' Everyone must have an equal access to the resources and experiences that make us all human.

Only those who shirk their responsibilities, deny or refuse (not 'fail') to use their gifts or who try to prevent others from reaching their full potential are seen as 'less than equal.' By compassionately shunning and/or chiding these individuals we hope to re-inspire them to take up the task of living their lives to the fullest. These people may also need spiritual direction or counseling, and if so we encourage them to go to the wise ones for such help. There are many reasons why people fail to live their lives to the full, some of which are remediable while others are not.

The Feast of Commonweal is a ritual expression of our hope for the realization of this ideal. It arises out of the 'spiritual logic' of the Thirteen Dayes of Yule and represents a fulfillment of all of the rituals, meditations and myths in which we have participated for the last two weeks. Remember the compassion of Saint Deirdre? Remember the indiscriminate generosity of Saint Nicholas? As we seek personal transformation we learn to become more human; more whole. Wholeness (i.e., *Slán*) implies a vision of how we might best – as human becomings – relate to other people, and this in turn leads us to the ideal of equality.

If you consider the myth of the Glastonbury Thorn in its ecumenical implications, you will see that such a Tree stands for the possibility that everyone who wants to realize their full humanity should be able to do so. How can we live our beliefs honestly and openly if we have to be worried about where our next meal is going to come from? How can we say to someone, "believe what you will and I will respect your beliefs," if we are living in ways that prevent them from making a living. Prejudice – whether carried out ideologically or in economic and social terms – has no place in the Light of Yule.

As the meal begins, toast each other's good health and say, "May we dwell together in love, hope and joy!" These words reflect our highest understanding of Life-Together-in-Earth-and-Spirit. At the table let everything be shared in common. Hospitality and prayerful humility are the hallmark of this meal. Relate to each other as 'equals' and make every attempt to eliminate the usual pecking order that emerges between people

196

when they gather. There is often one relative or friend who tends to get dumped on, just as there are always those who take charge and who – inadvertently or otherwise – frustrate other people's self-expression in their desire to make things 'run smoothly' according to their own vision of 'how it should be done.' At the Feast of Commonweal, try to imagine what it would be like for all of this vanity and abuse to vanish. Throw all inequalities and abusive behaviors onto the purifying pyre of the Fire in the Hearth and let them go! Imagine a new situation emerging based on the ideal of "equality with deference to difference," in which the main thing that matters is that everyone is able to become a friend of Wisdom on their way to Slán (wholeness).

After the meal, relax together near the hearth or meditate in your private place of prayer. Ask yourself, "Has the ideal of commonweal been made more manifest among us this year?" Evaluate the ways in which the ideals of the Thirteen Dayes of Yule have or haven't come to fruition. Ask yourself, "Have I contributed to the ideal of commonweal, or have I hindered its expression?" Finally, ask yourself, "How might I better approach the Thirteen Dayes *next year*, in order to make this ideal more manifest?" and "In what areas do I need to grow – and/or change – in order to better embody the ideal of commonweal?"

Once the sun sets, take a few minutes to reflect on this year's pilgrimage. Though you will be basking in the aura of the Season for the next twelve days, the Thirteen Dayes are at an end. Do you notice the difference that keeping the Yule has made this year in your awareness and wakefulness? If you don't, don't despair – you soon will! The pilgrim is always rewarded, in one way or another. On this day – or soon afterwards – the ordinary may begin to glow with an extra-ordinary aura. Pray that you will recognize this aura for what it is and not obscure it with false hopes and misguided intuitions of what 'is supposed to happen' by the end of Yule.

Glastonbury Thorn Day winds down into well-deserved rest, and – as you go to your bed – remind yourself that the Season of Yule is now past. There's no way of going back and doing it again. The next week or so will be lived out in the after-glow of Yulefire, and all that has been kindled in your own Heart and near your hearth will become your spiritual sustenance for the further pathing of Wisdom in life's sway.

Natural Meditation: Focus on the psychic resourcement inherent in the White Poplar. Meditate on its aspects and participate in its prophetic powers. Remember your climb up Glastonbury Tor last night! Go and re-visit the Glastonbury Thorn in your imagination, sending out a blessing on all those who have celebrated the Winter Solstice Season in whatever secular or religious tradition their steps are to be found.

Scriptural Meditation: Focus on an image of the infant Jesus (Luke 2:6-7, Matthew 1:25, 2:1), and imagine the Divine Mystery becoming dependent on human beings for survival in the world that was created by a 'divine hand' and that is still being creating. As with any other infant, Mary had to tend to Jesus' every need. Imagine the humanity of Jesus. Meditate on what it means for this humanity to be invested with the Divine Presence.

C. The Gifting of the Stag (26 December)

"The Stag of the Wildwood is the mentor of our Heart.
Deep in the strange barrows of our soul, Cernunnos runs
free and ever-haunted across the Fields of Love and Life.
... The gates of Paradise can be discovered in following the
Gifting Stag through the ever-deepening woods of our
imagined Inner Landscapes." (29)

- New Book of the Graensídhe (1968)

"The Stag of the Woods is the Deer of the Hearth. Coming
through from the Othersídhe, this wild animal of the Spirit
appears to mortals dwelling in Earth Peace and inspires
them with Earthen Power. Through this encounter we gain
the stamina to continue in life's quest for meaning, justice
and wisdom. Hail the Gifting Stag!" (109)

- Magdalena Ipswich
The Runes of Celtic Hearth Philosophy
(1992)

After White Poplar Day it's normal to experience either a sense of
relief or calm repose. If kept well, the Thirteen Dayes of Yule can be
alternately draining and challenging, centering and inspiring. By the time
it's over, we're either riding high in the Spirit or ready to really rest for a
few days, basking in the glow of the Season that has just passed.

The days following the Yule are generally characterized by a state of
lowered energy, a sense of repose, and – if we're not careful – signs of
impending depression. The Keltelven keeping of Yule is so potent that
when it's over there is a tendency to slip into a kind of numbed inactivity
and even to become moody. This happens after any "mountaintop
experience" in life, and in particular after Yule, as we emerge from the
season of lights into the wintry whiteness and seeming mundane doldrums
of January. Once the journey is over, therefore, we have to remember to

199

re-connect with daily life, carrying the fruit of our Yuletide pilgrimage back into the ordinary rounds of work, school, play and family life.

For this reason the Season does not end with 25 December. Glastonbury Thorn Day is the climax of Yule, and then, for the next twelve days, we bask in the glow of the Season and whatever we've experienced along the way. If we remain vigilant in the Spirit, the afterglow of the Winter Solstice Season won't finally fade away until Epiphany (6 January). During this time we walk with a memory of the Thirteen Dayes behind us, going forward with a renewed sense of how life might better be lived.

You might say that we've ascended a heath in order to enter the Cave of Rebirth, and now we must climb down the far side. We should climb down slowly and carefully from Glastonbury Tor so as not to spoil the spiritual rewards we've received. Yule has often been compared to a kind of retreat from the world in which people turn from rigorous schedules and the demands of daily living in order to recover their sense of well-being. After Glastonbury Thorn Day we begin to turn the other way, returning to the regular routines and more hectic schedules of daily life.

Many people have to go back to work on 26 December, if not on Glastonbury Thorn Day. Whenever you do go back to work, make every attempt to carry the positive fruits of your Yuletide experiences with you. Try to preserve the Spirit of Yule at your place of work or at school as long as it seems plausible. The Fires of Yule are elusive, however, and the presence that was so real on the 25th may seem to evaporate once we leave the quiet stillness and solace of the hearth. You must therefore seek runes of continuity as the Light of Yule's inspirations and visions fade away.

The Keltelven Calendar as a whole is structured so as to help us *internalize* the Fires of Yule. As we path through the Thirteen Dayes we are led to meditate on the most powerful symbols and icons of the Season, thereby internalizing the secrets and mysteries of the Winter Solstice. Now we must realize *outwardly* what has taken place *inwardly*. Each year, as we leave the place where Yule has been kept we should pray to become a lantern of authentic Pagan Light in the thick of the world. The Fires of Yule can be carried within us, and we can use them to cast sparks in the world where we work and play.

At dawn on this first day after Yule, go to the hearth or the Nativity scene. Kneel there and say the following invocation:

200

Hail Cernunnos, Stag of the Woods_
Come to us, we pray You!
Inspire our Hearts with Faith
and an adventurous love of life;
Lead us and we will follow You_
through the Wildwoods and to the Heaths
where the haunted ones of the Sídhe
worship in the Dark Night
of Mystery's Embrace! Amen.

The Stag of the Woods is known in the shining shadowy Light of Yule as **the Gifting Stag;** a mystical animal whose antlers symbolize all of the innate powers of the Winter Solstice Season. On this day we seek to be "horned like the Gifting Stag" (<u>Yuletide Grimoire</u>, 1898). By invoking the Stag's ever-potent presence we are aspiring toward a recognition of the Presence of Mystery in our daily rounds during the sacred time immediately following the Thirteen Dayes of Yule.

The myth of the Gifting Stag arose out of the old intuition that Cernunnos is the guide of those devoted to Wisdom. Thus he came to be seen as leading pilgrims to Glastonbury Tor on Matrum Noctem. He is the Stag we envisage on the eve of Glastonbury Thorn Day, eyes shining and antlers flailing in the last light of dusk near the Tor.

Some stories intimate that he has been manifest in the Yule Tree – symbolic of the Glastonbury Thorn – ever since the 14th of December. After leading us to the Tor, he enters the Cave of the Nativity and is one of the animals at the Nativity during the Vigil of Expectant Repose. Then, on the 25th of December, he may appear to devout seekers in the form of a great white or gray Stag, inspiring meaningful interpretations of Commonweal in their hearts when they meditate.

The Gifting Stag shows us hints of ways to put into practice the insight we have gleaned from pathing wisdom in and through the Thirteen Dayes. He has been known to inspire practitioners of the Yule to give away what they've received on the 25th of December, distributing their gifts among those who are less fortunate than themselves. He has inspired others to simplify their lives and receive the Illumination of Pine Wisdom, which is a kind of 'gift' of lunar insight connected with Winter's Solstice.

During the days after the Yule this strange Stag may be glimpsed here and there as we return to work and school. The Gifting Stag is a symbol of the Fires of Yule extending their power beyond the Season. The inspiration we experience through imagining the presence of the Gifting Stag as being *with us* will help us render out all of those ideals that are implicit in the Keltelven Yule more tangibly, making of these ideals poetic guidelines for the illumination of daily living. The Gifting Stag is thus a "translator of our ideals into the kindling of practical ethics" (Yuletide Grimoire, 1898).

The Gifting Stag tarries near those homes where the hearth is burning bright with love, hope and joy. He may leap suddenly back into the Strangewood of the Othersídhe, however, if people too quickly extinguish the Fires of Yule in their hearts! Otherwise he may stay for as long we live in the light of the mystery of Yule. Ultimately – and rightly – though, people's sense of Yule's mystery *will* wane, at which point the Gifting Stag leaves us. This parting is inevitable, yet we can put it off for a week or two if we remain *waeccan*.

The Gifting Stag has usually departed by Epiphany (6 January), though there are stories that indicate that he may return on the Eve of Imbolg, (1 February) the Eve of Beltaine (1 May), the Eve of Lughnassadh (2 August) and at the Autumnal Equinox (22 September), visiting those who are keeping the ideals of the Yule alive throughout the year. Wherever the ideals of equality, justice, compassion and commonweal erupt as runes of new possibilities out of the mundane milieu in which we usually strive, the Gifting Stag appears to help mortals fan the embers of these ancient and worthwhile icons of our humanity. When we turn to the presence of Cernunnos as the Gifting Stag in such situations and invoke his help, we may well find ourselves becoming the facilitators of personal and social change, becoming ambassadors of Yuletide Spirit in the world.

On the 26th of December the Gifting Stag finally becomes manifest. We have long been hoping for spiritual rebirth and personal transformation. The Gifting Stag usually 'appears' to us in an imaginative vision or perhaps through a two-fold vision inspired by the actual sighting of a deer in the woods. He comes as a tangible spiritual symbol of our progress, and through envisioning him we should hope to come to a tangible expression of what we've gathered from the runes of Yule. Those who shun the keeping of Winter's Solstice will not see the Gifting Stag.

Throughout this day, anticipate seeing Cernunnos in this mystical disguise. The Gifting Stag might well become present in the sighting of an actual deer. If you live in the country you might see a deer standing near a wooded area or browsing along the edge of a field or road or you might see the Gifting Stag while out on a hike today.

If you don't live in the country, look for a picture of a Stag in a book and meditate on it as an icon. Take an image that represents to you what the Gifting Stag would look like and set it up on the Yule Table. If you dream of the deer, elaborate an edifying story from the details of this dream and then record the tale in a journal and/or share it with others. Stories that we are inspired or 'compelled' (by some inner impulse) to tell, reveal the heart of our coích anama (soul house) and its condition. Stories that we connect with reveal the inner workings of our experiences and tell us where we are.

Dreams of the Gifting Stag may follow one of several traditional scenarios, or they might reveal something totally new and as yet unheard of. One typical dream is of a pack of deer running through a snowy field, with a Great Stag in the lead. This Stag then comes to an open window in your house and blesses you for the coming year. The Gifting Stag may gift you with a small box. When opened, it is found to contain nothing but a golden or silvery dust, almost like sand. When you run your hands through the dust, though, everything you've experienced during the Yule becomes a reality in your own Cromlech[54] of Meath (i.e., another metaphor for your Inner Hearth)! If you dream this dream, meditate on the experiences of Yule today as the Spirit prompts your Earthen Heart with possibly new insights!

You might start the day by imagining the Gifting Stag standing outside your house, shimmering in the glow cast from windows, hooves cloaked in new-fallen snow. This is an iconic image, so it doesn't matter where you live; he still stands there in the cold snow, eyes glowing and mouth mumming ancient tunes of benevolence or prophetic intention. These tunes are often thought to be 'borrowed' from the Elves of Saint Nicholas and are thus of the style known to Celtic musicians and poets as the *Ceól Sídhe*; the Faery Music that haunts mortals into dreams of renewal, often drawing them across the Sídhe on adventures of self-understanding and transfiguration. This music, however, can also lead you away from *this life* into an otherworldly adventure from which you may not return; so you must remain mindful of yourself and your present life when you hear it! If you *hear* this music as you imagine a sighting of the Gifting Stag, be certain that you are being haunted by the Spirit and that the emissaries of the Divine – the Faeryfolk themselves – are seeking you out for purposes that will lead to transformation!

On the 26th of December the Gifting Stag waits near the portals of human dwelling in order to make sure that his mortal friends have all that they need before he departs. Some stories tell of him leaving a flagon of red wine on the Yule Table at dusk on White Poplar Day. If you find such an archaic container, invite everyone dwelling and keeping Yule with you to take a sip out of it before dusk today. Then set the container – part or wholly empty – on the hearthstones or by the Yule Tree. If you want, make a ritual meal of the wine, partaking of small sweet cakes or good home-baked bread along with the wine. Thus the body and blood of the Gifting Stag is symbolically partaken of by you and, thereby, a portion of the life-force and earthen power of the Stag himself becomes yours.[55]

Feel free to imagine the Gifting Stag as you like and make up stories about him. The only prerequisite of these tales is that they strike you as somehow meaningful in the shimmering glow of the residual Light of Yule. They may be humorous, tragic or playful, serious or lighthearted. The Stag is always close by, and his ears are open to our requests. He is ready to become the founder of our ongoing spiritual feast, if we will gift ourselves to him.

As we receive gifts on White Poplar Day, we should *become* gifts on the day after, giving of ourselves to others in service, humility and hospitality. If we tell genuine stories of the Gifting Stag, we will experience an inspiration to self-giving, having been loosed from some of the chains that have veiled our vision until now, keeping us chained to the rough and splintered fence-posts of selfishness. Our keeping of the Yule begins in a sumptuous yet innocent self-indulgence in the rich ambiance of hearth-fire, the glowing lights of trimmings and the illumination of old stories. As the Yule proceeds we must learn to give more and more of ourselves until we reach the threshold of the ideal of Commonweal on White Poplar Day. After this, it is up to us to rune out the Heart of the Spirit of Yule in our own lives. We begin this process of outward expression on the 26th of December.

This working out of the inward meaning of the Yule involves our ongoing meditation on the Nativity scene, which has long been a focal point of humanizing Pagan Wisdom. The Nativity scene will undergo two additions over the next twelve days, and then after Epiphany it will be vacated.

Sometime during the day add the figurines of **the shepherds** to your Nativity Scene. These figures represent the second set of seekers to arrive at the holy scene (Mary & Joseph being the first seekers to arrive). You may want to spend a little time in the morning or at eventide meditating on what it means for these rustic characters to visit the Nativity. Reflect on the biblical story of the Shepherds (Luke 2:8-20). How are they different from the Magi who will arrive on the 6th of January? How are they different from Joseph and Mary? How are they different from you? How are we all – as seekers – the same in our approach to the Nativity as a pagan Icon of Rebirth and Transformation?

As a general practice, keep the Nativity illuminated from 26 December until Epiphany (6 January). The diorama embodies and re-interprets all of the primary Pagan symbols of the Yule, and it transmutes what has happened to us during our pilgrimage this year into a polyvalent spiritual illustration that cannot be literalized and that cannot be turned into a justification for religious exclusivism (as no one who visited the Nativity in the biblical story were 'Christians.' Some were Jews and others – like the Magi – were Pagans).

Yet as we meditate on the Nativity during the twelve days after White Poplar Day, the Star in the heavens fades from view and the light of the incarnation (the event of a god taking on human flesh) dwindles away, becoming one with the ordinary background lighting of our mortality. As such the Nativity Scene is a viable focus for the post-Yule season, when the festive lights begin to be turned off and when the decorations begin to be taken down. All of our experience now comes to be understood in the context of the Nativity as a place of Pagan Rebirth.

While many of the trimmings may be left up for the next few days – even until Epiphany (6 January) – and while seasonal music may still be played or sung or listened to, the externals of the Season should now begin to be internalized. You've witnessed your world transfigured by trimmings, evergreens, candles and other symbols of Yule's wintry mystery long enough! It's now time to internalize the meaning of these trimmings. Begin by taking down and putting away all of your icons of Santa Claus and Saint Nicholas before dusk on 26 December, as his day has passed.

The Yuletide imagination moves on, now that the long-expected shift has taken place. Whereas, from 6 December until 25 December, we lived in a cumulative sense of anticipation, from 26 December until 6 January we partake in the fruit of our spiritual labors, enjoying whatever illumination and enlightenment we may have reaped, meditating on the renewal and awakening we may have experienced. Cultivate a sense that you've completed a journey; it's now time to relax. Sometimes we make great strides during the Yule, while in other years it may seem we've not gotten anywhere. Our situation in life and the things going on around us can leave us feeling like the Hearth of Yule is reduced to rubble. If so, we may yet find something of value by sifting through the ashes and broken bricks.

Anyone grieved by something that's happened during the Yule along with anyone who has become dissatisfied with how it has turned out for them, should voice their concerns to the Gifting Stag. Some people wish that their families kept Yule better, or that quarreling in the family and among friends & acquaintances could be lessened more from year to year. For some, gatherings with relatives have always been a chore more to be endured than enjoyed. For such people the Yuletide journey will be more of a quest for wellbeing than it is for others.

The better we prepare ourselves for the Yule, the more enabled we will be to accept whatever has been given us this time around. The fact that we live in this as yet un-awakened world, however, means that we will always – no matter how good Yule is kept – find ourselves challenged to dream of a better world still to come. Therefore, no matter what the Winter Solstice Season has been like, dream on!

Some people find it necessary to get away from all the decorations in the house and even from the glow of the Yulefire after it's all over, at least for an hour or two. Hiking is good medicine for the soul, as you may feel cooped-up after the luxuriance of White Poplar Day! For some people, the intensity of the place of dwelling – strewn with decorations and the vividly colored lights, the uplifting music and stories – may push them further into wakefulness than they are willing to go just yet. To get away, if only for an afternoon, is a good way to disarm spiritual tension and begin to reap the actual rewards of our Yuling.

At dusk on 26 December, the Gifting Stag leaves the place of mortal dwelling, returning to the Wildwoods of the Spirit. This is the ultimate symbol that the Winter Solstice is past and the Yule is over. The Gifting Stag will stay with us as long as we live in the aura and memory of Yule's Fires resourcing ourselves out of Santa Claus' sack of wonders. Yet at twilight or perhaps just after supper, you must imagine the Stag taking one last look at your place of dwelling, and then, turning on his hind legs, bounding off into a deep and haunted forest! There He will stay until Yule comes around on the Wheel of the Year once more.

Act this ritual out by going to a back porch or to a door or window that looks out across fields to a snow-covered wood – even if this scene is imagined – and watching the god depart. Describe the scene as you imagine it and then wave goodbye as the Stag bounds away. Reminisce about former years when you saw the Stag leaving, and remember to invite him back! If you forget to invite him back before he bounds out of sight, the <u>Yuletide</u> <u>Grimoire</u> (1898) says, you must "go after him – ever playfully – and let him know that you desire his return, waving your hands after him and saying, aloud and with a childlike spirit, 'We will miss you! Remember to come ye back again!' – or some such address."

This is the first formal end of the Season of Yule. By observing it ritually we can pass out through the back door of the Thirteen Dayes into more or less ordinary time once again. It's important to bring seasons of celebration to an end, with all of their holy significance, as this provides a sense of spiritual, emotional and aesthetic closure. Only then can we really get on with the routines of daily life! Sacred Seasons are 'times apart' when the powers of life are intensified and when the ordinary births extra-ordinary experiences and understandings. During such times, insight flows forth from unforeseen sources.

If we don't leave strangetime behind in a tangible way, anxiety may mount and frustration will supervene, allowing free-floating tensions to weigh us down. By imagining the presence of the Gifting Stag on 26 December, and then by bidding him farewell at dusk, everyone gets a tangible, symbolic signal that Yule has passed, and that it's now time to gather up the baggage of life and move on.

When you go to bed on 26 December, remember to pray the "Prayer to Christ our Stag," which is a Christ-centered version of the invocation you used in the morning:

> Hail Jesus, Stag of the Woods_
> Come to us, we pray You!
> Inspire our Hearts with Faith
> and an adventurous love of life;
>
> Lead us and we will follow You_
> through the Wildwoods and to the heaths_
> where the haunted ones of Earth & Spirit
> worship in the Dark Night
> of Mystery's Embrace!
> Amen.

This prayer reminds us that the Gifting Stag is still with us in spirit – even if he's not visibly present to our heart – and that it's only the festive Season of Yule that's passing. Pray this prayer (or the invocation of Cernunnos as the Gifting Stag) each day until the day called "the Hinterlands" (6 January). Strive to live in the aura that has been generated by the Fires of Yule this year each and every day as you return to work and your normal routines. By so doing, your keeping of Yule will continue to impact your life.

> **Natural Meditation**: Focus on the meaning of the visitation of the Gifting Stag. Meditate on the mystical character of the deer; their persona in myths, their mystery and power. Meditate on the myth of Cernunnos and the wisdom of encounters with the Ancient Stag of the Celtic Tuath.

> **Scriptural Meditation**: Focus on the visit of the shepherds to the manger (Luke 2:8-20). Imagine their astonishment when the Angel appears to them in the night. Chant the song of the heavenly host: "Glory to GOD in the Highest, and on Earth, peace among all people with whom GOD is

pleased!" Meditate on the arrival of the shepherds at the manger, and the reaction of Mary and Joseph to these visitors and their story.

The Runes of Saint Stephen (26 December)

"Let me tell you a tale, now, my child,
as we wait upon the goose_
for on this day of Good Saint Stephen,
we let our sins go loose!   1

Once upon a time, I tell you_
I was as wild as birds were free,
but then I learned to love another,
with the stalwartness of a tree!   2

I loved her long and wayward went
into the bowers of the sated saints!
I loved her hard and fell down spent,
upon the boards of lesser taints!   3

We ventured through long seasons gone
a-picnicking on lone beaches,
where we spent our youth's insurance
in taking off our breeches!   4

Child, now hear me, innocent twig –
I laugh not at your ponies of glee!
I chide you not for your many toys,
just let my confession fly free!   5

Here upon the Roods of Olde Saint Stephen,
I remember not with pain
the way we went lusting abroad
in terror of mortality's dogged stain!   6

Six times we wed ourselves anew
upon the Heaths of summers come and gone,
Nine times we conceived our love's child,
in barrows beneath the Christian lawn!   7

Ancient of Ways we went, to and fro_
chasing mirth 'til the angels did know
that we were children of sweetest Earth,
living life for all 'twas worth!   8

Hear me now, Child, don't you cry_
for I'm settled to this consignment!
I've lent you all these words, and now,
I'll make my designs and repent!   9

We wandered through this life unlearned,
tearing fortunes from the dirt!
Tethered to our souls were the powers
which we'd gathered in Life's skirt!   10

But now that Christmastide has passed,
you must know that our love was true;
for we've conceived and now've birthed you,
in the Runes of Saint Stephen, drawn anew!   11

We went away and returned, once & again,
in our love's long lusting_
'Til we found the gates of homesteading,
which took our souls to dusting!   12

All for you_ Child, all for you,
have we settled down at last,
and the sins, which we've long enjoyed,
are a worthy pence of our final repast!   13

Hear me now, child, the goose is cooked,
and we'll soon be gone to table_
So take my confessions, bury them deep,
within your flesh; as you are able!   14

We've gathered home and barn and fields
and now we've called you to us!
Flesh of flesh and bone of bone,
may you always be ever near us!   15

We've raised our hopes and settled down
within the vale of Stag and Bear_
we've given all we have left to sell
_so do not sneer, nor snitch on us!   16

You are the fruit of loins long spent,
and of the passages of love!
You are the child of Saint Stephen's Runes,
as innocent as God's own Dove!   17

Take my sins then, and bury them, please,
within your eyelids' folds_
cherubic are your consolations, child_
as balmy as Winter's marigolds!   18

I trust you smell the roasted bird,
and will forgive me now my leave_
these are my confessions on poor Saint Stephen's,
which time shall never hence retrieve!"   19
Amen.

D. The Hinterlands (6 January)

"The Elves who visit us at Christmas may seem to move in with us, but they're not really at home here. They *have* a home, back in the hinterlands of Ancient Dayes. At the end of the Twelve Dayes of Christmas, therefore, we must encourage the little rascals to get out of our closets and pantries and find their way back to the Hinterlands where they can dance the night away!" (99)

- Catharine Abbot
A Yuletide Handbook (1986)

"Like the Magi from the East, let us come to the Nativity one last time this day, seeking an epiphany of Christ our Teacher and Wildwood Guide." (343)

- Geoffrey Whittier
The Whittier Hearth (1992)

It's been eleven days since the formal departure of the Gifting Stag back into the wildwoods of the Mystic Earthen Imagination. During this time the embers of the Fires of Yule have been burning down and fading away, ebbing now to ash as the fire of the new solar year is kindled and increases in potency and virility day by day. The days are now getting perceptibly longer, while the nights are shortening. Winter's Solstice is past. Now comes the time for clearing away all of the outward signs and symbols of the festivity of the preceding month.

For some people, the celebration of Yule ends on 25 December and life returns to normal more or less immediately, while for others the vestiges of Yule's power and the resplendency of the Solstice Season persist through the twelve days from the 26th of December to Epiphany. Whether you experience an immediate departure from the Fires of Yule on the Day of the Gifting Stag or not until Twelfth Night (the Eve of 6

January), all of the outward evidence of the Winter Solstice Season must now be put away.

The runes of "Twelfth Night" may be found in the symbolism surrounding the numeral 12; which is the Keltelven number of the fruition of the manifest universe. It's a sign of completion and is connected with the Sun. Most all religions have some fundamental solar dimension. All of the great world religions (Judaism, Islam, Buddhism, Hinduism, Confucianism, Taoism and Christianity) are primarily solar in orientation. The number twelve recurs again and again in the history of religions and has come to be invested with auspicious oracular powers.

The lives of the founders of great secular as well as religious movements have often been linked with the mythology of the Sun. There were 12 sons of Jacob, who founded the 12 tribes of Israel. There were 12 princes of Ishmael, 12 Olympian deities, 12 priests of Osiris, 12 apostles of Jesus, 12 Knights of the Round Table, and many more such instances of the importance of the number twelve in the lore of religions and charismatic movements around the world. These twelves all correspond to the signs of the Zodiac with the Sun – the leader of the movement or religion – seated at the center of the circle.

A god or goddess born at Winter's Solstice (Christmas) was often believed in ancient mythologies to appear to people in some way on Twelfth Night. The Keltelven god Hesus becomes visible at dawn on the Twelfth Day after the Longest Night. MABON – whose name is an anagram for the divine family (MA = Mother, AB = Father, ON = Son) – visits his home and his descendants on the Twelfth Night after the Winter Solstice. These appearances can be thought of as "epiphanies" of deity; moments in which mortals glimpse the actual presence of the one they are worshipping. It's on this day that the Astrologers from the East glimpsed the presence of divine mystery in the infant Jesus. As this moment was deeply epiphanic for all involved, 6 January has long been called "Epiphany" in the Christian calendar.

As you get up this morning, ring the Solstice bell one last time to signify the clarity of vision that we expect on this last day of the Season. The bell is then put away in its box where it will stay for eleven months. The ringing of the bell stirs up the last embers of the Fires of Yule in the Hearth of the Heart of human dwelling. It awakens us to the imminent visit of the Magi-Astrologers, who will arrive from the East sometime during the day. As the Magi are coming to see the child Jesus, so we should turn our hearts and minds to the Nativity Scene and to the artifacts of our own rebirth one last time.

Going to breakfast, nurture a sense of closure in your heart. Greet others with the acclamation, "A blessed Epiphany to you!" – which either betrays our relief that the Season is finally over or else conveys an assurance that we are now, at last, blessed by what we've gone through in the previous month. To signify the solar significance of the day, use something gold-colored along with small samples of Frankincense and Myrrh to decorate the breakfast and meditation tables.

As twelve is a number of completion and consummation, this is the day when we look to experience the final epiphanic evidences of our Yuletide pilgrimage. Yule formally comes to a close only by reaching a degree of mystical fruition. Its power will now reside in our hearts for the next eleven months. We bring an end to the season formally by (1) taking down decorations and (2) saying good-bye to the Elves who have haunted us and our abode since the eve of Nicholas' feast. During these activities we anticipate possible epiphanies connected with our pathing of the Yuletide Mystery. We might well divine a peculiar gift of Wisdom in our Hearts today; one that will stimulate our minds and open our wills to the guiding presence of the Spirit in the Earth.

An **epiphany** is an "appearance," and in both Pagan & Christian traditions this word generally refers to an event that heightens human consciousness to the Presence of Mystery among us. An epiphany can result in a sudden gift of insight, or it may enhance our intuitions concerning the magical nature of the events and various symbols we've been meditating on for a month. It might also show us possible paths to take as we leave the environs of the Nativity behind and return to the ordinary world.

An epiphany may happen in a moment, yet it can lift a person out of ordinary consciousness into another realm. By meditating on the epiphanic impetus we can return to the luxury of a heightened state of mind for days or even weeks. An epiphany is unbidden and unexpected and cannot be generated much less predicted. Nevertheless, because of the logic inherent in the mysteries of Yule, we have come to anticipate epiphanies on 6 January, remaining open to whatever might transpire at the crosstroads.

As the Magi visit the manger in Bethlehem, so we now return to the Nativity scene, seeking enlightenment. For the Magi, seeing the divine child in the manger for the first time is an epiphanic moment. They give him valuable gifts, thus acknowledging what their astrological knowledge has shown them: that they are present at the birthplace of a divinely chosen Teacher of Wisdom. This is how Keltelvens see Jesus of Nazareth (not to mention Buddha, Mohammed, Sri Krishna, Confucius, and others). We don't treat him as some "one and only" sign of the God in the flesh, nor can we allow that he is even the 'best' embodiment of Divine Wisdom. Jesus represents universal Pagan wisdom.

To have an epiphany is to have a profound experience of "Oh, *now* I see!" It's an event overflowing with new awareness of truth. As pilgrims to the Hearth of the Fires of Yule, what we're seeking today is some glimmer of the truth of the events we have witnessed, meditatively and in daily experience, throughout the preceding four weeks. We're hoping to glean the meaning of both positive and negative experiences, just as the Magi were seeking to understand why they had come all that way across the fertile crescent from Persia in order to wonder at a newborn boy and offer him symbolic gifts. We're likewise hoping that some wise Pagan ranns will be intuited during our final visit to the Nativity scene today as we go about taking down the last of the trimmings.

Those who have kept the Winter Solstice should be alert to the possibility of mysterious encounters with Saints, Angels, and the Faeryfolk, in which our highest ideals and our own innate divinity may be discerned today. Read mythic stories, cast runes, pray a pagan version of the rosary, do tarot readings or simply meditate in a circle in front of the hearth or Yule Table. As the day passes, finish undecorating and prepare to say good-bye to the Elves, as they must return to their home in the Hinterlands before mid-night tonight.

If the Yule tree has remained healthy and has continued to give you joy, go and sit beside it one last time. Appreciate the colored lights and shiny ornaments before you begin to untrim it. If this is a school/work day, the children should bid farewell to the Evergreen Guest in the morning, as by suppertime it may well be untrimmed and ready to be carried out of doors. There should be some conscious and formal recognition that the Season is over. If the tree dried out and had to be taken down before 6 January, say your farewells to the Season at the Yule

Table, which is probably still decorated with some of the remnants of greenery and gutted candles from Matrum Noctem. If you used live pine boughs in your decorations, the fact that they have now gone dry and brittle is a sign that all things perish and pass-away in time. As the greenery dries up, so the Season of Yule passes, leaving mortals to carry on with their lives, having imbibed deeply of the powers of the Fires of Yule. The externals (candles, electric lights and other decorations) are now the décor of the hearth of our own internal hearts. Only in this sense can we keep Yule all year long! We have created an inner reality out of all the glitter and symbolism of Yule, and in this way the Spirit of Yule survives past 6 January *in us.*

Some people are never really ready to take the decorations down. If you're one of these people, this may perhaps be a sign that the spiritual work of the season is still not complete. As you take down the decorations *anyway*, meditate on what you need to do to be able to move on. Perhaps you were too engrossed in worldly responsibilities, things happening at your workplace or else otherwise distracted to get the full benefit out of the Season while it was happening. Now is the time to reclaim what you have lost, dedicating yourself to enjoying whatever embers of the Yulefire still burn in the Hearth of your own Heart. Just as there is no way to prevent the Winter Solstice from arriving, so there's no way to 'make it stay' longer than its due season. By the day after 6 January, you will have returned to ordinary time. You must take with you whatever memories of the Fires of Yule are now within you.

The act of undecorating is symbolic of chasing all of the reticent spirits of the Season back into the **Hinterlands**, where they will remain until the Feast of Nicholas next December! Egbert Whittier said in The Thirteen Dayes of Yule (1800) that:

> "The Hinterlands are a place behind the real world where Elves, Faeryfolk, Dwarves and all other helpful and nastie spirits do reside, from time to time in holy tines. From thence do they plan their revels and benevolences toward humanity!" (183)

For the last month, the Christmas Elves have virtually had the rule of the house. They came from the North Pole on 6 December during the first of

Nicholas' visits. They have inspired us and teased our imaginations toward an appreciation of the mysteries of the Yuletide, and they have stirred our hearts to random acts of benevolence and disciplined goodwill. They have played, danced, and schemed magical acts of kindness with you and your family or housemates as accomplices for a month now. They have intimidated those who were reluctant to celebrate the Yule, teasing unwilling Hearts to open up and approach the Cave of the Nativity. They have put on imaginative plays of the Heart for those entering into the glow of the Yuletide Hearth. Now, at last, they must return home. On this day they know that their reign among us is over. They are, at least for the most part, ready to return whence they came.

When you think you've finally gotten all of the trimmings down, make a search of your place of dwelling, from top to bottom, looking for any remaining tinsel, ornaments or other evidences of the Yule. Pack away renegade holiday toys and Yuletide icons. There's usually one ornament or strand of tinsel left somewhere, and if you can find it before mid-night, so much the better.

During this search someone may playfully declare "I've found an Elf!" Such an announcement usually rouses everyone to vigilance! This "Elf" is seeking to remain *with* you, stowing away for the whole year. It must be *chased out*, both playfully and deliberately, in order that some mischief may not befall those living in the house. Keltelven lore says that the woman in charge of the keys of the house must fetch a broom and then go find the Elf. Upon seeing it, she declares:

"There you are! What in the world are you still doing here?! Get on with you! Get thee back to the hinterlands – now! – before I am forced to take this broom to you!"

She then pretends to chase the laggard out, running down hallways, into and out of bedrooms, and making riot of the event! The Elf must be chased out for your own good! You should bid it a fond farewell, however, and, at the last moment before it scampers off over the horizon – perhaps at a fence behind your place of dwelling – remember to invite it back! Without the presence of the Elves, Yule would be a much less magical and mysterious time. We need them, but they *cannot* stay all year long!

This ritual can be a lot of fun, especially if one of the more elfish children wants to play the part of the stow-away. Let the child get into the role by dressing up like an Elf while others are taking down the trimmings, and then hiding somewhere – in a closet or under a bed, perhaps – where they will be 'discovered' during the last search for decorations. When found, the elfish-impostor will try to lead his or her pursuers all over the house, if possible, before heading for a door and fleeing out of the house!

Once the chase is on, younger children may cheer for the Elf, hoping that it will stay. Adults must be sure, however, that the Elf is chased out and sent back to the Hinterlands. When the Elven imitator comes back in, they should be rewarded with milk & cookies, as this is a favorite food of all Elves! Thus you will never quite know for sure if *all* the Elves have fled or not, as one *may* have come back into the house in the guise of this child who played the part of the Elf who was chased out!

Shortly after dusk, enact the arrival of the Magi at the manger. Set out the figurines of the Magi at the Nativity scene, and then reflect on their story for a while. They have come with royal gifts to bestow on Jesus: Gold, Frankincense and Myrrh (Matthew 2:1:12). The Magi – like the shepherds before them – had an epiphanic moment when they finally saw the newborn infant lying in the manger. Joseph & Mary were then lifted into prophetic consciousness by hearing the tale these travelers told of their journey, the astrological sign (the star) in the sky that they followed, and their encounter with King Herod, who represents all those forces in the world that seek to suppress wisdom.[56]

Imagine the impact of this visit on Mary & Joseph. It's apparent from their own account that these foreigners are Persian astrologers. Most likely they are also practitioners of ceremonial magick. Given the social and political context, their tale of an encounter with Herod would probably have put the parents of Jesus on guard, especially when they recognized that the Magi described their newborn son as a king (Matthew 2:2). This recognition would have deadly political repercussions.

The Nativity may be left set up for a week and a day after the rest of the trimmings have been taken down. This scene becomes the focus of ongoing meditations on the mysteries of our own rebirth during the Winter Solstice Season. Remove the figures of the Magi in a couple of days, as they must have embarked on their return journey back to their own land rather quickly, having been warned in a dream not to go back to Herod.

The brevity of the Magi's stay is indicative of the danger that pursued the holy family after the birth of Jesus. Joseph and Mary then fled to Egypt to escape persecution. Therefore, remove the figures of Mary, Joseph and the Infant a couple days or so after removing the figures of the Magi. By the time you take down the Nativity scene, all human characters will be gone.

For one last meditation of the Season, imagine – before you go to sleep – all of the Elves of Yule reaching the Hinterlands. There they are dancing around their fires, carousing, and singing mystical jigs and reels. This is the traditional **Dance of the Elves**. Go to sleep with this image in mind, bidding final farewell to the last embers of the Winter Solstice Season and preparing yourself to enter into the Winterwood Season that will last until the Vernal Equinox (20 March). Amen.

Endnotes

[1] *Remember* that in this book, you are listening to characters and traditions from the world where Ross County is real. *That* is the world in which the Keltelven Traditions exist. These endnotes are – more often than not – expressed in the terms that characters in Ross County – especially Cornelius Whitsel and others – would use for grounding, defining and defending the Keltelven Traditions. However I do – as when I teach the Thirteen Dayes of Yule – refer to other *actually published texts in our world* to show how the Keltelven Traditions are actually linked back into Celtic or Euro-Pagan traditions. Reading The Fires of Yule you are engaged with a fictional world!

Though there is no certain or 'positive' proof of surviving ancient Pagan traditions in the Middle Ages, there are hints here and there. Ward Rutherford, in Celtic Lore (1993; pp. 131, 132), discusses whether druidism may or may not have survived under edict when the Romans made druidism 'illegal' in Gaul. He mentions how druids may have passed as bards at the beginning of the Middle Ages in order to avoid scrutiny and how the bards thereby came into possession of what seems like druidic teaching. Other scholars – include Peter Berresford Ellis and Jean Markale – have also hinted at the possibility of the survival of ancient pagan traditions.

[2] There are many books that have sections in them dealing with the "Wheel of the Year." You might check out Starhawk's The Spiral Dance (1989; ch. entitled "Wheel of the Year"), A. & B. Rees Celtic Heritage (1966; pp. 83-94), John King's The Celtic Druids' Year: Seasonal Festivals of the Ancient Celts (Blandford, 1995), and Caitlín Matthews' A Celtic Book of Days (Inner Traditions, 1998), as well as relevant entries in Nigel Pennick's The Pagan Book of Days (Destiny Books, 1992).

[3] **Cernunnos** – The Stag God of the Continental Celts. He often appeared to people in the form of a huge Stag with thirteen points on his rack. As such he often stood thirteen feet high at the crown of his head. He was

sometimes seen as an albino with red eyes, though an ordinary looking Stag might just as well turn out to be Cernunnos. The Stag Hunt – in which mortals go out tracking and following Cernunnos wherever he may lead – was a common story in Celtic folklore. On Cernunnos, see Gerhard Herm's The Celts (1975; pp. 124-125, 130 and 157), Peter B. Ellis' The Druids, (1994; p. 123), Cowan's Fire in the Head (1993; pp. 116-121) and Miranda Green's The Gods of the Celts (1986; pp. 182-184).

[4] **Bran the Blessed** – A Celtic sea-god who became one of the early heroes of Welsh mythology. He was considered 'blessed' because he was of a gentle heart and practiced the runes of hospitality with deep sincerity. Bran died in battle, after which he ordered his warriors to behead him and carry the head to London, where they were to bury it facing out to sea. They did so, and along the way the head prophesied. The buried head was said to protect Britain from invasion until Arthur dug it up. As a dying-hero, Bran's story is often seen to prefigure that of Christ, who also gave his life for his people.

[5] **Cú Chulainn** is the central character in the myth of the Irish Ulster Cycle. He is the greatest hero in all of Irish literature. He is one of the three great heroes of early Ireland. He is the child of a human mother and a divine father. There are at least two stories of his birth, in one of which he is the son of the god Lugh and a human mother named Dechtire. Many of his feats during life indicate that he was not merely human.

[6] see John Matthews' The Winter Solstice: The Sacred Traditions of Christmas (Quest Books, 1998) for an excellent survey of traditions surrounding the Winter Solstice in many cultures.

[7] I first read about this in Hans Kung's On Being a Christian (1976; pp. 436-437). Many books on comparative religion will make similar observations about gods of light and their connection with the Winter Solstice. In the Celtic world it was the god Mabon who was born on Alban Arthuan.

Part I:

221

[8] **Sídhe** – A name for the stone barrows and long-burial mounds that are found in Britain, Ireland, Wales and Scotland, it is a term from the ancient Celtic world carrying a multitude of meanings. Sídhe (pronounced "Shay" or "Shee" and sometimes like "Side") were thought of as crossroads between this world and the Otherworld. Celts saw them as mystical "way-stations" for the souls of the departed, and thus they were treated as permanently haunted! Sídhe may also refer to the Faeryfolk. Though the word is pronounced like "shay" in some Celtic tongues, Keltelven practitioners tend to pronounce it "side." Thus all kinds of metaphors are possible, such as "Over the Sídhe and Far Away," which is a paradoxical way of speaking about the nearness of those who've died and crossed✜over into the Aether.

[9] **Otherworld** – The "Land beyond Death." The "Land on the Otherside." The "Land of Youth." Refers to the place where the souls of the dead go to continue life's quest. Celts believe that life is a gift and that death is a door that leads one to another stage of life in the Aether.

[10] **Shunnache** – An Old Faery name for the most basic energy underlying all life and presence. Out of it comes the biological life-force and all physical energies, such as electricity and radiation. It is the "energy" tapped into by the practice of draíocht (magick).

[11] **Dolmens** – pre-Celtic stone structures consisting of three standing stones across which a large flat stone has been placed. The larger ones are uncanny "shelters" where those passing by can get out of the rain, snow or hot sun, and which have long been associated with spirits, haunting, and visitations from angels, saints and the Divine TRIBANN. It used to be thought that the smaller dolmens were "druidic altars," but this view has been rejected. Archaeology suggests that they were originally places where the leaders of tribes were buried. The body was placed within the dolmen, and earth was heaped up over it. Over the millennia the earth washed away, leaving only the mysterious standing stones. The Celts thought of Dolmens as places where the living were often encountered by the discarnate souls of heroes, saints and animal-guides. They became potent places for meditation, sojourning and vigils.

[12] On the role of women in Celtic society, see Jean Markale's <u>Women of the Celts</u> (1972), Mary Condren's excellent study <u>The Serpent and the Goddess: Religion and Power in Celtic Ireland</u> (1989), Moyra Caldecott's <u>Women in Celtic Myth: Tales of Extraordinary Women from the Ancient Celtic Tradition</u> (London: Arrow, Book, 1988; Rochester, VT: Destiny Books, 1992; 1988),and Lisa Bitel's <u>Land of Women: Tales of Sex and Gender from Early Ireland</u> (Ithaca: Cornell University Press, 1996)

[13] For a discussion of the Celtic reverence for Nature, see Bamford & Marsh <u>Celtic Christianity: Ecology and Holiness</u> (1987; especially pages 12-13, 19, 21, etc.). For a Celtic spiritual philosophy of Nature as a sacred landscape, see Nigel Pennick's <u>Celtic Sacred Landscapes</u> (Thames & Hudson, 1996).

[14] Celtic society – being tribal and pastoral-agrarian – had a low level of social stratification and inequality. Like many other tribal societies, there wasn't much of a socioeconomic difference between the farmers and the chieftains, though the Celtic world was not 'egalitarian.' For some clues as to the Celtic ideal of justice and social equality see Jean Markale <u>Merlin: Priest of Nature</u> (1995; p. 40) and Peter Berresford Ellis <u>The Druids</u> (1994, pp. 20, 141, 169).

On the radical nature of Celtic society and spirituality, see Jean Markale's excellent study <u>Women of the Celts</u> (1972; esp. pages 21-40). There he describes the absolute threat that the druidic vision of social and political order posed to Roman patriarchy (p. 15). See also relevant excerpts from Monica Sjoo & Barbara Mor's <u>The Great Cosmic Mother</u> (Harper & Row, 1987; pp. 258-259) and Marie-Louise Sjoestedt's <u>Gods and Heroes of the Celts</u> (1982); this latter text explores the balance of male and female power in Celtic mythology. She argues that the early Celtic worldview was actually matrifocal and was only later assimilated to patriarchal patterns.

[15] **Gwrach** – A Keltelven wisewoman, the equivalent and complement of a druid, whose equal she is. The term comes from the Old Welsh and later referred to any old craefty, uncanny woman of deep experience and reputed wisdom, though she was described as 'weird' in her ways.

[16] The story of Cú Chulainn can be found in many texts. See Cross, T. P. & C. H. Slover, eds. Ancient Irish Tales (New York: Barnes & Noble; 1996; originally Henry Holt and Company, Inc., 1936; pp. 134-136), Lady Gregory's Cúchulainn of Luirthemne: The Story of the Men of the Red Branch of Ulster (Gerrard's Cross: Colin Smythe, 1970) and Eleanor Hull's The Cuchullin Saga in Irish Literature (London: David Nutt, 1898; Dublin: M. H. Gill & Son, 1923) for classic treatments.

[17] Matthew 2:7-12
[18] Luke 2:33-38
[19] Luke 2:4-5
[20] Luke 2:8-20
[21] On "thin places," see Edward Sellner's Wisdom of the Celtic Saints (1993, p 11).

[22] Obviously this tale has evolved rather recently in Keltelven Circles, as the stories of the Reindeer of Santa Claus comes from Clement Clark Moore's "A Visit from Saint Nicholas" (1822) and the 9th Reindeer is obviously Rudolf, who was first imagined by Robert L. May – an employee of the Montgomery Ward department store – who wrote an inspired story-poem called *Rudolf the Red-Nosed Reindeer* in 1939 and distributed it to the children of his customers.

The Legend of Nicholas as I now tell it incorporates all of the major popular elements of the story of Santa Claus as well as lesser known elements of the Nicholas hagiography. Being a storyteller with a very Celtic sense of reality, I am able to move back and forth quite freely between history and myth, as what is *really* important in a spiritual narrative is whether it tells us something 'true' about life, not whether it corresponds literally to 'something that *actually* happened.'

[23] **The Daghda** – the "All-Father" of the Tuatha Dé Danann, the gods and goddesses of Ireland who were the "children" of the Goddess Danu.

[24] The Yuletide Grimoire (1898) is not published, nor is it known to exist any more on this side of the Sídhe. The quotes from it cited in the present

text come from imaginative interaction with Cornelius Whitsel and through psychic dictation given by my Keltelven spirit guides; Alcuin Englewood and Marion of Stonehenge.

[25] There are thousands of Celtic saints mentioned in literature and in place-names through the Celtic countries. Though Deirdre's story is typical of many saints, I have never found her mentioned outside of the imagined world of Ross County where Keltelven spirituality is practiced.

[26] **Samhain** – The "Night of the Dead," 31 October, when the Sídhe open up. A time for respecting and remembering the dead as well as meeting with the souls of people and animals you have known in this life. As such it is a haunted night between the old year (which ends at dusk on 31 October) and the beginning of a New Year (which commences at dawn on 1 November). It is a time for practicing forgiveness, reconciliation and repentance, and praying for a "new start" or a personal transfiguration.

[27] **Aether** – A Keltelven name for the Otherworld; the place where those who have discarnated work, play and adventure, learning more and more, until they either come back into the vales of mortal incarnation or go on to Paradise of the "Isles of the Blest." Keltelven mysticism knows of no place called "heaven" where life stops and people sit around in the dull cacophony of endless silence for all eternity, listening to angels play blithe, spineless music. If Heaven is where 'GOD' is, then – so reason the Keltelven Druids and Gwrach – Heaven is everywhere, except that we don't see it, being lost in waking-slumbers. When we begin to awaken spiritually – following Christ or in some Old Pagan Way – we begin to become aware that 'Goddess' is here, and therefore that Heaven is everywhere. This world (of incarnate mortals) as well as the Otherworld (where we go after we die) are both encompassed within the mysterious Presence of 'GOD' who is Here, There and Everywhere.

[28] For the use of Cedar in the Jewish Temple in Jerusalem, see I Kings 5:6-10, 9:11, and 2 Chronicles 2:3. For its symbolic meaning in Biblical mythos, see Ezekiel 31 and Psalm 92:12, wherein it is connected with divine power and natural strength.

[29] The ancient Celts were fascinated with triads, and many of their deities were triple; three characters linked together, their three-fold name alluding to the Mystery beyond the naming itself. I imagine Keltelvens in Ross County honoring the Mystery by naming it ANU—DANU—TAILTIU – where ANU is the name of the Goddess of Cosmic Horizons and Primeval Origins, DANU is the Goddess of Rivers and water in general, and where TAILTIU is the Goddess of Earth.

The TRIBANN is a non-personal mystical Keltelven name for the Mystery meaning "THREE RAYS." The name was later adopted as an epigram for the Trinity by Celtic followers of Christ. The word refers to a mystical encounter in which three rays of light fall from the heavens onto the earth either marking a destination or surrounding the seeker.

[30] **Ceugant**—This is the realm in the tops of the tree of being-becoming – the place of twigs and leaves – that could never support the weight of our bodies but which surrounds us and is yet within the cosmos, while being the place of immanent transcendence. We dwell in this tree – which is Earth infused with Spirit (it is *not* 'beyond' the cosmos) – and it is *in this tree* that we find our way into the meaning of the deepest Runes of Mystery that we – as human becomings – are able to comprehend.

[31] **Annwn**— the unseen roots of the World Tree and also of the Cosmic Tree of Life. These roots lie beneath Abred and also correspond to the unconscious realm of the psyche. Annwn is the realm of primal matter and energy; the Abyss out of which all true magic and mystical enlightenment are both sourced. It is out of Annwn that we may consciously draw up primal psychic and spiritual sustenance. Annwn is also the "underworld" in Bardic Philosophy, a place where the more frightening beings of the cosmos dwell; demons, furies, wraiths of self-forgetfulness, etc. When we settle down in anal-duccaid (meditation), entering the Cromlech of Meath, Annwn becomes accessible to us.

[32] **Gwynnyd**— the 'location' in the tree of the self (i.e., also the cosmic tree of the Bard Llewellyn Sion's 16th century cosmology) to which we are sometimes lifted up out of Abred and where enlightenment and illumination become possible. This level corresponds to the first levels of

vision in traditional Christian mystical praxis (such as that outlined by Teresa of Avila in her autobiography). We meditate and pray in Abred and then – when moved by Spirit – our minds are elevated to an inspired state where we are still "in the body" and yet where we are traveling beyond it's limitations.

[33] **Abred**—the place of ordinary consciousness and ordinary daily life. The lower trunk of the Tree of Life. The place where – when we center down in meditation and prayer – we find ourselves in the Cromlech of Meath; our own Internal Nemeton. Within the Cromlech of Meath we enter inward to find the Runes of Mystery. Here – if we are graced with an Invitation to the Hero's Table – we come to dwell at **Uisnech.** This is an indescribable, unnamable place within the Dolmen of the self; the ultimate Centre – the Non-Place where we cannot arrive by our own effort, but where the Mystery we call "God" or "Goddess" may call us to dwell deep in our-selves for a time/moment. Once in Abred, we are in the place of earthen power.

[34] **Waeccan** – An Anglo-Saxon word meaning "to be awake" or to "wake up." Keltelvens use the word to name that state of consciousness we are hoping to nurture by seeking Wisdom in the midst of life. To be "waeccan" is to be alert to (1) the way the world is around us, (2) the presence of 'GOD' in Nature, and (3) the ways in which people distort their own consciousness of reality. Those who are not "waeccan" are "slumbering in the sleep of ordinary consciousness."

[35] **Draíocht**—One of the three primary Keltelven Arts referring to what we would now called "magick" (in both the simple and the ritual sense). The term comes from the Irish Gaelic and refers – in common usage – to the magic associated with Druids. Keltelvens, however, use it to mean "the use of powers to effect ends." Spell-casting, the use of evocations and invocations, the practice of chanting, circle dancing (to effect a particular end) and other arts are all a part of draíocht.

[36] **Taghairm**—A word from the Irish Gaelic that in Keltelven usage refers to a primary art of the wise; that of 'determining the nature of things.' The word is related to an Old Irish word *toghairm*, which referred to what we

would call an act of "incantation." In its etymology the word carries intimations of mystic sleep or "the summoning of spirits." This refers to the art of sleeping on an earthen mound in order to discover some truth. As such the word has come into Keltelven use as a general word for divination. It involves the use of oracles or the interpretation of natural events in an attempt to figure out "what's going on" and "what a mortal should do." It also has to do with discerning one's way. Runes, Tarot cards, astrology, and scrying in a crystal or in the face of a pool of water are all methods used in Keltelven Taghairm.

[37] **Corrguine**—A word from the Irish Gaelic usually meaning a general form of magick but which Keltelvens have adopted to refer to "herbal magic" and in general "herbal arts and craefts." A primary art of the wise (along with Taghairm and Draíocht), Corrguine is usually defined as meaning "the use of natural substances to effect ends." The symbol of those who are proficient in the arts & craefts of Corrguine is the Heron.

[38] **Faery Light** – The light that emanates from Faery-haunted places and that signifies the presence of wise spirits in the woods as well as places where wisdom may be sought by mortals. Faery Light is said to 'glow incandescently' all around us in holy or enchanted seasons of Earth & Spirit, though it cannot usually be seen except by those whose senses have opened to the invisible reality behind the surfaces we normally perceive. Sitting in a dark room with just three small candles burning is said by some to be a Faery ritual for opening the senses to the invisible.

[39] This is not a grammatical mistake; I intended to say it this way, as Keltelvens always assume that some of those gathered near their hearth at Winter's Solstice may be on the Otherside. Keltelven metaphysics also assumes that the dead can still see physical objects when they're on this side of the Sídhe and can even read books.

[40] For one discussion of Celtic storytelling see Alwyn & Brinkley Rees Celtic Heritage (1961; pp. 11-25, 207-212).

[41] When I refer to 'our grandparents' generation' I realize that this is a relative term. My own grandparents were born in the late 19th century and

lived until the 1960's. My parents have often spoken of storytelling sessions held on the front porch of their respective homes in the summer and around the hearth or the wood-burning stove in the winter months, at get-togethers usually also involving music played by anyone who brought an instrument. For the younger students I've had since 1990, the generation that participated in storytelling as a regular pastime was that of their great-grandparents or even their great-great grandparents'.

[42] A **Grimoire** is a book of secrets, traditional lore and magical practices. It is usually kept by the adepts of a tradition and is used to teach advanced arts & craefts.

[43] **Shunnache** – see note 10, above.
[44] **Nemeton** – A sacred earth-place. It radiates Earth-power and is a place where Earth-peace becomes possible. Saints and Pagans have used nemetons as 'destinations' for pilgrimage and have meditated and prayed within the aural bounds of certain favorite nemetons. No structures may be built at a nemeton, as it should be left in its natural state. Its "power" may wax and wane during different times of the year, and it may cease to radiate earth-power from time to time.

[45] **Groves** – Circles of sacred trees wherein an open green was tended. Here the Druids traditionally met for worship and seasonal celebrations in pre-Christina times.

[46] **Cauldron** – A vessel in which to cook food, make medicinal concoctions or prepare sacrifices (especially sacrificial food). They were also used in rituals of divination. There are many Cauldrons in Celtic lore, most notable among which are (1) the cauldron of Ceridwen, (2) the Cauldron of the Daghda, and (3) the Cauldron of the People of Partholon. Drinking from a cauldron could bring a person to the precipice of divine or psychic sight or induce a transformation.

[47] **The Aether** – A Keltelven name for the Otherworld; the place where those who have discarnated work, play and adventure, learning more and more, until they either come back into the vales of mortal incarnation by way of the Tales of the Blest or go on to Paradise.

[48] "Three Rays" refers to the primary Keltelven metaphor for the Divine Mystery – i.e., the **TRIBANN** – a mystical name meaning "Three Rays." The word refers to a mystical encounter, in which three rays of light fall from the heavens onto the earth, either marking a destination or surrounding the seeker, bringing their journey to a standstill, rendering them fecund of mystic wonder. The name was later adopted as an epigram for the Trinity by Keltelven followers of Christ.

[49] While when I first wrote this I took the expression "cast the runes of guidance" to be metaphorical, it could also be taken to refer to the method of taghairm in which we use stones engraved with the Norse or Anglo-Saxon Runes to discern our path and help us navigate through difficult times. A Rune is a "symbolic letter" that carries a deep meaning. "To rune" is to seek out the mystery of life. "Runing" is the actual process of seeking & interpreting life, which unveils Mystery in our midst; in the very traces of our experiences.

[50] The basic texts of these stories are to be found in the first two chapters of the Gospel of Matthew and the first two chapters of the Gospel of Luke in the New Testament of the Bible.

[51] These would include the birth of Cú Chulainn and Mabon as well as the births of several of the more or less well-known Celtic saints, who were often born under unusual circumstances. In many ways you will find that the Celtic saints – especially those who are said to have lived in the 4th through the 6th centuries – were attributed with the same or similar aspects as the gods and goddesses whom their cult was to replace in local religious culture.

[52] On the use of 'Christian' hymns: Remember that many of the themes of the Christian celebration of Christmas were drawn from Paganism to begin with and that these are often still imbedded in the folk expressions of Christian faith; and this includes hymns and carols. What we need to avoid when using Christian sources is falling into the *exclusive* nature of many of the claims that are made about Jesus by Christians; i.e., that he is the *only* Son of God and that the 'God' of whom he is the *only* Son is the

only true God. When singing carols we should hear these assertions as reflections of the enthusiasm of Christians and not as absolute claims.

[53] **Spirit Guides**—The ancient Celts were a traditional, tribal people, and as such were very much in-touch with their ancestors. A person's family tree was their way of understanding how they were related with other people in the tuath (i.e., "tribe"). Druids and Gwrach (wise-women), Bards and warriors all derived personal power and authority as well as wisdom from communion with their ancestors. The wise ones – including the later Celtic saints – often had contact with particular ancestors who came to them from across the Sídhe and who functioned as mentors or *anamchara* (soul-friends) in life.

[54] **Cromlech** – A circle of stones surrounding a Dolmen (see endnote 11). The "Cromlech of Meath" is a Keltelven metaphor for the "sacred space" at the existential center of our being; what in other spiritual traditions is called "the Heart" or "the Center." The Keltelven mystics of Ross County journey 'down' in meditation to this Inner Cromlech. There they find empowerment, traces of the Divine Mystery and the spoor of the Stag who reveals Wisdom to us in strange and often obscure runes.

[55] Though Christians use bread and wine in their ritual of worship as symbols of Christ's body and blood, wine and bread have been used in various religious traditions – even in certain Neo-Pagan circles and in Goddess spirituality – as symbols of the Divine Presence. The Bread and Wine ritual outlined here is not meant, therefore, to be a token of Christianity but rather is intended as a reclaiming of ancient symbols in a Pagan context.

[56] **King Herod** was a puppet ruler; a Jew put on the throne of Judea by the Romans and as such is often seen as a traitor to his own people. He was desperate to maintain control and reap the 'advantages' of his office. He is deeply threatened by the message of the Magi, who tell him that a *real* king – a Son of God – has been born in his country.

Because of the prophecies that a Messiah would come to liberate Judea from foreign control, Herod according to the Gospel of Matthew has all of the infants in his territory slaughtered, thus making sure that this newborn god-child is destroyed.

Glossary of Keltelven Terms and Yuletide Symbols

This glossary contains terms linked to the Keltelven Season of Yule that have been used in this book and that may not be found in ordinary dictionaries. It also lists the primary meanings of decorations and symbols prevalent in this Calendar of the Thirteen Dayes. Other general Keltelven words may be found defined in the Endnotes.

Acorns – Symbolic of wisdom in Celtic and other Euro-Pagan traditions, they represent the difficulty of digesting wise teachings. Acorns must be cooked long and well before their 'meat' can be eaten. In the same way we must prepare the Wisdom we receive by making it palatable to our spiritual digestion. When we become like the god or goddess whose path we are following, we no longer have to cook the Acorns of Wisdom in order to digest them.

Acorns have long been used in Yuletide decorations. They are strung on garlands and tied into wreaths. They may be placed in bowls on the Yule Table on the morning of White Poplar Day as a symbolic manifestation of the rebirth we have undergone during Matrum Noctem.

Alban Arthuan – An old druidical name for the Winter Solstice, now celebrated during the night between dusk on the 21st and dawn on the 22nd of December. It is the Ninth Night of Yule.

Angels – "Messengers of God" in Christian tradition who come to visit human beings for a variety of reasons. There are a number of angels traditionally associated with the birth of Jesus. Gabriel visited the Virgin Mary (Luke 1:26-28) and then her husband to be (Matthew 1:20), to announce the miraculous conception of their son. Angels appeared to the shepherds in the fields, telling them of the birth of Jesus (Luke 2:8-20). An Angel warned Joseph and Mary that they were in danger, and sent them fleeing to Egypt (Matthew 2:19-20).

Apples – A fruit sacred to the Triple Goddess ANU—DANU—TAILTIU. Apples are symbolic of Wisdom. The Apples of Paradise bring health and lead mystics to the next crossroads of their journey. If you want to find the Nativity of Rebirth in your heart, eat a red apple each day during Yule while meditating on the holy story of his birth. Eat an apple while meditating on the habits, faults and tendencies from which you want to be delivered. When you reach the core, extract the seeds and name each one after the root of one of your imperfections. Then dispose of the seeds by throwing them in a stream of flowing water.

Apples are also symbolic of the Presence of Mystery. Their fleshy red skin symbolizes blood and life. The watery white flesh of the apple symbolizes the nourishing nature of Wisdom. Apple seeds, being hidden within the core, are symbolic of Mystery's Source, which is revealed only to those who have received enlightenment in the Earth & Spirit.

Apples are among the most common gifts children in Ross County receive from Saint Nicholas. Apples as Christmas gifts represent the gift of life and health. They are also set out on the breakfast table on 25 December as icons of the rebirth we have experienced by that point.

Avalon – The mystical "Land of Apples" where Celtic priestesses were said to live in pre-Christian times. The area around Glastonbury Tor is the legendary location of the magical doorway leading over into Avalon. Keltelven traditions say that the Virgin Mary became an initiate in one of Avalon's order of priestesses after her arrival in England. Avalon remains a sacred Keltelven symbol of Paradise.

Balsam – A straight-growing evergreen tree with a 'conical' outline when freestanding. Their branches splay out in whorls from the trunk. The cones, which stand erect on the branches when mature, are composed of thin, closely packed scales. The tree can grow from

40 to 60 feet in height when mature. Its needles are fragrant and resinous.

To hold a small branch of Balsam Fir in your hands while meditating during the Yule is said to restore creative energies and connect you with the deep flowing power of the Spirit. A wild Balsam Fir found standing in a clearing in the woods is a place where the Elves may be found dancing on Winter Solstice Eve before beginning their night-long ministry with Nicholas. Seek out Balsam Fir groves in the woods as nemetons of inspiration and creative meditation.

Bayberry – A popular name for the Myrtle Wax tree; an evergreen that grows to about 4 to 12 feet in height. It has fragrant stems and branches on which berries grow. These berries are covered with a fragrant green or yellow substance called Bay Wax, Candleberry Wax or Bay Tallow, which is an edible, compound botanical fat.

Bayberry wax has been harvested in North America since early colonial times. Some American Indians used it in tonics. It has long been used in making candles. A bushel of berries yields about five pounds of wax, and these make richly aromatic candles. The bark is used in folk teas to aid internal healing. The Myrtle Wax tree grows primarily in North America.

Bay Leaves – Symbolic of strength, victory, and integrity. They are used in divination. They are thought to enhance clairvoyance. They are decocted in oil and put on salads as a way of blessing a guest's wish for Wisdom. They are used in spells of protection and in purification rites. They are linked with the Winter Solstice as a symbol of the victory of the Sun over darkness and death.

Bells – Bells have long been considered sacred instruments of invocation and blessing, annunciation and declaration. The sound of the bell clears the air of unwanted influences and spirits. Bells have long been used for purification in Christian liturgy. Keltelvens use bells to purify a place where prayer or magick is to be engaged in.

Mystics associate the ringing of a bell with an awareness of the Presence of Mystery.

1. Silver bells symbolize the intuitive powers and the clarity of inspirations. They are iconic of the festivity of Yule and are associated with the night flight of Santa Claus across the sky.
2. Gold bells are connected with rebirth, the coming of Wisdom's teachers and solar prophecy.
3. Brass Bells clarify the mind and the spirit.
4. Bronze Bells drive away evil spirits.

Bethlehem – A town near Jerusalem where Joseph and Mary went to keep the census that Christian texts say was imposed on the Jewish people at the time of Jesus' birth. The Hebrew word "Bethlehem" means "House of Bread." Bethlehem was the city of King David's birth. Joseph and Mary were unable to find a room at the "inn" in Bethlehem and were forced to spend the night outside in a "stable" which may have been in a small cave behind the "inn."

Bonfire – (a "Sun-fire") A large fire lit on each of the eight festivals of the Pagan year (Solstices, Equinoxes and also the Cross-Quarter Days). The bonfire symbolizes life's power, the spirit of the Earth and the presence of divine mysteries among us. It is kindled with seven sacred woods.

Brand – A piece of wood saved from the previous year's Winter Solstice fires and used to light the bonfire as well as logs in the hearth. The goddess Nerthus is considered to be the "keeper of the Brand."

Brighid – Goddess of Craeft, Art and Music and the "Mistress of the Hearth" in Keltelven myth. Along with Nerthus and Coventina she watches over and orchestrates Yuletide preparations and celebrations. She protects the Hearth and all those gathered around it. She encourages, uplifts and cultivates positive, humanizing lifestyles. She will not stand for any of her children to be harmed, and she protects anyone who petitions her for refuge.

Salt and milk are her symbols, along with the chalice, which may be filled with mead (a heavy beer) and raised in her honor. She despises vulgar drunkenness. To bring Ivy into the house was to seek her patronage. She plays a Celtic harp and wanders along the borders of the property to encircle it with protection.

She sometimes appears as a dairymaid and at other times as the Great Grandmother of a kin-group. She is imaged as a dark, statuesque woman of middle age, mature and strong, carrying her own mystical source within herself. At Yule She is often dressed in russet and faded green farming clothes, bearing a basket of vegetables and un-husked corn on her left arm. Ivy is draped across her shoulders, and an anklet of bronze bells may be seen hanging around her right ankle. These bells jingle as she walks, driving away evil spirits and negative influences from the place of dwelling! She is buxom and on her head is a crown with 4 towers symbolizing the 4 Sídhe (Falias = North, Murias = East, Finias = South, and Murias = West). Her eyes are dark blue (sometimes black), and her hair is usually red or reddish blond. Wherever she walks, peace and harmony follow!

Candles – A candlestick symbolizes the potency of divine power that is always being gifted to devout human beings in the Earth. Fire is related to spirit, breath and life. The lit candle represents a fire controlled by the human will and ingenuity. The candle flame symbolizes the soul while the wax symbolizes the body. Candles also symbolize the triple nature of the Goddess of Inspiration (Boann—Brighid—Ceridwen). The candle is composed of three parts (the wax, the wick and the flame) and if you take any one of these away, you no longer have a candle.

Used as Yuletide decorations, candles symbolize the presence of various helpful spirits among us. "Each candle is a spirit or soul" (<u>Yuletide Grimoire</u>, 1898). On the Christmas tree they represent stars in the heavens. Candles are put in windows to indicate that there is a spare room set aside for travelers. The light of the window candle guides guests to the house. We put candles in our windows on Matrum Noctem to guide Nicholas/Santa Claus to the house and also to illumine the house of our own souls in preparation for the rebirth we hope to experience.

Caroling – An old term referring to the singing of "carols"; i.e., songs sung about the mysteries of the Yule and Winter's Solstice. Originally caroling referred to a song sung to facilitate round- or circle-dancing. "To carol" was to dance in a circle.

Cedar – An evergreen often used as a Yule Tree. Cedar boughs are used for decking the halls and as swags on the doors of the house. Cedar chips are aromatic and symbolize protection and healing. The box in which the Magi brought gifts to Jesus was made of Cedar.

Cernunnos – God of the Wildwood. He often appeared in the form of a Stag. He is lord of wildlife and functions as a guide to travelers. He is also a Guide of the Dead, leading souls through the veil and across the Sídhe into the Otherworld. Following him through the wildwood, Keltelven mystics hope to discover the runes of earthy wisdom. Cernunnos functions as a guide to those participating devoutly in the Thirteen Dayes of Yule. He guides pilgrims to Glastonbury Tor and to the Thorn, which stands outside the Cave of the Nativity on the Tor. On the day after Matrum Noctem he comes among us as "the Gifting Stag."

Cherry Tree – It has long been a custom among Keltelvens to place a small cherry branch in a container of water at the beginning of the Yule Season. This branch often buds and breaks into bloom by White Thorn Day. This branch is sometimes called the "Cherry Rose." It is thought of as prefiguring the new life of the coming year.

There is a legend relating that on the way to Bethlehem, Mary asked Joseph to pick some cherries for her from a tree that had bloomed miraculously by the side of the path. Joseph was not tall enough to reach the branches, so the tree bent down and let Mary –

who was nine months pregnant – pick as many cherries as she wanted. As the tree bent before Mary, adoring the divine child in her womb, so Joseph knelt before the tree, adoring the One who made the tree and who had caused Mary to become pregnant.

Cinnamon – An herb of knowledge. At Winter's Solstice it stands for the heightening of our earthen awareness of the mystery of birth and rebirth. It is used in magical spells and rituals of prayer to enhance our mortal ability to see into the mystery of ordinary things. As well as being put in candles to scent the place of dwelling, it can also be used to flavor food. Leaves from the Cinnamon tree can be added to wreaths that decorate the doors and windows of the house.

Colors – The colors with which we surround ourselves have a dramatic impact upon consciousness. We should use colors in order to uplift & empower ourselves to keep sacred seasons and be "awake" to what is going on around us in Earth & Spirit. Colors are connected with light and the way in which we 'see' the world. Colors have their own spiritual energy and as such conscious employment of various colors can enhance our experience of the Yule Season. The primary colors of the Yule are red and green, silver and gold, and white.

Crabapples – These small fruits are connected with the deer and the groves in the wildwood where deer sojourn in colder weather. To have pickled crabapples at your table on Nicholas Eve (6 December) is to invite the deer to come near and visit your place of dwelling. This is also an implicit invitation to the Reindeer of Nicholas.

Cranberries – One of the red berries associated with the Celtic Goddesses at Winter's Solstice, as they ripen at the end of Autumn. As they grow in bogs, they symbolize the way in which spiritual Wisdom must be procured near waters. Keltelvens see Cranberries as a manifest fruit of the Wisdom of the Earth Mother, Tailtiu, who is sometimes considered to be the Mother of Brighid, the Goddess of the Hearth.

Decorations – We decorate our places of dwelling during Yule in order to transform them into an intimation of Paradise. Shining lights represent the presence of spirits and souls, angels and saints. Garlands represent the ways in which all living things are connected to each other in the Earth & Spirit. Wreaths represent the circle of the worlds in which we live, as well as completion and hope. Tinsel and other glittering decorations indicate the nearness of Paradise and the doorways into Spiral Castle.

Deer – These animals – widely venerated in the Celtic world – are visible incarnations of the god-force in Nature. The Stag in particular is thought of as a mystical manifestation of earthen power and god-centered Wisdom. Deer foraged near farms, huts and fields in Celtic days thus becoming symbolic of the mysterious presence of the Divine. The image of the silent doe or buck standing within range of the lights of the Hearth, yellow eyes reflecting in the Moonlight and tail flicking back and forth in nervous curiosity, is one of the iconic images of the Keltelven Yule.

Wild deer were once kept on sacred isles where mystics went to path Cernunnos as the Great Stag. Encounters with deer are still considered auspicious during the Yule. By leaving apples and other food out for them, deer are encouraged to tarry near the homes of those who live near the woods and who desire the presence of these mysterious animals. To feed the deer is a ministry to the gods.

Dolmens – Small stone structures erected by placing a large flat stone across three standing stones. A dolmen looks like a chamber with open walls. Historic dolmens come in many sizes, and are found throughout Celtic lands. Mystics go to dolmens to pray and commune with their gods and goddesses. Saints and angels have long been known to visit the followers of Christ at dolmens in Celtic landscapes. During the Yule a dolmen is seen as symbolic of the place where the ancestors enter the world. It may also be seen as a womb-symbol representing birth and rebirth. A small dolmen may be set up on the Yule Table during Yule.

Elves – According to Keltelven myth-history, the Elves are the remnants of the Neolithic (New Stone Age) people of Britain who lived on the haunted isle before Iron Age peoples began arriving. They were driven back into the hinterlands (un-arable land or wastelands) by the invading Celts in the 3rd to the 1st centuries BCE. Elves were hunter-gatherers, and became nomadic pastoralists after the Celtic invasion. In Ireland they were known by various names, including the *Sluagh Sídhe* (the people of the Sídhe). Keltelvens in Ross County believe they remained a thriving sub-culture until the 9th or 10th century CE.

The Elves of Saint Nicholas are the most well known elves of the Winter Solstice Season. They were originally from a ráth called Tara Lough in Ireland. They set out on a quest across Europe and found the wisdom they were seeking once they encountered the young Nicholas in Myra. Today these Elves live with Saint Nicholas "at the North Pole" in the Otherworld.

Epiphany – An "epiphany" is an experience of personal insight arising out of a coincidence of events. It is often sparked by the experience of a dynamic tension between different feelings or other sensual factors. The appearance of a god is an epiphany, and as such the birth of Jesus of Nazareth was considered to be an epiphany.

Evergreens – The idiom "ever-green" refers to any plant or herb that keeps its green leaves or needles through the winter months. As such, Pine and Fir Trees, Holly, Myrtle, and Ivy are all "evergreens." Evergreens symbolize the tenacity of life. They have long been seen as signs that life survives the death of the body.

Fires – There are many symbolic fires connected with the Winter Solstice. Bonfires may be lit in Pine Groves on Solstice Night. Hearthfires are lit in houses and communal halls. Bonfires and Hearthfires are thought of as "gifts of the Sun" and as manifestations of divine power at the tides of Winter's Solstice. All fires connected with the Winter Solstice and then with Christmas are called "Yulefire" by Keltelven practitioners. Fire is generally symbolic of Divine Presence indwelling the coích anama (soul-house) of the human being and thus is a metaphor for the life-force. To be "en-fired" is a way of describing the inspiration of poets and mystics. To have "Fire in the Head" is a metaphor for being spiritually "awake."

Frankincense (*franc* ["pure"] + *encens* ["incense"]) – A gum resin exuded as a milky colored liquid from trees belonging to various species of the genus *boswellia*. This white liquid soon solidifies and may be collected in the form of grainy "tears" which can then be melted down and turned into sticks. It is usually left in its pure state, but may also be mixed with other ingredients.

Frankincense yields a balsam-like fragrance when burned. It has been used for at least 4,000 years in embalming, fumigation and in the making of perfume. Ancient Egyptian recipes for mummification (dating to the 3rd millennium BCE) include Frankincense as an ingredient. The ancient Jews burned Frankincense in their temple. The historian Josephus (1st century CE) wrote that two golden chalices were filled with Frankincense and set beside the "Bread of Presence" (Leviticus 24:7) in the Holy of Holies; the most sacred precinct of the Jewish Temple in Jerusalem. Its fragrance was said to be "pleasing to the Lord" (Exodus 30:34-38).

Gifts – The original Yuletide gift-givers were the three Magi who visited the Nativity of Jesus soon after he was born. The tradition of giving gifts on 25 December also arose in imitation of the charity of Saint Nicholas. Gift-giving is a sign of reconciliation. It also affirms another person's worth and may act as an offer of forgiveness or as a declaration of love. To give a gift may be seen as an overture to friendship.

Glastonbury Thorn – An ancient tree growing near Glastonbury Tor in England, a place long connected with Avalon. The tree is a Keltelven version of the Norse World Tree (the *Yggdrasil*). Joseph of Arimathea is said to have planted the original Thorn, which is thought to have been a Hawthorn or Blackthorn. All Glastonbury Thorns are thought to be descended from this original tree. Keltelven spirituality treats the "Glastonbury Thorn" as the "destination" of the Yuletide journey. Pilgrims who follow Cernunnos to Glastonbury Tor then find the entrance to the Cave of the Nativity near the Thorn.

Glastonbury Tor – A sculpted hill riddled with caves and located in County Somerset in western England. On its terraced slopes are ancient maze-like paths etched into the rocks. Following these paths takes a pilgrim from the flatland around the Tor up to the top, where a small hermit's cell stands. The Tor is rumored to be the burial place of Arthur & Guinevere. It has long been haunted by Elvenfolk and is where Joseph of Arimathea planted the Glastonbury Thorn. As such, the Tor is symbolic of the deep, ancient link between Pagan and Christian mysticism. Both Pagan and Christian mystics used to path the Tor's maze on Matrum Noctem.

Gold – An almost universal symbol for enlightenment, intellectual refinement and mystical power. It is connected with the sun, and when worn or held enhances the powers of logic, rationality and deduction. It also brings out the innate power of leadership in those who have the gift to rule and administrate political power. It is one of the gifts the Magi gave to Jesus (Matthew 2:11).

Gospel, The – A name for the teachings of Jesus of Nazareth. It means "Good News," but in Keltelven interpretation it portends the mysterious paths mortals must take to Wisdom's Door. It refers to the stories told about Jesus and to the adventures that must be undertaken if his followers are to come into the Illumined Circle of Wisdom. Keltelvens understand "the Gospel" as one of the *many* dreams of a better world encoded in the tales and mythologies of human religions.

Green – The primary color of living things in the plant world, green symbolizes the sustaining power of the Spirit of Life. Nicholas alternately wears green and red coats as a sign of his identification with the natural powers of life. Cernunnos is seen as the "Green Man" in the summer months.

Hearth – A fireplace in the house where all the cooking was done and where all of the magical practices associated with *Corrguine* (herbalism) used to be practiced. The fire of the hearth heated the place of human dwelling. The hearth symbolizes the presence of life's vitality in our midst. The hearth is where the Goddess Brighid becomes manifest to her mystics. She is "Mistress of the Hearth" and as such keeps an eye on all those who live near the hearth. She is the patroness of children's welfare in the home.

Heath – An exposed hilltop from which the circle of the horizon can be seen. Ancient peoples worshipped their gods & goddesses on heaths, earning the title "heathens." Heaths are potential sites for spiritual encounters, epiphanies and revelations. On the morning after Winter's Solstice Keltelvens still go out to a heath to watch the sun rise. Keltelvens also make pilgrimages out to heaths on Silver Fir Day (23 December).

Hemlock – An evergreen tree connected in Keltelven lore with the Bards. It is a very stable tree with a generally straight trunk. It has supple branches and soft needles. Its strength is its flexibility; like the Willow its boughs rarely break in the wind, and storms do not usually damage it.

The Hemlock has small, papery cones. Owing to its thick foliage and supple branches, the wind blows through Hemlock trees in a sometimes eerie and musical way. This fact may have resulted in its becoming associated with the Bards of the Keltelven traditions of Ross County. During Yule its "wind music" is thought of as the music of the Spirit of Life.

Holly – An herb associated with the presence of the god-force in Nature, Holly has been connected with the Winter Solstice since ancient times. It symbolizes the very essence of biological life: the green leaves with their pin-like tines represent the fecundity of the flesh, while the red berries, which are brightest near the Winter Solstice, represent blood, which remains red and flows throughout the cold, dark winter. Holly is associated with the Daghda; who is the "All-Father" in ancient Celtic and contemporary Keltelven mythology.

Immanuel – A Hebrew word meaning "God with us." In Christian terms, Jesus is Immanuel, as he is "God" born in human flesh. Though this was unusual in Jewish religion the ancient Celts were quite familiar with virgin births and god-men (e.g., Cú Chulainn – the Ulster hero – was conceived in his mother's womb by the mystical influence of the god Lugh).

Incarnation – A pagan term used in Christian theology to refer to the event of God taking on human flesh in Jesus of Nazareth. As with the term "Immanuel," the incarnation of divinities in human form was nothing unusual in Celtic traditions.

Ivy – A symbol of (1) tenacity in life, (2) the deep and viney connection between all living things, and (3) protection. Ivy is difficult to destroy, once it gains a foothold. Ivy vines anywhere, climbing buildings and even making its way into fissures and cracks in solid stone, breaking the rock open. Thus, Ivy is both a protector and a destroyer. If the house is sound the Ivy tendrils will not harm it; the vines will actually protect the structure against the effects of weathering and keep a house moist in dry weather! If the house is unsound, however, the Ivy will widen cracks and fissures, eventually undermining walls and foundations. Ivy is sacred to Brighid and is a symbol of fidelity. It is symbolic of Spiral Castle. It has long been known to bring spiritual cleansing to a house when it is grown or brought indoors. Some Ivy plants live to be 500 years old.

Juniper – An evergreen with a potent life-force, Juniper's herbal property is to make the house secure. Hanging it over the hearth symbolizes a dedication to the welfare of the occupants. When hung by doors it is a hex against thieves. To wear Juniper on your lapel or attached to a coat or dress symbolizes the security of your heart, and your dedication to Wisdom.

Ley-Lines – Mysterious lines 'etched' into bedrock by some unknown force at some indeterminate time in the past. Following ley-lines can lead you to answer questions of divine import and magical potentiality. The expression "the ley-lines of Yule" refers to the paths we must discern if we are to celebrate and observe the season well, arriving at the Nativity by mid-night on Matrum Noctem.

Lugh – The omnicraefty god of the Irish Celts, he comes on Balsam Fir Day (15 December) to help those who are keeping the Yule finish their arts & craefty work before Winter's Solstice.

Magi – A title for the wise men who visited the manger in Bethlehem where Jesus was born (Matthew 2:1-12). They gave him three gifts – Gold, Frankincense and Myrrh – adoring him as a Child of Divine Wisdom. They were obviously well versed in astrology as they had followed a Star all the way from their homeland (Persia?). Their visit to Bethlehem may be seen as evidence that one does not have to become a "Christian" (in the narrow sense of the term) in order to worship Jesus and find the runes of Wisdom in his teaching, as the Magi returned home without undergoing any kind of "conversion."

Mary – (see, "Virgin Mary")

Matrum Noctem – Keltelven name for the Eve of 25 December meaning "Night of the Mother." It originally referred to the presence of the Earth Goddess at the tides of Winter's Solstice.

245

Meditation Table – A table on which icons of the season are placed. Candles, stag's horns, and statues of gods and goddesses may be placed on the table. Images or statues of saints may be set out at their appropriate season, as well as artifacts of nature (leaves, pine cones, rocks, etc.). During Yule it is called a "Yule Table" and may serve as a substitute for the hearth; the candles lit on the table taking the place of hearth-fire if there is no hearth in your place of dwelling. Keltelvens often build a small dolmen on their meditation table during Yule to signify the place of divine-human encounter.

Menhir – A stone (usually between two and three feet tall) erected at a place in the woods where you have encountered the Presence of Divine Mystery. A Menhir symbolically represents the way-stations we pass on spiritual journeys or on pilgrimages to sacred places. During the Yule menhirs may be seen as symbolic markers of the paths we take on our way to the manger of transformation and rebirth.

Mistletoe (*Uchelwydd*) – An herb traditionally known as "All Heal," it has white, poisonous berries that ripen in early winter and as such was held to be sacred as a solar herb in Northern Europe in Pagan times. The role of Mistletoe in Yuletide celebrations may be older than that of pine trees. Many of its earliest associations were carried over into Christian symbolism.

Mistletoe imbibes the "Three Rays" of the Sun deity at the Summer Solstice. By the time the berries ripen as Winter's Solstice approaches, they contain the mystical essence of the Sun. Mistletoe grows on solid foundations and thus it gives the one who finds it a psychic/symbolic intuition into what is built upon the foundations. Mistletoe reveals the inner meaning of things. Hanging mistletoe in a doorway or on your front door is a sign that you forgive anyone who comes to your house of any wrong they may have done to you in the past. This is the original meaning of kissing beneath the Mistletoe.

246

Myrrh – An herb that grows in the Middle East, it has fragrant wood and resinous bark. The sap-like yellow gum that flows from it is used in perfumes, magical ointments, anointing oils and in burial salves. It was one of the three gifts brought to the infant Jesus by the Magi (Matthew 2:11). It generally symbolizes the death and rebirth we hope to undergo at Winter's Solstice.

Mysterious Stranger, The – A title for the god of Wisdom who often comes to visit us in a stranger's guise. Mortals may encounter him out on the open road. Christ, the Daghda and Cernunnos may come to our doors during the Yule as the "mysterious guest" asking for a meal and shelter. Having been invited to our hearth and table, the stranger will reveal his true identity. (This story was known in Jewish and early Christian circles; see Hebrews 13:1 and Luke 24:13-35)

Nativity – A word referring to the place of birth, the birth event, or the record of a birth. It has come to refer almost exclusively to the birth of Jesus of Nazareth in Bethlehem. Keltelvens understand it as "a place of birth and rebirth" in the Season of the Winter Solstice.

Nativity Scene – A diorama depicting the scene in the stable-cave where Jesus of Nazareth was born. It is usually set up after Winter Solstice Night. The figures of Mary and Joseph are added on the 23rd or 24th of December and then the figure of the infant Jesus is placed in the manger at midnight on Matrum Noctem. On the 26th of December the shepherds are added and finally, on 6 January, the figures of the Magi are added. The Nativity Scene is a primary icon of spiritual birth and rebirth during the later days of Yule. It represents the drama of our own transformation and rebirth during the devout observance of Matrum Noctem.

Nemeton – A sacred place in the wildwoods where mystics go for solitude, to pray and perform magick, seek direction in their lives and celebrate minor sacred days (such as New Moons). The nemeton is the place where shunnache (the primeval energy of the universe) becomes manifest to Keltelven shamans, Druids, Gwrach and Bards. A nemeton might be discovered in a wooded grove or in a natural clearing created when a tree fell, opening a hole in the forest canopy. Springs, bogs, and the estuaries of streams or rivers also make fecund nemetons.

Nerthus – The Keltelven Goddess of Winter Solstice and the Mistress/Driver of the Yuletide Wagon, Nerthus is the elder-mother of the two other goddesses – Brighid and Coventina – who together constitute the Triple Yuletide Goddess. As part of this Triad, Nerthus watches over the community in the form of the Night Owl and the Gray Wolf, and is often present as the Hind that runs with Cernunnos, bearing his offspring. Her presence becomes manifest during the Yule in wild rabbits. She is heard whispering in root cellars and caves and anywhere where water is running in the dark (though in this last place She is more likely known as Coventina). She lives on an island-grove during the year and drives a magical wagon from her abode to where Keltelvens keep the Yule.

Nicholas, Saint (380-452 CE) – A native of Asia Minor, the historical Nicholas was orphaned at birth and grew up in the house of his aunt and uncle in Myra, on the southern shores of Asia Minor. He was soon graced with the precocious habit of begging coins from the rich and giving these to poor children in the streets, asking alms as well to feed other orphans.

He later became known for his anonymous gift-giving and, by the time he was an adult, he had been declared a "living saint." He is the historical figure behind all of the gift-giving figures of various Christian traditions, including Sinter Klaas, Father Christmas, and Santa Claus.

North Pole – The legendary place where Nicholas/Santa Claus lives with his Elves. It was originally called "the top of the world," a term from late Celtic myth alluding to the realm of the gods in the

Otherworld. "North" was always a mystery direction. In the "North" many divinities set up their Ice Castles. Thus it became a fitting place for Nicholas to dwell. Keltelven legends say that Santa's Workshop, located at "the top of the world," was called Tara Lough.

Nuts – Like apples, nuts are symbolic of divine triads. The hard outer shell indicates that the wisdom contained in the nut is for the initiated. The inner skins represent the divine vehicle in which Wisdom is communicated to mortals, while the actual nut represents the flesh of knowledge. Nuts of all kinds are used as decorations during the Yule.

Ornaments – Any shiny seasonal objects used to adorn the place of dwelling at Winter's Solstice may be called "ornaments." They have various cultural origins. The glass or metal balls we now use as ornaments symbolize the spirit-worlds of Faery and Elves. When hung on the Yule tree, they represent the greater spirits of benevolence and charity – such as saints – who wander through the world during Yule. As shiny, reflective objects, they may be used in oracular divination (like crystal balls, specula or "witch balls").

Otherworld – The Celts believed that after the death of the coích anama (soul house) a person enters the "third way" and passes into another realm (neither "heaven" nor "hell"), where life continues in another 'mode' and where souls are able to continue their pursuit of Wisdom. The Otherworld is 'right next' to our world. It does not exist 'above' or 'below' the world of incarnate souls. It is no better or worse to live in the Otherworld than in this world.

Paradise – The Celts believed that beyond the Otherworld was the realm of perfection and fruition; a land of perpetual bliss and happiness called "Paradise." This realm could become manifest on Earth especially at Winter's Solstice. Many of the decorations of Yule – which shine, glitter and give off light – are symbolic of the breaking-through of Paradise into our own mortal time.

Rabbits – The manifest power of the Earth Goddess Tailtiu in Nature, they are symbolic of the potency and fertility of the Goddess. When rabbits are seen in the woods, Keltelven mystics stop to pray for the guidance of the Spirit. Rabbits make the goddess-force manifest just as Stags make the god-force manifest in the Earth.

Ráth – A name for the semi-subterranean houses of the Elvenfolk. Ráths were usually circular, covered with sod and well-ventilated with a smoke hole at the top of the conical roof. Saint Nicholas is said to live in a ráth at Tara Lough at the top of the world. A ráth is also what Keltelvens call a house where community business is taken care of and where festivals are celebrated.

Red – The color of blood and therefore the primary symbol of animal life. Red symbolizes the richness of life and the power of the life-force flowing through us, both in our blood and in our spirit. It symbolizes the blood of dying-gods such as Jesus and Bran, who sacrificed themselves for the sake of their people. Red is one of the two primary colors of Yule. Decorations for Yule should be replete with both Red and Green (not one or the other).

Reindeer – Relatives of the common White-tailed deer, these large herbivores live in the far northerly climes of the world and have therefore come to be associated with the mystery of the "North" (see **North Pole**). Magical reindeer pull Nicholas' sleigh through the skies on his annual visits. Keltelvens imagine that the original eight reindeer – named Dasher, Dancer, Prancer and Vixen, Comet, Cupid, Donder and Blitzen – whose names were first published in Clement Clark Moore's poem "A Visit from Saint Nicholas" (1822), were gifted to Nicholas and his Elves back in the 4th century. They are able to fly through the air on account of their originally being inhabitants of the Celtic Otherworld.

Rosemary – A fragrant herb primarily found in southern Europe and Asia Minor. Mary is said to have placed Rosemary beneath the head of her newborn son to give him gentle sleep and aid his memory of his own divine identity. Rosemary was also added to the water

Mary used to bath Jesus, as this would keep him free of disease and hidden from the prying eyes of evil spirits.

Joseph and Mary then burned Rosemary incense on their flight into Egypt, where they went to hide their son Jesus from the murderous madness of Herod. The name was later believed to have come from "Mary's Rose." It is still used as an ingredient in Yuletide incense.

Rune – A magical letter. Runes were first introduced in Celtic lands by the Norse. Keltelvens later adopted them as a form of mystical and magical writing. There are several ancient runic alphabets. "**To Rune**" means to encode something in runes or to work toward an understanding of a mystery. "**Runing**" is either the process by which we "write out" a series of runes that touch upon the essence of some mystery, or a process of en-coding something in runes.

Santa Claus – The primary American manifestation of the myth of Saint Nicholas. Santa Claus emerged from the Christmas Imagination during the 19th century through the work of Washington Irving, Clement Clark Moore and Thomas Nast. His lore continues to be expanded today through contemporary stories, films and images generated by the media.

Silver – A color representing ice and shiny surfaces, sparkling cold streams, and the glistening of falling snowflakes. It is the color of illumination and is associated with the Moon. Silver reflects our true nature.

Spiral Castle – A mythic archetype of the spiritual journey in Keltelven spirituality. Spiral Castle refers to (1) the spiral nature of our life's paths as well as (2) the spiral path leading into the next life and finally to Paradise. A Spiral is not a "vicious circle." Rather, it's a circular pattern in which we return to the same places, in different cycles, but further along in our spiritual growth. To move in a spiral implies cyclic progress. "Spiral Castle" is therefore a symbol of spiritual growth. Spirals are prominent in Celtic art and lore.

A "Spiral Castle" is also an edifice built by a divine agency and empowered with strange-magick (i.e., magick coming from a divine source), wherein the pilgrim or quester can seek the divine Source of their lives. Spiral Castle is symbolized in the Yule Tree. By following the lines configured by the garlands and light strings decorating the Tree, we engage in a meditation on our pilgrimage to Spiral Castle. In Keltelven lore Nicholas' 'residence' at the top of the world is to be identified with Spiral Castle.

Spirit of Yule, The – A name for the Presence of Mystery in the Cosmos as it is manifest among us during the Season of Yule. It inspires hope, charity, generosity and acts of hospitality in human hearts. The Spirit of Yule invites us to enter into the Yule and celebrate the inner spiritual meaning of the Winter Solstice in our hearts, near the hearth, and out in the world where we live and work. The Spirit of Yule 'lights' the Fires of Yule.

Star of Yule – A name for the heavenly beacon that the Magi followed from their homeland to Judea and then from Jerusalem to the Nativity in Bethlehem. The star is often seen as having four-points and shaped irregularly in the basic figure of a cross.

Keltelven mystics have long believed that the star the Magi followed was not some brilliant astronomical event – a quasar or an exploding supernovae – but rather an ordinary star that the Magi – because of their astrological prowess – saw as an extra-ordinary sign. Those keeping Yule today often follow the Star on their pilgrimage to the manger of their own rebirth.

Tinsel – Anything that glitters and shines, reflecting firelight, moonlight or some other source of illumination. Its sparkling and shining is symbolic of the sparks of Divine Nearness.

Virgin Mary – A title of the human mother of Jesus, Mary was an unwed woman who, while she was still betrothed to her future husband was told by an Angel of her God that she would bear a child. This child was to be the "messiah" (i.e., an anointed teacher of Wisdom long awaited by certain sects of Judaism). Her story is told primarily in the first two chapters of the Gospel of Luke in the New Testament. Mary accepted the invitation of the Angel to become pregnant with a divine child. She is called "Virgin" because she had no sexual intercourse before becoming pregnant with Jesus and because she was in charge of her own sexual destiny.

Mary is a symbol of human stamina, faith-in-life in the face of impossible odds, and a resolve to embody the Divine Will in life, regardless of the consequences. In Keltelven lore, the Virgin Mary is seen as a sister of the ancient goddesses of Wisdom. Mary is given the title of the "Mistress of Virtues." She is also connected with the Moon and with the Muse in Keltelven mysticism. Keltelvens associated Mary with Roses, pools of water and the various fish who utter words of wisdom in the ears of awakened mystics. These fish are usually sacred trout or salmon and are kept by mystics devoted to Mary in pools high up in the hills. The fish symbolize her Son, who was Wisdom incarnate.

Mary was the mentor of many of the early Celtic followers of Christ. She led them into devout paths and taught them how to live out the wisdom embodied in the life—death—resurrection of her son. The Celts prayed to Mary as to an elder sister of faith, and also as one who was exalted to the Table of the Heroes in paradise. Today Keltelvens revere her in the same company as Dechtire (the mother of Cú Chulainn), Ceridwen (the mother of Taleisin) and other women who gave birth to divine sons after experiencing unusual mystical means of conception.

Walnuts – Symbols of the seeds of Wisdom offered to mortals in this life. Wisdom is always "a hard nut to crack." The outer shells of Walnuts represent the difficulty of penetrating the meaty marrow

253

of a parable, rann or sacred riddle, and their fruit represents the nutritious and sustaining power of true wisdom. To see Walnuts – and other nuts – on the table after Nicholas Eve (6 December) is to be reminded of the wisdom that is waiting to be discovered within the paths of Yule.

White – A color symbolizing the Sun at Winter's Solstice, which often seems to lose its color, becoming pale. Keltelven mystics call the Winter Solstice Sun the "Pale White Eye of She Who Is," as in Celtic myth the Sun was often imaged as feminine rather than masculine. White is also a natural color of Winter, bringing to mind the snow that covers the ground in northerly climes. White snow may refer to "psychic sleep" which brings rebirth.

World Tree (*Yggdrasil, Bilé*) – Norse and Celtic mythology both represented the world as a tree growing inside the horizons of an inscrutable mystic sphere. The roots of the tree were grounded in the Earth, from which all life springs. The branches of the tree represent the heavens. The trunk of the tree represents the world in which we live, which holds up the heavens. The Yule Tree is often likened to the World Tree in the Light of the Fires of Yule.

Wreaths – A circular swag of evergreens. The circle represents the worlds we inhabit ("Every world is circular," Keltelvens say). As a circle, the wreath also represents harmony and eternity. The circle is a symbol of perfection, completion, and the cycles through which Creation passes. The Wheel of the Year, which turns once from one Winter Solstice to the next, is the cosmological circle. The wreath symbolizes this "primeval circle" in Yuletide decorations.

Wreaths are often decorated with nuts and fruits tied on with bows and fine twine. These illustrate – to the symbolic imagination – that the Circle of the Earth and Life is rich with treasures and bounty. When you make a wreath and hang it up, see yourself in the center of it with the fecundity and mysteries of Nature surrounding you, your soul extending out in all directions in the empowerment of the Spirit. This is an icon of the Mystery of the cosmos as ever-present. The richness of Divine Life knows no limit or end. When you carry a wreath to the house of a neighbor or friend, you are seeking to inspire a desire to participate in the circle of the cosmos.

A wreath decorated with Rosemary and Sage is often set out on Keltelven tables where the Feast of Nicholas is eaten on the 6th of December. Four candleholders are set into the wreath, and the candles in these holders represent the spirits of the cardinal directions (North = Falias, East = Gorias, South = Finias, West = Murias). As these candles burn down during the Yule, participants 'map' their own progress to Glastonbury Tor.

Yew (*Ioho*) – Keltelven mystics think of the Yew tree as symbolic of immortality and reincarnation as well as a psychic gateway into the Otherworld. The Yew renews itself and is "born again" from its own death.

It is believed that the spirits of the dead are able to pass back and forth between the worlds via the branches and roots of these strange trees. A Yew may be planted near sacred nemetons, groves and dolmens. Touching a Yew puts a grieved person in contact with a loved one who has recently crossed❖over to the Otherworld. Celtic Christians interred their dead near old Yews. As a Christian symbol, the Yew is connected with heaven and resurrection.

Yggdrasil – (see "World Tree")

Yule Log – A fragrant-burning log brought into the house as a symbol of the dying of the old solar year. As the Yule Log burns away in the Hearth, so the old year passes away and a new one is born out of its ashes. Often a piece of the Log is kept and saved until the next year, when it will be used to light the next Yule Log. The piece saved from one year to the next was called a "brand." This ritual act symbolizes the continuity of experience from one year to the next.

Keltelven followers of Christ see in this rite of burning the Yule Log a symbol that the Old World of ignorance is coming to an end as Jesus is born in the hearts of his friends each year at Winter's Solstice. Out of our psychic and symbolic death comes the birth of a New World.

Yule Tree – During the 1st millennium BCE, European peoples venerated trees as wise elders and living beings in the Earth. The origin of the Yule Tree is to be found first in Germanic folklore. The Christian use of the Yule Tree goes back to at least the 8th century CE. The legends say that as St. Wilifrid (later also called Saint Boniface) traveled through the northern woods of what is now Germany, he dedicated some of the old sacred trees to Jesus. The Germanic people cut these trees down and took them into their huts as a sign that Christ was present with them during the cold winter months.

The Anglo-Saxons brought the Germanic practice of setting up a Yule Tree with them to Britain. By the early Middle Ages the "English" were cutting evergreens and bringing them into their houses at Winter's Solstice. The tree was usually left undecorated. It stood in the middle of the room in which it was set up so that people could dance in circles around it.

The Yule Tree is an icon of the "World Tree." The roots of the Tree are in the earth, the trunk and boughs represent the Spirit of Life while the needles represent the lives of mortal beings. The top of the tree is thought of as representing "the realms of the gods" or as the entrance to the Otherworld.

Bibliography (Fictional & Seasonal Sources)

This bibliography includes two kinds of sources. First there are the fictional sources, which arise from my visionary visits to Ross County. Secondly, I offer a list of sources that may help you deepen your appreciation of the spiritual paradigm presented in this book.

A. Quotes from Fictional Sources

As a Celtic poet I have created my own fictional geography that by the mid-1980's was being called **Ross County**. Here live all of the characters that populate my stories. My imagination has free play in this parallel realm, and it is from delving into this landscape and dealing with its inhabitants that I draw up water from the wellsprings of mused inspiration.

Over the years a cast of characters has emerged to whom I refer often when teaching Keltelven and Celtic Christian spirituality. **All of the 'quotes' in The Fires of Yule are from texts 'written' by these characters who are even now living in Ross County**. A few of these texts actually 'exist,' though most of them have yet to be brought to any concrete manifestation.

Characters such as **Cornelius Whitsel** and **Robert Werner** are prolific 'writers' who live on Deer Hill; a mysterious, thickly forested heath located about 2 miles south of Wickersfeld, the County seat of Ross County. **Egbert Whittier** is an ancestor of the Whittiers of Deer Hill. His book – The Thirteen Dayes of Yule (1800) is one of the key touchstones for the present text. The other major touchstone has been the Yuletide Grimoire, which Cornelius Whitsel told me was composed in 1898 by a Keltelven community living in Ross County. While I have no manuscript of this book, various Keltelven characters in Ross County have dictated quotes from it to me over the years.

The symbolic and spiritual mythology of the "Thirteen Dayes of Yule" has been evolving – in the fictional time of Ross County – since about 1800. In *my* authorial time it has been coming together since about 1974-1976, when I first began to imagine the characters whose books I am today quoting in the texts I create. The book-length 'sources' quoted from in The Fires of Yule include the following texts:

Abbot, Catharine	A Yuletide Handbook (1986) What is Decorating? (1987) Weaving the Christed Way (1989)
Hester, Mabel	The Veil in the Well (1993)
O'Donoghue, Damion	Patterns of Soul Friendship (1994)
Sackneuseum, Judas	The Celtic Crossroads (1985)
Smythe, Gawain	The Way of the Bards (1996)
Werner, Robert	Wintering Upon the Way (1970) The Way of the Poet (1971) Tales from the Seasons (1985) Fire in the Shadows (1989)
Whitsel, Cornelius	The Keltelven Traditions: A History (1982) Earthen Meditations (1986) Table of the Sacred Dayes (1990) The Keltelven Grimoire (1993)
Magdalena Ipswich	The Runes of Celtic Hearth Philosophy (1992)
Whittier, Bedlow	The Celtic Constitution (1990)
Whittier, Egbert	The Thirteen Dayes of Yule (1800)
Whittier, Geoffrey C.	The Whittier Hearth (1985) The Whittier Hearth (1992)
Whittier, Hildegard	The Elf Plot (1992)
Whittier, Susan Jean	The House Upon the Hill (1973)

B. Bibliography of Seasonal and Celtic Sources

While I have tried to include in the text of this book everything you need to begin celebrating the Thirteen Dayes of Yule, you may eventually want to go deeper into the spirituality represented here. This bibliography contains sources that will facilitate your quest for depth. It is comprised of two lists. First, a list of studies of 'Christmas' that will provide background for the customs and folklore of the Winter Solstice Season from both Pagan and Christian perspectives. Second is a list of sources that will help you to broaden your own understanding of Celtic religious & cultural heritage.

(1) Christmas Sources

Auld, William Muir Christmas Traditions
(New York: MacMillan, 1931)

Coffin, Tristam Potter The Illustrated Book of Christmas Folklore
(New York: Seabury Press, 1974)

Count, Earl Wendel 4000 Years of Christmas
(New York: Rider, 1953)

Crippen, Thomas George Christmas and Christmas Lore
(Detroit: Gale Research Co., 1971)

Dickens, Charles Christmas Stories and Christmas Books
(Oxford University Press, 1987; Oxford Illustrated Dickens)

Foley, Daniel J. The Christmas Tree: An Evergreen Garland Filled with History, Folklore, Symbolism, Traditions, and Stories
(Philadelphia, PA: Chilton Co., Book Division, 1960)

Halpert, Herbert Christmas Mumming in Newfoundland: Essays in Anthropology, Folklore and History
(Toronto: Toronto University Press, 1969)

Hole, Christina Christmas and its Customs: A Brief History
(New York: M. Barrows, 1957)

Matthews, John The Winter Solstice: The Sacred Traditions of Christmas
(Wheaton, IL: Quest Books; Theosophical Publishing House, 1998)

[A book encompassing all of the various customs of the Winter Solstice and written from an informed, open-minded perspective! John Matthews is a scholar of Celtic spiritual traditions, both Pagan and Christian, with a perceptive approach to symbols and ritual meanings that makes his texts refreshing to read and ponder!]

Miles, Clement A. Christmas in Ritual and Tradition, Christian and Pagan
(London: T.F. Unwin, 1912; Detroit: Gale Research Co., 1968)

Restad, Penne L. Christmas in America: A History
(Oxford: Oxford University Press, 1995)

Shoemaker, Alfred Lewis Christmas in Pennsylvania: A Folk Cultural Study
(Kutztown: Pennsylvania Folklife Society, 1959)

Wilkinson, M. Yule Fire
(New York: Mac Millan, 1925)

(2) Celtic Sources

Brenneman, Walter L. and Mary G. Crossing the Circle at the Holy Wells of Ireland
(Charlottesville & London: University of Virginia Press, 1995)

Cahill, Thomas How the Irish Saved Civilization: The Untold Story of Ireland's Heroic Role from the Fall of Rome to the Rise of Mediaeval Europe
(New York: Doubleday, 1995)

Caldecott, Moyra   Women in Celtic Myth: Tales of Extraordinary Women from the Ancient Celtic Tradition
(Rochester, VT: Destiny Books, 1992; 1988)

Cowan, Tom Fire in the Head: Shamanism and the Celtic Spirit
(HarperSanFrancisco, 1993)

Cross, T. P. & C. H. Slover, eds. Ancient Irish Tales
(New York: Barnes & Noble; 1996; originally Henry Holt and Company, Inc., 1936)

Dames, Michael Mythic Ireland
(London: Thames and London, 1992)

Ellis, Peter Berresford The Druids
(Grand Rapids, MI: William B. Eerdmans Publishing Company, 1994)

Ellis, Peter Berresford   The Chronicles of the Celts: New Tellings of their Myths & Legends
(New York: Carroll &Graf Publishers, Inc., 1999)

Gregory, Lady Visions and Beliefs in the West of Ireland
(New York: Oxford University Press, 1970)

Gregory, Lady   Cúchulainn of Muirthemne: The Story of the Men of the Red Branch of Ulster
(Gerrard's Cross: Colin Smythe, 1970)

Gregory, Lady   Gods and Fighting Men: The Story of the Tuatha Dé Danann and the Fiana of Ireland
(Gerrard's Cross: Colin Smythe, 1976)

Glass-Koentop, Pattalee   Year of Moons, Season of Trees: Mysteries and Rites of Celtic Tree Magic
(St. Paul: Llewellyn Publications, 1991)

MacManus, Dairmaid Irish Earth Folk
(New York: Devon-Adair, 1959)

Markale, Jean Women of the Celts
(Rochester, VT: Inner Traditions International, LTD, 1986; 1972)

Matthews, Caitlin & John The Encyclopedia of Celtic Wisdom
(New York: Barnes and Nobles Books; 1994)

Murray, Liz and Colin The Celtic Tree Oracle: A System of Divination
(New York: St. Martin's Press, 1988)

O'Donoghue, Noel Dermot Aristocracy of Soul: Patrick of Ireland
(Wilmington, DL: Michael Glazier, 1987)

Pennick, Nigel Celtic Sacred Landscapes
(New York: Thames and Hudson, 1996)

Pennick, Nigel The Celtic Saints: An Illustrated and Authoritative
Guide to these Extraordinary Men and Women
(New York: Sterling Publishing Co., Inc., 1997)

Pennick, Nigel The Celtic Cross: An Illustrated History and
Celebration
(London: A Blandford Book; A Cassel Imprint, 1997)

Rees, Alwyn & Brinkley Celtic Heritage: Ancient Tradition in Ireland
& Wales
(London: Thames & Hudson, 1961)

Rutherford, Ward Celtic Mythology
(New York: Sterling Publishing Company, Inc., 1987)

Ryan, John Irish Monasticism: Origins and Early Development
(Ithaca, NY: Cornell University Press, 1972)

Sellner, Edward Wisdom of the Celtic Saints
(Notre Dame, IN: Ave Maria Press, 1993)

Sheils, W. J. and Diana Wood (Eds.) The Churches, Ireland and the Irish
(Oxford: 1989)

Scherman, Katharine The Flowering of Ireland: Saints, Scholars and Kings
(Boston: Little, Brown & Company, 1981)

Van de Meyer, Robert Celtic Fire: The Passionate Religious Vision of Ancient Britain and Ireland
(New York: Doubleday, 1991)

About the Author

Montague Whitsel has lived most of his life in western Pennsylvania becoming a Poet as well as a devout student of both Celtic and Biblical mythology. His undergraduate work was in Anthropology, History and Philosophy, after which he pursued Masters degrees in History, Sociology and Theology. He has been fascinated with religion since he was a teenager and has looked at it from both the inside (as a participant in wicche and goddess spirituality and later as a member of Catholic and Lutheran churches) and from the outside (as an historian and philosopher trained in the social sciences).

Montague Whitsel first became interested in the Celts in the early 1970's. Since then anything Celtic – whether culture, music, mythology and religion – has fascinated him. While pursuing his various degrees he took any opportunity that presented itself to do research on the material culture, history, mythology and religion of Celtic peoples from their obscure 'origins' in central Europe around 1000 BCE down through the Celtic Iron Age and into the period of Celtic Christianity. More recently he has sought to understand the literature of various Celtic countries and influences.

Mr. Whitsel eventually began giving private instructions in what became a **contemporary Celtic spirituality**. As some of his students were more or less involved in Christianity while others were either Pagan (practitioners of Wicche, etc.) or Secular in their orientation, he was soon led to put together *two different paradigms* of Celtic spirituality, one Pagan and the other Christian. The Celtic Christian paradigm came together as a series of "Nine Ways" in and through which one could "follow Christ *today* as a Celt." The Pagan Celtic paradigm was put together under the fictional umbrella of what he calls "the Keltelven Traditions" and brought forth in several texts, of which The Fires of Yule is the first to be published.

With the publishing of The Fires of Yule, Mr. Whitsel hopes that many more people will be able to experience the unique vision of the celebration of the Winter Solstice Season that has evolved out of his own and his students' desire to live a more interesting, richly symbolic life in the 21st century.

Printed in the United States
68284LVS00004B/85-99